4-5-73

P J Proudhon

GENERAL IDEA

OF THE

REVOLUTION

IN THE

NINETEENTH CENTURY

BY

P.-J. PROUDHON

TRANSLATED FROM THE FRENCH
BY JOHN BEVERLEY ROBINSON

GORDON PRESS

New York

1972

Originally published 1923

GORDON PRESS
P. O. Box 459
Bowling Green Station
New York, N.Y. 10004

Library of Congress Catalog Card Number 79-188095

International Standard Book Number 0-87968-009-1

Printed in the United States of America

GENERAL IDEA
OF THE
REVOLUTION
IN THE
NINETEENTH CENTURY

BOOK
REVIEWS

The General Idea of the Revolution in the 19th Century, by
P. J. Proudhon.   Reviewed by Robert Anton Wilson.

Benjamin Tucker considered this Proudhon's best book—
"the most wonderful of all the wonderful books of Proudhon"—
and he may well have been right in that judgment. Like many of
the greatest works of the last century this "most wonderful book"
comes to us from a prison cell; a fact which is probably far from
insignificant. It is not without cause that the letters of Bartolomeo
Vanzetti, the *Pisan Cantos* of Ezra Pound, "The Ballad of Reading
Gaol," Nietzsche's *Antichrist,* the best poems of Antonin Artaud,
Van Gogh's two or three greatest canvases, Koestler's *Darkness at
Noon,* and several other of the most significant cultural products
of this age, were produced by men who were at the time unwilling
"guests of the State." Nor is it idle to note that some time has
been served (unproductively, alas!) by Ford Madox Ford, Nijin-
sky, Seymour Krim, Allen Ginsberg, William Burroughs, Jim
Peck, and almost everybody else worth a damn as a serious thinker or artist. It is getting to the point where, as Eustace Mullins
noted in his biography of Ezra Pound, lack of a police or psychi-
atric record is looked on, by avante garde, as a sign that a
man has sold out.

The General Idea of the Revolution in the 19th Century was
written while Proudhon was serving three years "of enforced leisure" (his own phrase) for something he had written that of-
fended Louis Bonaparte. He doesn't tell us much about his prison,
so maybe it wasn't as bad as some of the others that the great
minds of our time have been confined in; but it was evidently bad
enough, for the next time Proudhon was sentenced to prison
(again for something he had written), he fled to Belgium and accepted exile rather than the regime of sadism-and-sodomy we inflict on the great minds which society imprisons to protect itself.

The background of *The General Idea of the Revolution in the
19th Century* was the abortive Revolution of 1848 in which Proudhon had participated and which ended with Reaction entrenched
more firmly than ever. Writing in an exalted and prophetic vein,
Proudhon sees clearly that the Revolution is not dead and fore-
shadows the Paris Commune twenty years in the future. He fore-
tells many victories still ahead for the *status quo,* he has moments
of doubt and almost Reichian pessimism about the masses: "But
reasoning will avail nothing," he writes once. "The eagle defends
his eyrie, the lion his den, the hog his trough, capital will not relinquish its interest. And we, poor sufferers, we are ignorant, un-

armed, divided: there is not one of us who, when one impulse urges him to revolution, is not held back by another."

The structure of this book is as block-like and monolithic as Euclid or Spinoza: a fact sometimes hidden by the wit, brilliance and poetry of the style. But beneath all the rapier-thrusts of his hyperbolic and eclectic polemic, Proudhon builds as carefully and logically as a mathematician. Each demonstration proceeds from the demonstration before it, and the cumulative effect is breathtakingly irresistible.

Chapter One, "Reaction causes Revolution," studies the methods by which the entrenched bourgeoisie, attempting to stifle rebellion, directly increased it and created the Revolution of 1848. Bringing the study up to the time of writing (1851), Proudhon shows, in detail, how the subsequent oppressive laws, aimed at preventing further revolution, are instead making further revolution inevitable. For instance, he points out that the teachers, with their usual conservatism, mostly opposed the Revolution of 1848, but have become, by 1851, quite revolutionary because of the thought control imposed upon them by the reactionary government.

Chapter Two, "Is there sufficient reason for a revolution in the 19th Century?" is a study of economic life in France from the fall of the Bourbons to 1851. The general impression is like that of Engels' *Condition of the Working Class in England*. Proudhon shows that, with such misery being almost universal, the laws made to prevent revolution can only inflame the people and bring revolution closer. Proudhon's special emphasis, however, is on the various "reform" movements which attempted to better the lot of the people. It is sixty years since feudalism was replaced by capitalism in France, he argues, and all the attempts to "reform" capitalism only prove that the original Revolution is unfinished. The death of the old privileged class has not brought freedom, but a new tyranny; it has not brought order, but more chaos. The Revolution of the 19th Century is inevitable, Proudhon argues, because the Revolution of the 18th Century was incomplete. Here he sounds strangely contemporary; as he elsewhere preceded Marx in discovering the labor theory of value, he here precedes Paul Goodman in the concept of social chaos being caused by an "unfinished revolution."

Chapter Three, "The Principle of Association," argues that capitalist society is *structured* in a topsy-turvy and cock-eyed way. Here he begins to introduce his concept of *anarchy*, and his chief (but not only) argument for it is that it will be less chaotic, more orderly, than capitalistic democracy. Under the facade of equality and representational government in our system Proudhon sees the ancient relationship of Master and Slave not basically abolished. Land tenure and the banking monopoly both come down to us from the Roman slave state, he says, and as long as they last we will always be basically slaves. Here he offers his new model of non-governmental society: anarchism, which he defines as a system "based not on *force* but on *contract*." Here also he criticizes the Blanquist socialists (the forerunners of modern Communism) for their attempt to create a new society in which *force* will still be a State monopoly thus producing a new form of tyranny where the abolition of tyranny is called for. They, too, he predicts, will make an unfinished revolution.

Chapter Four, "The Principle of Authority," is probably the most devastating attack ever written on parliamentary democracy, and should be compulsory reading for those "liberals" who keep complaining that Cuba hasn't had elections since her revolution. With blistering sarcasm Proudhon writes of how "laws, decrees, edicts, ordinances, resolutions . . . fall like hail upon the people. After a while the political ground will be covered with paper, which the geologists will put down among the vicissitudes of the earth as the *papyraceous formation.* . . . At present, the Bulletin of Law contains, it is said, more than fifty thousand laws; if our representatives do their duty, this enormous figure will soon be doubled, Do you suppose that the people, or even the Government itself, can keep their reason in this labyrinth?" Here his attack on the *chaos* of capitalist-democracy comes to its culmination. The whole idea of the State is wrong, upside-down, irrational; it has its origin in theology and demonology; there is no place for the Principle of Authority among those who pretend to democracy and equality. The State is an invention of the kings, he adds angrily, and should have been abolished when they were. We are still suffering chaos because the Revolution of the 18th Century was unfinished.

Chapter Five, "Social Liquidation," considers the "divine rights" which should have been abolished along with royalty but weren't: the money monopoly, by which a handful of bankers control the monetization of credit; the land monopoly, by which a handful of landlords "own" the earth and force the rest of us to pay tribute for living and working on it; and the system of laws by which these monopolies are protected against free competition. Proudhon shows how poverty, crime, disease and war are caused directly by these monopolies; and he shows how they can be abolished, without violent revolution and without expropriation. Here it is especially difficult to summarize his thinking briefly; the basis of it all is his "Bank of the People," which lends *without charging interest.* (Douglas's Social Credit League which worked so successfully in Alberta, Gesell's stamp scrip which performed social miracles in Worgle until the bankers" monopoly had it suppressed by the State, the Credit Unions now pioneering non-usurious finance in Nova Scotia and elsewhere, are all offshoots of the basic Proudhonian concept.) Proudhon shows how the abolition of interest by the People's Bank will force universal abolition of interest through that free competition which is supposed to be, but isn't, a feature of capitalism. Nobody will borrow at interest, when he can borrow without interest; the capitalist banks will not be able to compete with the People's Bank. Next, Proudhon turns to the land monopoly, and proposes a solution much more rational than Henry George's (or the socialists'): after a certain date, he says, let all rent payments be considered as installments toward purchase, and let the price of all land be fixed at the traditional twenty times the annual rent; within twenty years, the workers will own the land, and the landlords will not have been forcibly expropriated. Following the abolition of the money and land monopolies, prices will automatically fall to a level near the cost of production, since the manufacturer, not having to add rent and interest to his overhead, will not be able to pocket the difference either, due to competition. Thus, the basic aims of socailism will be achieved without a tyrannical bureaucracy and without violent expropriation of present proprietors.

Chapter Six, "The Organization of Economic Forces," presents the total anatomy of a society based on contract instead of force. In its amazingly logical structure and its painstaking attention to detail, this chapter is impossible to summarize, even more so than Chapter Five. Instead, I quote a brief passage giving the general conception without the details:

"That I may remain free; that I may not have to submit to any law but my own, and that I may govern myself . . . everything in the government of society which rests on the divine must be suppressed, and the whole rebuilt on the human idea of CONTRACT.

"When I agree with one or more of my fellow citizens for any object whatever, it is clear that my own will is my law; it is I myself who, in fulfilling my obligation, am my own government. . .

"Thus the principle of contract, far more than that of authority, would bring about the union of producers, centralize their forces, and assure the unity and solidarity of their interests.

"The system of contracts, substituted for the system of laws, would constitute . . . the true sovereignty of the people, the REPUBLIC . . .

"The contract, finally, is order, since it is the organization of economic forces, instead of the alienation of liberties, the sacrifice of rights, the subordination of wills."

The final chapter, "Absorption of Government by the Economic Organism," deals with the peaceful dissolution of the State into the system of contractual associations. Each such association might, in a sense, be called a small government; but it would be different in essence from traditional political government in that membership is voluntary instead of compulsory. The possibility of tyranny—even of the tyranny of the majority—will become zero. It is important not to misunderstand Proudhon here: don't think of the Shoemakers' Association planning long-range programs to which the individual shoemaker must submit. *Contract* implies a specific agreement for a specific purpose, to which all parties to the contract agree from motives of rational self-interest. It is not to be confused with a *law* binding upon an indefinite number of cases unto infinity. Proudhon is so aware that "each case is unique" one almost suspects he has been studying general semantics. There simply is no possibility, under his system, for a man getting trapped into compulsory obedience to a condition he didn't voluntarily accept by signing a contract.

What can we say of this magnificent edifice of creative and constructive social thought? There is no way to do justice to the mind which saw through the errors of all the other reformers of its age and clung stubbornly to the idea of freedom against all the blandishments of "State planning"; there are no words to praise the originality, precision, imagination and logic of this man, Proudhon. The only fitting comment is that, one hundred and eleven years after he wrote, the chaos he dreaded is still in action everywhere, and the concept of orderly contractual society which he invented is still not understood by either conservatives or radicals. The only way to honor him is to forget all about praising his obvious genius and to make his dream come true. The unfinished revolution has been unfinished for too long.

* * *

TO BUSINESS MEN.

T O you, business men,[1] I dedicate these new essays. You have always been the boldest, the most skilful revolutionaries.

It was you who, from the third century of the Christian era, drew the winding-sheet over the Roman Empire in Gaul, by your municipal federations. Had it not been for the barbarians, whose coming suddenly changed the aspect of affairs, the republic which you established would have ruled the Middle Ages. Remember that the monarchy in our country is Frankish, not Gallic.

It was you who later vanquished feudalism, arraying the town against the castle, the king against the great vassals. Finally, it is you who, for eighty years past, have proclaimed, one after the other, all the revolutionary ideas — liberty of worship, liberty of the press, liberty of association, liberty of commerce and industry: it is you who, by your cleverly drawn constitutions, have curbed the altar and the throne, and established upon a permanent basis equality before the law, publicity of State records, subordination of the Government to the people, the sovereignty of Opinion.

It is you, you alone, yes, you, who have set up the principles and laid the foundation for the Revolution of the Nineteenth Century.

Nothing survives of the attacks which have been made upon you.

Nothing which you have undertaken has fallen short. Nothing at which you aim will fail.

Despotism has bowed its head before Business: the victorious Soldier,[2] the legitimate Anointed,[3] the citizen

---

All footnotes are the Translator's.

[1] Bourgeois. This untranslatable word and its kindred have been translated by different approximations, all inadequate.
[2] Napoleon Bonaparte.
[3] Louis XVIII.

King[4] glided away like phantoms as soon as they had the misfortune to displease you.

Business men of France, the initiative in the progress of humanity is yours. The untutored workingman accepts you as his masters and models. Is it possible that, after having accomplished so many revolutions, you have yourselves become counter-revolutionaries, against reason, against your own interest, against honor?

I know your grievances: they do not date only from February.[5]

One day, the 31st of May, 1793, you were taken by surprise and were supplanted by the shirt-sleeved brigade. For fourteen months, the most terrible period that you have ever encountered, the helm was in the hands of the leaders of the mob. What could they do for their unfortunate supporters during those fourteen months of popular dictatorship? Alas, nothing! Presumptuous and boasting, as usual, their effort reduced itself to continuing as well as they could, your task. In 1793, just as in 1848, those elected by the people — who for the most part were not of the people — cared for nothing but for preserving the rights of property: they cared nothing for the rights of labor. The whole power of the government, outside of its resistance to foreign enemies, was devoted to maintaining your interests.

None the less, you were wounded by this assault upon your ancient privileges. Because the people, through inexperience, did not know how to continue the revolution which you had begun, you seemed, from the morrow of Thermidor[6] on, to oppose this new revolution. This was a halt in progress for our country and the beginning of our expiation. The people thought to avenge themselves by voting for the autocracy of a hero as a curb to your insolence. You had sowed resistance, you reaped despotism. Glory, the most

---

[4] Louis Philippe.
[5] 1848: The establishment of the Second Republic.
[6] 9 Thermidor (27 July, 1794): Execution of Robespierre and installation of the reactionary régime.

foolish of divinities and the most murderous, took the place of liberty. For fifteen years the tribune was silent, the upper classes humiliated, the Revolution blocked. At last, thanks to you, the Charter of 1814[7], extorted, not conceded, whatever they may say, launched it again upon the world; fifteen years had not passed when the old regime met its Waterloo in those July days.

In 1848, the people, supported, as in '93, by your bayonets, drove an old knave[8] from the Tuileries, and proclaimed the Republic. In so doing, it only made itself the interpreter of your sentiments, drawing the legitimate conclusion from your long opposition. But the people had not yet been initiated in political life: for the second time they failed in controlling the revolution. And, as in '93, their presumption again aroused your wrath.

Nevertheless what evil had the inoffensive people done during their three months interregnum, that you should show yourselves such ardent reactionaries when you had scarcely been restored to power? The Provisory Government had done nothing but try to soothe your vanity, to calm your disquiet. Its first thought was to recall you to the family council: its only desire to make you the guardian of the lower classes. The people looked on and applauded. Was it then in reprisal for this traditional goodfellowship, or on account of their usurpation of your place, that, when you had been reestablished in your political preponderance, you treated these simple revolutionaries like a pack of rascals and criminals, that you shot, transported and sent to the hulks poor workmen who had been driven to revolt by starvation, and whose sacrifice served as a stepping stone to three or four intrigues in the Executive Commission and the Assembly? Gentlemen, you were cruel and ungrateful. Moreover the repression which you enforced after the events of June cried for vengeance. You became accomplices of reaction; you ought to be ashamed of yourselves.

---

[7] At the first Restoration under Louis XVIII.
[8] Louis Philippe.

And now, corrupt political schemers of every stripe, the objects of your eternal hatred have reappeared. The clericals have clapped their extinguisher on you: friends of the foreigner have made you finance their anti-national policy: the hangers-on of all the tyrannies which you had overthrown make you their associates daily, in their liberty-destroying vengeance. In three years your pretended saviors have covered you with ignominy, exceeding the wretchedness which half a century of failures has left to the workers. And these men, whom your blind passion has permitted to grasp unlimited power, scorn you and deride you; they call you enemies of order, incapable of discipline, infected with liberalism and socialism: they look upon you as *revolutionaries.*

Gentlemen, accept this name as the title of your glory and the pledge of your reconciliation with the workingmen. Reconciliation is revolution, I assure you. The enemy has established himself in your domain, let his insults be your rallying-cry. You, the elder sons of the Revolution, who have seen so many despotisms born and dead, from the Caesars to the last of the Bourbons, you cannot escape your destiny. My heart tells me that you will yet accomplish something. The people are waiting for you, as they did in '89, '93, 1830, 1848. The Revolution stretches out her arms to you; save the people, save yourselves, as did your fathers, through the Revolution.

Poor Revolution! everybody throws a stone at it. They who do not slander it distrust it, and strive to divert it. One talks of extending the powers of the President: another discourses upon the fusion of the two branches, and of the necessity of putting an end to the choice between monarchy and democracy. One pleads for the Constitution of 1848; another demands direct legislation. You might call it a conspiracy of empirics against the idea of February.

If this policy could serve any purpose; if it were endowed with the smallest power for restraint and peace, I should remain silent: I should not care, gentlemen, to disturb your peace. But, admit it or deny it as you like, the Revolution is rushing upon you with a speed of a million leagues a second. It is not a question for discussion: it requires preparation to receive it, and above all, to understand it.

During the leisure given by a long imprisonment, when Power, breaking my journalist's pen, held me aloof from the polemics of the day, my revolutionary soul betook itself to travels in the realm of Ideas.

From my wanderings I have brought back from beyond the prejudices of our worn-out world, a few seeds which cannot fail to grow, if planted in the soil that we have prepared for them. You, gentlemen, may have the honor of first planting them: the first fruit will be to remind you of the only thing with which it is worth while at this time to concern yourselves — the Revolution.

And may bolder explorers than myself, encouraged by my example, at last complete the discovery, of which men have dreamed so long, of the Democratic and Social Republic!

Greeting and fraternity.

P. J. PROUDHON.

Conciergerie, 10 July, 1851.

GENERAL IDEA

OF

THE REVOLUTION

IN

THE NINETEENTH CENTURY.

———

IN every revolutionary history three things are to be observed:

The preceding state of affairs, which the revolution aims at overthrowing, and which becomes counter-revolution through its desire to maintain its existence.

The various parties which take different views of the revolution, according to their prejudices and interests, yet are compelled to embrace it and to use it for their advantage.

The revolution itself, which constitutes the solution.

The parliamentary, philosophical, and dramatic history of the Revolution of 1848 can already furnish material for volumes. I shall confine myself to discussing disinterestedly certain questions which may illuminate our present knowledge. What I shall say will suffice, I hope, to explain the progress of the Revolution of the Nineteenth Century, and to enable us to conjecture its future.

FIRST STUDY,   *Reaction causes Revolution.*

SECOND STUDY, *Is there sufficient reason for a revolution in the Nineteenth Century?*

THIRD STUDY,   *The Principle of Association.*

FOURTH STUDY, *The Principle of Authority.*

FIFTH STUDY,   *Social Liquidation.*
SIXTH STUDY,   *The Organization of Economic Forces.*
SEVENTH STUDY, *Dissolution of Government in the Economic Organism.*

This is not a statement of facts: it is a speculative plan an intellectual picture of the Revolution.

Fill it in with data of space and time, with dates, names, manifestoes, episodes, harangues, panics, battles, proclamations, manipulations, parliamentary man= oeuvres, assassinations, duels, &c. &c., and you will have a flesh and blood Revolution, as described in the pages of Buchez and Michelet.

For the first time the public will be able to judge of the spirit and form of a revolution before it is accomplished: who knows whether our fathers might not have avoided disaster, if they had been able to read in advance their destiny, in a general abstract account of the dangers, the parties and the men.

In this account I shall endeavor as far as possible to adduce facts as proofs. And among facts I shall always choose the simplest and best known: this is the only method by which the Revolution, hitherto a prophetic vision, can become at last a reality.

FIRST STUDY.

Reaction Causes Revolution.

1. The Revolutionary Force.

IT is an opinion generally held nowadays, among men of advanced views as well as among conservatives, that a revolution, boldly attacked at its incipiency, can be stopped, repressed, diverted or perverted; that only two things are needed for this, sagacity and power. One of the most thoughtful writers of today, M. Droz, of the Academie Francaise, has written a special account of the years of the reign of Louis XVI, during which, according to him, the Revolution might have been anticipated and prevented.

And among the revolutionaries of the present, one of the most intelligent, Blanqui, is equally dominated by the idea that, given sufficient strength and skill, Power is able to lead the people whither it chooses, to crush the right, to bring to nought the spirit of revolution. The whole policy of the Tribune of Belle-Isle — I beg his friends to take this characterization of him in good part — as well as that of the Academician, springs from the fear that he has of seeing the Reaction triumph, a fear that I am not afraid to call, in my opinion, ridiculous. Thus the Reaction, the germ of despotism, is in the heart of everybody; it shows itself at the same moment at the two extremes of the political horizon. It is not least among the causes of our troubles.

Stop a revolution! Does not that seem a threat against Providence, a challenge hurled at unbending Destiny, in a word, the greatest absurdity imaginable? Stop matter from falling, flame from burning, the sun from shining!

I shall endeavor to show, by what is passing before our eyes, that just as the instinct for conservatism is inherent in every social institution, the need for revolution is equally irresistible; that every political party may become by turns revolutionary and reaction= ary; that these two terms, reaction and revolution, correlatives of each other and mutually implying each other, are both essential to Humanity, notwithstanding the conflicts between them: so that, in order to avoid the rocks which menace society on the right and on the left, the only course is for reaction to continually change places with revolution; just the reverse of what the present Legislature boasts of having done. To add to grievances, and, if I may use the comparison, to bottle up revolutionary force by repression, is to condemn oneself to clearing in one bound the distance that prudence counsels us to pass over gradually, and to substitute progress by leaps and jerks for a continuous advance.

Who does not know that the most powerful sovereigns have made themselves illustrious by becoming revolutionaries within the limits of the circumstances wherein they lived? Alexander of Macedon, who reunited Greece, Julius Caesar, who founded the Roman Empire on the ruins of the hypocritical and venal Republic, Clovis, whose con= version was the signal for the definite establishment of Christianity in Gaul, and to a certain extent, the cause of the fusion of the Frankish hordes in the Gallic ocean, Charlemagne, who began the centralization of freeholds, and marked the beginning of feudalism, Louis the Fat, dear to the third estate on account of the favor he extended to the towns, Saint Louis, who organized the corporations of arts and crafts, Louis XI and Richelieu, who completed the defeat of the barons, all performed, in different degrees, acts of revolution. Even the execrable Bartholomew massacre was directed against the lords, rather than against the reformers, in the opinion of the people, agreeing in that respect with Catherine de Medicis. Not until 1614, at the last meeting of the States General, did the French monarchy seem to abjure its function of leadership and betray its tradition; the 21st of January, 1793[9] was the penalty for its crime.

It would be easy to multiply examples; anybody with the slightest knowledge of history can supply them.

A revolution is a force against which no power, divine or human, can prevail: whose nature it is to be strengthened and to grow by the very resistance which it encounters. A revolution may be directed, moderated, delayed: I have just said that the wisest policy lay in yielding to it, foot by foot, that the perpetual evolution of Humanity may be accomplished insensibly and silently, instead of by mighty strides. A revolution cannot be crushed, cannot be deceived, cannot be perverted, all the more, cannot be conquered. The more you repress it, the more you increase its rebound and render its action irresistible. So much so that it is precisely the same for the triumph of an idea, whether it is persecuted, harassed, beaten down during its beginning, or whether it grows and develops unobstructed. Like the Nemesis of the ancients, whom neither prayers nor threats could move, the revolution advances, with sombre and fatal step, over the flowers cast by its friends, through the blood of its defenders, across the bodies of its enemies.

When the conspiracies came to an end in 1822[10], some thought that the Restoration had overcome the Revolution. It was at this time, under the Villèle administration, and during his expedition to Spain, that insults were hurled at him. Poor fools! The Revolution had passed away: it was waiting for you in 1830.

When the secret societies were broken up in 1839, after the attacks of Blanqui and Barbès, again the new dynasty was believed to be immortal: it seemed that progress was at its command. The years that followed were the most flourishing of the reign. Nevertheless it was in 1839 that the serious disaffection began,

---

[9] The date of the execution of Louis XVI.
[10] After the second Restoration of Louis XVIII.

among the business men by the coalition, among the people by the uprising of the 12th of May, which ended in the events of February. Perhaps with more prudence, or with more boldness, the existence of the monarchy, which had become flagrantly reactionary, might have been prolonged a few years: the catastrophe, although delayed, would have been only the more violent.

Following February, we saw the Jacobins, the Gi= rondists, the Bonapartists, the Orleanists, the Legitimists, the Jesuits, all the old parties, I had almost said factions, that had successively opposed the revolution in the past, undertake, by turns, to put down a revolution which they did not even understand. At one time the coalition was complete: I dare not say that the Republican party came out of it well. Let the opposition continue, let it persist: its defeat will be universal. The more the inevitable overthrow is put off, the more must be paid for the delay: that is as elementary in the working=out of revolutions as an axiom in geometry. The Revolution never lets go, for the simple reason that it is never in the wrong.

Every revolution first declares itself as a complaint of the people, an accusation against a vicious state of affairs, which the poorest always feel the first. It is against the nature of the masses to revolt, except against what hurts them, physically or morally. Is this a matter for repression, for vengeance, for persecution? What folly! A government whose policy consists in evading the desires of the masses and in repressing their com= plaints, condemns itself: it is like a criminal who struggles against his remorse by committing new crimes. With each criminal act the conscience of the culprit upbraids him the more bitterly; until at last his reason gives way, and turns him over to the hangman.

There is but one way, which I have already told, to ward off the perils of a revolution; it is to recognize it. The people are suffering and are discontented with their lot. They are like a sick man groaning, a child crying in the cradle. Go to them, listen to their troubles, study the causes and consequences of them, magnify rather than minimize them; then busy yourself without relaxation in relieving the sufferer. Then the revolution will take place without disturbance, as the natural and easy development of the former order of things. No one will notice it; hardly even suspect it. The grateful people will call you their benefactor, their representative, their leader. Thus, in 1789, the National Assembly and the people saluted Louis XVI as the *"Restorer of Pubilc Liberty."* At that glorious moment, Louis XVI, more powerful than his grandfather, Louis XV, might have consolidated his dynasty for centuries: the revolution offered itself to him as an instrument of rule. The idiot could see only an encroachment upon his rights! This inconceivable blindness he carried with him to the scaffold.

Alas, it must be that a peaceful revolution is too ideal for our bellicose nature. Rarely do events follow the natural and least destructive course: pretexts for violence are plentiful. As the revolution has its principle in the violence of needs, the reaction finds its own principle in the authority of custom.

Always the *status quo* tries to prescribe for poverty; that is why the reaction has the same majority at first that the revolution has at the end. In this march in opposite directions, in which the advantage of the one continually turns into a disadvantage for the other, how much it is to be feared that clashes will occur! . . .

Two causes are against the peaceful accomplishment of revolutions: established interests and the pride of government.

By a fatality which will be explained hereafter, these two causes always act together; so that riches and power, together with tradition, being on one side, poverty, disorganization and the unknown on the other, the satisfied party being unwilling to make any con≠ cession, the dissatisfied being unable to submit longer, the conflict, little by little, becomes inevitable.

Then it is curious to observe the fluctuations of the struggle, in which all the unfavorable chances at first seem to be for the progressive movement, all the ele≠

2

ments of success for the resistance. They who see only
the surface of things, incapable of understanding an
outcome which no perspicacity, it seems to them, could
have anticipated, do not hesitate to accuse as the cause
of their disappointment, bad luck, the crime of this one,
the clumsiness of that, all the caprices of fortune, all
the passions of humanity. Revolutions, which for intelligent contemporaries are monsters, seem to the
historians who afterwards recount them the judgments
of God. What has not been said about the Revolution
of '89? We are still in doubt about that revolution, which
asserted itself in eight successive constitutions, which
remodelled French society from bottom to top, and
destroyed even the memory of ancient feudalism. We
have not compassed the idea of its historic necessity:
we have no comprehension of its marvellous victories.
The present reaction was organized in part through
hatred of the principles and tendencies of the Revolution. And among those who defend what was accomplished in '89, many denounce them who would
repeat it: having escaped, they fancy, by a miracle from
the first revolution, they do not want to run the risk
of a second! All are agreed then upon reaction, as
sure of victory as they are that they are in the right,
and multiplying perils around them by the very measures
which they take to escape them.

What explanation, what demonstration can turn them
from their error if their experience does not convince
them?

I shall prove in the different parts of this work, and
I am now about to establish in the most triumphant
manner, that for three years past the revolution has
been carried on only by the red, tricolor, and white
conservatives who welcomed it: and when I say, carried
on, I use the expression in the sense of the determination
of the idea, as well as the propagation of the deeds.
Make no mistake, if the revolution did not exist, the
reaction would have invented it. The Idea, vaguely
conceived under the spur of necessity, then shaped and
formulated by contradiction, is soon asserted as a right.

And, as rights are so bound together that one cannot
be denied without at the same time sacrificing all the
rest, the result is that a reactionary government is drawn
on, by the phantom which it pursues, to endless arbitrary
acts, and that, in endeavoring to save society from
revolution, it interests all the members of society in
revolution. In this way the ancient monarchy, dismissing
first Necker, then Turgot, opposing every reform, dissat-
isfying the Third Estate, the parliaments, the clergy,
the nobility, created the Revolution, I mean to say,
caused it to enter into the world of facts — the
Revolution, which since then has not ceased to grow in
extent and in perfection, and to extend its conquests.

2. Parallel Progress of the Reaction and of the Revolution
since February.

In 1848 the lower class, suddenly taking part in the
quarrel between the middle class and the Crown, made
its cry of distress heard. What was the cause of its
distress? Lack of work, it said. The people demanded
work, their protest went no further. They embraced
the republican cause with ardor, those who had just
proclaimed the Republic in their name having promised
to give them work. Lacking better security, the people
accepted a draft on the Republic. That was sufficient
to make it take them under its protection. Who would
have believed that the next day those who had signed
the agreement thought only of burning it? Work, and
through work, bread, this was the petition of the
working classes in 1848; this was the unshakeable basis
given by them to the Republic; this is the Revolution.
Another thing was the proclamation of the Republic
on the 25th of February, 1848, the action of a more or
less intelligent, more or less usurping, minority; and yet
another, the revolutionary question of work, which gave
to this republic an interest, and alone gave it real value,
in the eyes of the masses. No, the Republic of February
was not the revolution; it was the pledge of revolution.
2*

It is not the duty of those who govern this Republic, from the highest to the lowest, to see that the pledge is not broken: it is for the people, at the next election, to determine on what further conditions they will accept it.

At first this demand for work did not seem exorbitant to the new officials, of whom not one up to this time had cared anything for political economy. On the contrary, it was the subject for mutual congratulations. What a people was that which, on the day of its triumph, asked for neither bread nor amusements, as formerly the Roman mob had demanded, — *panem et circenses* — but asked only for work! What a guaranty among the laboring classes of morality, of discipline, of docility! What a pledge of security for a government! With the greatest confidence, and, it must be admitted, with the most praiseworthy intentions, the Provisory Government proclaimed the *right to labor!* Its promises, no doubt, bore witness to its ignorance, but the good intention was there. And what cannot be done with the French people by the manifestation of good intentions? There was not at this time an employer so surly that he was not ready to give work to everybody, if the power were granted to him. *The Right to Labor!* The Provisional Government will claim from posterity the glory of this fateful promise, which confirmed the fall of the monarchy, sanctioned the Republic, and made the Revolution certain.

But making promises is not all: they must be kept.

Looking more closely, it is easy to see that the right to labor was a more ticklish business than had been suspected. After much debate, the Government, which spent 300 million dollars annually to preserve order, was forced to admit that it had not a cent left wherewith to assist the workers; that in order to employ them, and consequently to pay them, it would be necessary to impose additional taxes, making a vicious circle, because these taxes would have to be paid by those whom they were intended to assist. Moreover, it was not the business of the State to compete with private industry, for which already consumption was lacking and an outlet was demanded; and, still further, for the State to take part in production could only end in aggravating the condition of the workers. In consequence, for these reasons, and for others not less peremptory, the Government made it understood that nothing could be done, that it was necessary to be resigned, to keep order, to have patience and confidence!

It must be admitted that the Government was right to a certain extent. In order to assure work, and in consequence, exchange, to all, it becomes necessary, as we shall show, to change the course and to modify the economy of society; a serious matter, quite beyond the power of the Provisory Government, and upon which it became its duty to consult the Country as a preliminary. As for the plans which were thereupon proposed, and the semi-official conferences with which the lack of work of the laborers was beguiled, they merit the honor neither of record nor of criticism. They were so many pretexts of conservatism, which soon showed itself, even in the bosom of the Republican party.

But the mistake of the men in power, which exasperated the working class, and which turned a simple labor question in less than ten years into definite revolution, was when the Government, instead of inviting the researches of publicists, as did Louis XVI, instead of appealing to the citizens, and asking them their wishes upon the great questions of labor and poverty, shut itself up for four months in a hostile silence; when it was observed to hesitate about granting the natural rights of men and citizens, to distrust liberty, even liberty of the press and of assembly, to refuse the petitions of patriots relating to bail bonds and the stamp tax, to spy upon the clubs instead of organizing and directing them, to create for emergency from the volunteer guard a body of praetorians, to intrigue with the clergy, to recall the troops to Paris, that they might fraternise with the people, to arouse hatred against *Socialism*, the new name for the Revolution; then, whether from recklessness, or incapacity, or misfortune, or plotting and treachery, or all these together, to force penniless crowds at Paris and at Rouen into a desperate struggle; finally, after victory, to have but one thought, one idea, to smother the cry of the workers, the protest of February, by any means, lawful or unlawful.

It is enough to glance over the series of decrees of the Provisory Government and of the Executive Committee to convince oneself that during this period of four months repression was planned, prepared, organized, and revolt was provoked, directly or indirectly, by Power.

This reactionary policy, let it never be forgotten, was conceived in the bosom of the Republican party, by men who were scared at the memory of Hébert, of Jacques Roux, of Marat, and who believed themselves in good faith to be aiding the Revolution by combatting all manifestations to the limit. It was governmental zeal which divided the members of the Provisory Government into two opposing factions, leading some to desire open conflict against the Revolution, in order that they might rule through the prestige given by victory; others to prefer the display of superior force and the distractions of politics and of war, in order to restore quiet by rendering agitation wearisome and futile. Could it have been otherwise? No, because each shade of opinion regarded its emblem as that of the true Republic, and devoted itself patriotically to the destruction of its rivals, whom it regarded as too moderate or too extreme. The Revolution could not fail to be caught between these rollers: it was too small then and too low down to be perceived by its formidable guardians.

I recall these occurrences, not for the empty pleasure of stigmatizing men who were more ill-advised than culpable, and whom the course of things, it seems to me, restored to power: but rather to remind them that, as the Revolution defeated them once, it will overcome them a second time, if they persist in the course of distrust and of secret defamation which they have hitherto adopted towards it.

Thus, through governmental prejudice and proprietary tradition, whereof the intimate union constitutes the

whole political and economic theory of the old liberal=
ism, the Government—I make no allusion to individuals,
I understand by this word the sum of powers, before
June and after — the Government, I repeat, through its
hatred of certain Utopians, more noisy than dangerous,
believed it had the right to withhold the most vital
question of modern societies, although justice and
prudence required an appeal to the country upon the
demands of the working classes. That was its mistake;
let that be to it also a lesson.

From that moment it was recognized that the Republic,
whether yesterday's or that of '93, could never be, in
the nineteenth century, the same thing as the Revolu=
tion. And if Socialism, so calumniated at that time by
the very persons who, since then, recognizing their
mistake, have come in turn to ask its alliance, if Social=
ism, I say, had aroused this quarrel, if, in the name of
the deceived workers, of the betrayed Revolution, it had
pronounced against the Republic, Jacobin or Girondin,
it is all the same, this Republic would have been
overwhelmed in the election of the 10th of December,[11]
the Constitution of 1848 would have been only a
transition to empire. Socialism had higher views; with
unanimous consent it sacrificed its own grievances, and
gave its voice for republican rule. By this it increased
its danger, for the moment, rather than strengthened
itself. What follows will show whether its tactics were
wise.

Thus was battle joined between all=powerful interests,
skilful and inexorable, which took advantage of the
traditions of '89 and '93, and a revolution still in the
cradle, divided against itself, honored by no historic
antecedent, rallying about no ancient formula, moved
by no definite idea.

In fact, what crowned the peril of Socialism, was that
it could not say what it was, could not phrase a single
proposition, could not explain its grievances nor support
its conclusions. What is Socialism? was asked. And

---

[11] 10th of December, 1848, when Louis Napoleon was elected President.

twenty different definitions at once vied in showing the emptiness of the cause. Fact, right, tradition, common sense, everything, united against it. Besides there was this argument, irresistible with a people brought up in the worship of the old revolutionaries, — a worship that is still murmured among them — that Socialism now is not that of '89 nor of '93, that it does not date from the great period, that Mirabeau and Danton would have disdained it, that Robespierre would have guillotined it, after having branded it, that it is the revolutionary spirit depraved, the politics of our ancestors gone astray!... If at that moment Power had found one man who could understand the Revolution, he might have moderated its impetus at his pleasure, profiting by the small favor which it encountered. The Revolution, if it had been welcomed by the ruling classes, would have slowly developed during a century, instead of precipitating itself with racehorse speed.

Matters could not happen thus. Ideas are made definite by their contraries: the Revolution will be made definite by the reaction. We lack formulas: the Provisory Government, the Executive Committee, the dictatorship of Cavaignac, the Presidency of Louis Bonaparte, have undertaken to provide them for us. The folly of governments makes the wisdom of revolutionaries: without this legion of reactionaries which has passed over our bodies, we could not say, my Socialist friends, who we are nor whither we are bound.

Again I declare that I make no charge against the intentions of anybody. I profess to believe still in the goodness of human intentions: without it, what becomes of the innocence of statesmen, and why have we abolished the death penalty in political cases? Soon the reaction will fall; it would be without moral justification as well as without reason, it would do nothing toward our revolutionary education, if its representatives, holding all sorts of opinions, did not form a continuous chain, extending from the peak of the Mountain, and ending among the extreme Legitimists.

It is the character of the Revolution of the Nineteenth Century to separate itself, day by day, from the excesses of its adversaries and from the mistakes of its defenders; so that no one can boast of having been perfectly orthodox at every moment of the struggle. We all, whatever we might have been, failed in 1848; and that is precisely why we have made so much progress since 1848.

Scarcely had the blood shed in the affair of June been dried, when the Revolution, overcome in the streets, began again to thunder through the newspapers and through popular meetings, more explicitly and more accusingly than ever. Three months had not passed when the Government, surprised at this indomitable persistence, demanded new weapons from the Constituent Assembly. The riot of June had not been put down, it asserted: without a law against the freedom of the press and against public meetings, it could not be responsible for keeping order and preserving society.

It is of the essence of reaction to show its evil tendencies under the pressure of revolution. The ministers of Cavaignac said aloud, what a certain member of the Provisory Government, now reinstated in favor with the people, had thought in his secret confidences.

But it is also natural to beaten parties to join the opposition; therefore Socialism might count on at least some of its former adversaries making common cause with it. This was indeed what happened.

The mechanics, together with a good many tradespeople, continued to demand work. Business was not good; the peasants complained of high rents and the low price of farm produce; they who had combatted the insurrection and pronounced against Socialism, demanded as a recompense subsidies for the immediate present, and guaranties for the future. The Government could see in all this nothing but a passing epidemic, the result of unfortunate circumstances, a sort of intellectual and moral cholera-morbus, which must be treated with bleeding and sedatives.

In this, the Government found itself hampered by limitations! The law no longer sufficed for its protection; it must have martial rule. Socialism, on the contrary, declared itself republican, and stood upon the law, in the most disquieting manner, as within a fortress. So it was that at every effort at reaction, the law was always with the revolutionaries, and against the conservatives. Never was such bad luck. The saying of a minister of the old monarchy, "Legality is our ruin!" became true again under the republican government. Either law must be done away with, or the revolution must advance!

Repressive laws were granted, and several times made more rigorous. As I write, freedom of assemblage has been abolished; the revolutionary press no longer exists. What fruit has the Government gathered from this antiphlogistic medication?

In the first place, the demand for liberty of the press has united with the assertion of the right to labor. The revolution has added to its ranks all the old friends of public liberty, who refuse to believe that gagging the press was a remedy for the contagion of ideas. Then, as propaganda through the press had been suspended, propaganda by word of mouth began; that is to say, the strongest revolutionary method was opposed to the violence of reaction. In two years the Revolution made more way through this intimate talk of a whole people than it could have made in a century by daily dissertations. While the reaction wreaks its vengeance upon type, the revolution wins by the spoken word: the sick man who was to have been cured of fever, is torn by convulsions!

Are not these the facts? Are we not all daily witnesses of them? In attacking, one after the other, all forms of liberty, has not the reaction as often reaffirmed the revolution? And is it not contemporaneous history, this romance that I seem to be writing, whereof the absurdity far surpasses those of Perrault's stories? The Revolution never prospered so much as since the most eminent statesmen conspired against it, and its organs disappeared from the stage. Moreover all that shall be undertaken against the Revolution will strengthen it: let us cite only the principal facts.

In a few months the revolutionary malady had infected twothirds of Europe. Its chief centres were Rome and Venice in Italy, and Hungary beyond the Rhine. The Government of the French Republic, in order to repress the Revolution at home with more certainty, did not hesitate to make a foreign conquest. The Restoration had made the Spanish war against the liberals: the Reaction of 1849 made the expedition to Rome against the *Social=Democracy* — I employ these two words as indicating the progress which the Revo= lution had made in one year. Certain descendants of Voltaire, heirs of the Jacobins, — could anything else be expected from Robespierre's acolytes? — had conceived the idea of bringing aid to the Pope, and thus uniting the Republic and Catholicism: the Jesuits carried it out. Beaten at Rome, the Social=Democracy tried to protest at Paris: it was dispersed without a struggle.

What did the Reaction gain? To the hatred of kings in the heart of the people was added hatred of priests; and the war against governmental authority throughout Europe was complicated by war against religious authority. In 1848, the only question, the doctors said, was of political excitement: very soon, through the futility of the remedies, it became an economic question; now it is called religious. Is not medicine useless? What further physic can we use?

Evidently it was a case when politicians of the smal= lest common sense would have retreated: it was just this moment that they selected to push reaction to its utmost. No, they said, a nation has no right to poison itself, to assassinate itself. The Government has charge of its soul: its duties are those of the guardian and the father. The safety of the people is the highest law. Do what you ought, come what may!

It was resolved that the Country should be purged, bled, cauterized to the limit. A vast sanitary system was organized and followed with a devotion which would have done honor to the apostles. Hippocrates, saving Athens from the plague, did not seem more magnanimous. The Constitution, the electorate, the National Guard, the municipal councils, the University, the army, the police, the courts, all were passed through the flames. The business world, that everlasting friend of order, was accused of liberal inclinations, and involved in the same suspicions as the working classes. The Government went so far as to say, by the mouth of M.Rouher, that it did not regard itself as sound, that its origin was a stain, that it carried in itself the revolutionary poison: *Ecce, in iniquitatibus conceptus sum!*[12] . . . Then it got to work.

Instruction, based upon reason only, by secular teachers selected by examination, could not be depended upon. The Government thought it essential to place teaching under the authority of the Faith. It was announced to the world that instruction, like the press, was no longer free, by the subjection of primary teachers to the priests and to the lay brothers, by handing the City Colleges over to the Congregationists, by placing public teaching in charge of the clergy, by astonishing dismissals of professors after their denunciation by bishops. What did the Government gain by this treatment? By its jesuitical annoyance it threw them all into the Revolution, men devoted as they were to the education of youth, with nothing timid about them.

Then it was the army's turn.

Coming from the people, recruited every year from among them, in perpetual contact with them, nothing would have been less certain than its obedience, in the face of an aroused populace and a violated constitution. An intellectual diet, together with complete isolation, and the prohibition of thought, of conversa-

---

[12] Lo, I was conceived in iniquity.

tion and of reading on political and social topics was prescribed. No sooner did the slightest sign of con‧tagion appear in a regiment, than it was at once purified, removed from the capital and from populous centres, and sent as discipline to Africa. It is hard to discover what the soldier thought: it is at least certain that the treatment to which he was subjected for more than two years proved to him, in the most unequivocal way, that the Government wanted neither the Republic, nor the Constitution, nor liberty, nor the right to labor, nor universal suffrage; that the plan of the ministers was to reestablish the old order in France, as they had reestablished the rule of priests at Rome, and that they counted on him! ... Will the suspicious soldier swallow this dose? The Government hopes so; that is the question! ...

It was to the National Guard that the party of order owed its first successes, in April, May, and June of 1848. But the National Guard, while it put down the riot, had no idea of aiding the counter‧revolution. More than once it said so. It was said to be sick. Of all the cares of the Government, that which most occupies its attention is the disbandment, or at least, the disarm‧ament, of the National Guard, gradually, not all at once, that would not do. Against a National Guard armed, organized, ready for battle, reactionary wisdom knows no protection. The Government cannot believe itself safe as long as a single citizen soldier remains in France. National Guards! You cannot be turned from liberty and progress, advance toward the Revolution!

Like all monomaniacs, the Government is perfectly logical in its idea. It follows it with wonderful punctuality and perseverance. It quite understood that the cure of the nation, and of Europe, of which it had constituted itself the physician, might not have reached the point where popular elections could be done away with, and that the unfortunate patient, driven crazy by his medicines, might break his bonds, overpower his guards, and in one hour of madness might destroy the fruit of three years of treatment.

Already an imposing majority, in voting upon the electoral question, in March and April of 1850, had voted for revolution — *monarchy or republic* — that is to say, revolution or *status quo*. How ward off such a danger and save the people from its own frenzy?

It is necessary now, say the wiseacres, to proceed indirectly. Let us separate the people into two categories, the one comprising all the citizens who, from their position, are presumed to be the most revolutionary; they are to be excluded from universal suffrage; the other, all those who, from their standing, are more inclined to keep things as they are: these will form the electoral body. What of it, that by this suppression we shall have eliminated three million individuals from the voting lists, if the seven remaining million accept their privilege? With seven million voters and the army, we are sure to overcome the revolution; and religion, and authority, and the family, and property, are saved!

Twenty-seven notabilities in political and moral science, they say, were present at this consultation of men of consummate skill in checkmating revolutions and revolutionaries. The ordinance was presented to the Legislative Assembly, and was confirmed on the 31st of May.

Unfortunately it was impossible to make a law of privilege which should also be a list of suspects. The law of the 31st of May, cutting right and left almost equally among Socialists and Conservatives, only served to stir up revolution the more, by rendering the reaction odious. Among the seven million voters who were retained, four million perhaps belonged to the democracy. Add to these the three millions of the discontented who were shut out, and you will have the relative strength of the revolution and the counter-revolution, at least as regards the electoral privilege. Moreover, see the folly of it! It was just the very voters of the party of order, in whose favor the law of the 31st of May had been drawn, who were the first to denounce it: they blame it for all their present evils, and for the greater ills which they anticipate in the future; they are loudly demanding its repeal in their newspapers. And the best reason for believing that this law will never be put into execution, is that it is perfectly useless, the interest of the Government being rather to withdraw from its support than to defend it. Is that enough of blundering and scandal?

The reaction has made the revolution grow as in a hotbed during the last three years. By its policy, at first equivocal, then veering, finally openly absolutist and terrorist, it has created an innumerable revolutionary party, where before not one man could be reckoned. And, good heavens! what was the use of all this arbitrariness? To what end all this violence? Against whom lay the complaint? What monster, inimical to civilisation and society, did they seek to combat? Did anybody know whether the Revolution of 1848 was right or wrong? This revolution that had never defined itself? Who had studied it? Who, with his hand upon his heart, could accuse it? Deplorable hallucination! Under the Provisional Government and the Executive Committee the revolutionary party did not exist, except in the air: the idea of it, with its mystical formulas, had yet to be discovered. By its declaration against this spectre, the reaction has converted the spectre into a living body, a giant, which with a single gesture may crush it. That which I myself could scarcely conceive before the day of June; which since then I have come to understand only gradually, and under the fire of the reactionary artillery, I dare now assert with certainty: the Revolution has taken shape, it understands itself, it is completed.

3. Weakness of the Reaction: Triumph of the Revolution.

And now, reactionaries, you are reduced to heroic measures. You have carried violence to a point where you are hated, despotism to where you are distrusted, the abuse of your legislative power up to disloyalty. You have lavished scorn and outrage: you have sought blood and civil war. All this has produced as much effect on the Revolution as an arrow upon a rhinoceros. They who do not hate you, despise you. They are wrong: you are honest people, full of tolerance and philanthropy, moved by the best intentions, but your mind and conscience are upside down. I disregard whatever you may resolve, whether you continue to attack the revolution, or determine to treat with it, as I expect you will do. But if you select the former course, I will tell you what you must do; you your‹ selves may judge what you have to expect.

The people, according to you, are affected by mental alienation. It is your mission to cure them: public security is your only law, your highest duty. As you are accountable to posterity, you would dishonor your‹ selves by deserting the post at which Providence has placed you. You are in the right; you have the force; your resolution is clear.

All the regular methods of government having failed, your further policy is comprised in one word: FORCE.

Force, in order to prevent society from committing suicide; that means that you must put a stop to every revolutionary manifestation, every revolutionary thought, that you must put the nation in an iron strait jacket, hold the twenty‹six departments in a state of siege, suspend the laws generally everywhere, attack the evil at its source by deporting from the country and from Europe the authors and fomenters of anarchical and antisocial ideas, prepare for the restoration of the old institutions by conferring upon the Government discretionary power over property, industry and commerce, &c., until a perfect cure is effected.

Do not bargain about the absolute rulership: do not dispute over the choice of a dictator. Legitimate monarchy, half legitimate, a combination of parties, imperialism, total or partial revision of the Constitution, all that, believe me, is of no importance. The promptest action is the surest. Remember that it is not the form of government that is in question: it is society. Your only care should be to take your measures prudently; because if at the last moment the Revolution gets away from you, you are lost.

If the prince who is now in power were president for life, if at the same time the Assembly, uncertain of the voters, could prorogue itself as the Convention used to do, until the convalescence of the invalid, the solution would perhaps seem to be discovered. The Government would only have to keep still and have masses celebrated in all the churches of France, for the restoration to health of the People. There would be little need of doing anything against insurrection. Legality, in this land of journalists, is so powerful, that there is no oppression, no outrage, that we are not ready to endure, as soon as they speak to us *In the Name of the Law.*

But by the terms of the fundamental agreement, Louis Bonaparte leaves office at the end of April, 1852; as for the Assembly, its powers expire on the 29th of May following, at the very height of revolutionary ardor. All is lost if things go as the Constitution prescribes. Lose not a moment: *Caveant consules!*

Then as the Constitution now is the cause of all the danger, as there is no legal solution possible, as the Government cannot count on the support of any part of the nation, as the gangrene has involved everything, you must take counsel only of yourselves and of the immensity of your duties, on pain of forfeiture and cowardice.

In the first place the Constitution must be revised by you, by AUTHORITY; at the same time Louis Bonaparte must be prorogued in his powers, by AUTHORITY.

This prorogation will not suffice, as the elections of 1852 may give a demagogic Assembly, of which the first act will be the impeachment of the reelected President and his ministers. Therefore the President, at the same time that he is prorogued by the Assembly,

3

will prorogue the Assembly in his turn, and by
AUTHORITY.

After these first acts of dictatorship, the General
and Municipal Councils, duly renewed, will be asked to
send in their adhesion, on pain of immediate dissolution
and of the dispatch of commissioners.

It is likely that this double prorogation of the
president and of the Assembly will be followed by some
disturbance; it is a risk to be run, a battle to be joined,
a victory to win.

"To conquer without danger is to triumph without
glory."

Decide.

Then you must abolish universal suffrage, as well as
the law of the 31st of May, and return to the system of
M. Villèle and to the double vote; better still, suppress
the whole representative system, while waiting for the
reclassification of the nation in orders, and the
restoration of feudalism on a more solid basis.

Suppose then that the Revolution, so violently
provoked, does not stumble, or that if it does stumble,
it is crushed; suppose that the two hundred republican
representatives do not answer the usurping acts of the
majority by a declaration that they are unlawful,
prepared, signed and published in advance; that,
following this declaration, the authors of the *coup
d'État* are not struck down in the street, in their homes,
anywhere that the avenging hand of patriotic bands
can reach them; suppose that the populace does not rise
in mass, at Paris and in the provinces; that a part of
the troops, upon whom the reaction places its hopes,
does not join the insurgents; suppose that two or three
hundred thousand soldiers are enough to hold down
the revolutionaries of thirty-seven thousand towns, to
which the *coup d'État* will serve as a signal; suppose
that, lacking relief, the refusal to pay taxes, the
stoppage of work, the interruption of transportation,
devastation, conflagrations, all the fury foreseen by the
author of *The Red Spectre*, do not block the counter-
revolution in its turn; suppose that it is enough for the

head of the executive power, elected by four hundred
conspirators, for the eighty=six prefects, the four
hundred and fifty=nine subprefects, the procurers=
general, the presidents, the councillors, substitutes,
captains of police, commissioners of police, and some
thousands of notabilities their accomplices, to present
themselves to the masses in order to make them return
to their duty.

Suppose, I say, that any one of these conjectures, so
likely, so probable, is not realized, it will be necessary,
if you expect your work to stand:

1. To declare the state of siege general, absolute, and for
an unlimited time;
2. To decree the deportation beyond the seas of a
hundred thousand individuals;
3. To double the effective strength of the army, and to
keep it constantly on a war footing;
4. To increase the garrisons and the police, to arm all the
fortresses, to build in each district a strong castle, to
interest the military in the reaction, by making the
army an endowed and ennobled caste, which can
partly recruit itself;
5. To rearrange the people in corporations of arts and
crafts, no one accessible to any other; to suppress free
competition; to create in commerce, industry, agri=
culture, property, finance, a privileged trading class,
which will join hands with the aristocracy of the army
and the Church;
6. To expurgate or burn nine=tenths of the books in the
libraries, books of science, philosophy and history; to
do away with every vestige of the intellectual
movement for four centuries; to commit the direction
of studies and the archives of civilization to the
Jesuits exclusively;
7. To increase the taxes two hundred million dollars, and
issue new loans, in order to cover these expenses, and
to erect a special and inalienable privilege for the
support of the new nobility, as well as of the churches,
seminaries and convents.

3*

That is an outline of the policy and of the measures for organization and repression which the reaction must adopt in order to carry out what it has undertaken, if it wants to be logical and to follow its fortune to the end. It constitutes a social regeneration which carries civilization back to the fourteenth century, and restores feudalism, with the aid of the new elements furnished by the modern spirit and by experience of revolutions. To hesitate or to stop halfway would be to lose disgracefully the fruit of three years of effort, and to rush to certain, irreparable disaster!

Have you thought of this, reactionaries? have you reckoned the power that has been acquired by the Revolution through three years of pressure? Have you realized that the monster has grown his claws and teeth, and that if you cannot strangle him he will devour you?

If the reaction counts on the prudence of the country, and waits for the elections of 1852, it is lost. Upon this point almost everybody is agreed, both in the Government and among the people, whether republicans or conservatives.

If it limits itself to proroguing the powers of the President, it is lost.

If, after having prorogued the powers of the Assembly by the same decree, it allows the law of the 31st of May to stand, it is lost.

If it permits the hundred thousand most active republican socialists to remain in the country, it is lost.

If it allows the present numerical weakness of the army, and its present mode of recruiting to stand, it is lost.

If, after having restored the military caste, it fails to reconstruct industry and commerce on feudal principles, it is lost.

If it does not reestablish large properties and the right of primogeniture, it is lost.

If it does not completely reform the system of instruction and of public education, if it does not efface the very memory of past insurrections from the minds of the people, it is lost.

If it does not double the taxes, and succeed in collecting them, to cover the expenses of such great undertakings, it is lost.

Are you able to attempt even the first of these indispensable measures, from which a single omission will plunge you into the abyss? Do you dare to proclaim to the people this unconstitutional resolution: *The powers of Louis Bonaparte have been prorogued*?

No, you can do nothing, you can dare nothing, royalists, imperialists, bancocrats, Malthusians, Jesuits, who have used and abused force against ideas. You have wasted time and lost your reputation, without advantage for your safety.

Prorogue or not; revise everything or revise nothing; summon Chambord and Joinville, or come over to the Republic; all that signifies nothing. You will hold a National Convention, if not in 1852, then in 1856. The revolutionary idea is triumphing; in order to combat it you have no recourse but to republican law, which you have not ceased for three years to violate. Your only refuge is in that make-believe republic, which in 1848 was forced to be honest and moderate, as if honesty and moderation could exist where principle was lacking — that republic whose ignominious nakedness you are now exhibiting to the world. Do you not see her, calling to you and stretching out her hands to you, sometimes under the appearance of the most pacific sentiments, sometimes under the mask of the most inflated orations. Go then, to this republic — this constitutional, parliamentary, governmental republic, steeped in Jacobinism and in religion, which is none the less ruled by the formula of counter-revolution, whether it invokes the name of Sièyes, or appeals to that of Robespierre. After you have exhausted violence, trickery remains to you: in that also we are ready to meet you.

But to the republicans of February I say, — to that party which, without distinguishing shades of opinion, the Revolution may reproach for some errors, but not for crime:

It was you who gave the signal for reaction in 1848, by your ambitious rivalries, by your routine politics, by your retrospective fancies, almost at the same moment that you proposed the revolutionary question, unknown to yourselves.

You see what the reaction has done.

Before the battle of June, the Revolution was hardly aware of itself; it was but a vague aspiration among the working classes toward a less unhappy condition. Such complaints have been heard at every period; if it was a mistake to despise them, it was unnecessary to fear them.

Thanks to the persecution which it has suffered, the Revolution of today is fully conscious of itself. It can tell its purpose: it is in the way to define itself, to explain itself. It knows its principles, its means, its aim; it possesses its method and its criterion. In order to understand itself, it has needed only to follow the connection of ideas of its different adversaries. At this moment it is discarding the erroneous doctrines which obscured it, the parties and traditions which encumbered it: free and brilliant, you are about to see it take possession of the masses, and drive them toward the future with irresistible inspiration.

The Revolution, at the point at which we have arrived, is completed in thought, and needs only to be put into execution. It is too late to give vent to the mine: if the power which has come back into your hands should change its policy toward the Revolution, it would obtain no result, unless it changed its principles at the same time. The Revolution, I have just told you, has grown its teeth: the Reaction has been only a fit of teething sickness for it. It must have solid food: a few fragments of liberty, a few concessions to the interests which it represents, will only serve to increase its hunger. The Revolution means to exist, and to exist, for it, is to reign.

Are you willing then to serve this great cause; to devote yourselves, heart and soul, to the Revolution?

You may, for there is still time, again become the chiefs and regulators of the movement, save your country from a serious crisis, emancipate the lower classes without turmoil, make yourselves the arbiters of Europe, decide the destiny of civilization and of humanity.

I know well that such is your fervent desire; but I do not speak of desire, I want acts —pledges.

Pledges for the Revolution, not harangues; plans for economic reconstruction, not governmental theories: that is what the lower classes want and expect from you. Government! Ah! we shall still have enough of it, and to spare. Know well that there is nothing more counter-revolutionary than the Government. Whatever liberalism it pretends, whatever name it assumes, the Revolution repudiates it: its fate is to be absorbed in the industrial organization.

Speak then, for once, straightforwardly, Jacobins, Girondists, Mountainists, Terrorists, Indulgents, who have all deserved equal blame, and all need equal pardon. Fortune again favoring you, which course will you follow? The question is not what you would have done in a former exigency: the question is what you are going to do now, when the conditions are no longer the same.

Will you support the Revolution — yes or no?

SECOND STUDY.

Is there Sufficient Reason for Revolution in the Nineteenth Century?

1. Law of *Tendency* in Society. — The Revolution of 1789 has done only half its work.

A revolution is an act of sovereign justice, in the order of moral facts, springing out of the necessity of things, and in consequence carrying with it its own justification; and which it is a crime for the statesman to oppose it. That is the proposition which we have established in our first study.

Now the question is to discover whether the idea which stands out as the formula of the revolution is not chimerical; whether its object is real; whether a fancy or popular exaggeration is not mistaken for a serious and just protest. The second proposition therefore which we have to examine is the following:

Is there today sufficient reason in society for revolution?

For if this reason does not exist, if we are fighting for an imaginary cause, if the people are complaining because, as they say, they are too well off, the duty of the magistrate would be simply to undeceive the multitude, whom we have often seen aroused without cause, as the echo responds to one who calls.

In a word, is the occasion for revolution presented at the moment, by the nature of things, by the connection of facts, by the working of institutions, by the advance in needs, by the order of Providence?

It should be possible to determine this at a glance. If a long philosophical dissertation were necessary, a cause might exist, but it would be only in the germ, only potentially. To weigh arguments in such a cause would be prophecy, not practical history.

To solve this question I will take a rule, as simple as it is decisive, with which the occurrences in past revolutions furnish me. It is that the motive behind revolutions is not so much the distress felt by the people at a given moment, as the prolongation of this distress, which tends to neutralize and extinguish the good.

Thus the trial which is instituted by a revolution, and the judgment which later it puts into execution, are related to *tendencies* rather than to the mere facts: society, as it were, paying little attention to principles, and directing its course solely toward *ends* . . .

Usually good and evil, pleasure and pain, are inextricably entangled in human dealing. Nevertheless, despite continual oscillations, the good seems to prevail over the evil, and, taking it altogether, there is marked progress toward the better, as far as we can see.

The reasoning of the masses is built upon this idea. The people is neither optimistic nor pessimistic; it admits the absolute not at all. Let is stay as it believes.

Always at each reform, each abuse to be destroyed, each vice to be combatted, it confines itself to seeking for something better, something less evil, and works for its own sanctification by labor, by study, by good behavior. Its rule of conduct is therefore: *A tendency toward comfort and virtue;* it does not revolt until it can see nothing for it but *A tendency toward poverty and corruption.*

Thus there was no revolution in the seventeenth century, although the retrograde feeling which was manifested in 1614 was already the principle of the royal policy, and although the poverty was frightful, according to the witness of La Bruyere, Racine, Fénélon, Vauban and Boisguilbert. Among other reasons for resignation was that it had not been proved that the poverty was anything more than the accidental effect of some temporary cause: the people remembered having been much more wretched not very long ago. The absolute monarchy under Louis XIV could not have appeared to them worse than feudalism.

Nor was there any revolution under Louis XV, except in the intellectual realm. The corruption of principles, visible to philosophers, remained hidden from the masses, whose logic never distinguishes an idea from a fact. Popular experience, under Louis XV, was far from being at the level of philosophical criticism. The nation still supposed that with a well-behaved and honest prince, its ills might have an end. Louis XVI too, was welcomed with fervor; while Turgot, the unbending reformer, was received without sympathy. The support of public opinion was lacking to this great man. In 1776, one might have said that a worthy man, who wanted to bring about reforms peacefully, had been betrayed by the people. It was not within his power to accomplish the Revolution by action from above without disturbance, I had almost said, without revolutionaries.

Fifteen years more of chaos were needed, under a monarch personally irreproachable, to prove to the most thoughtless that the trouble was not accidental but constitutional, that the disorganization was systematic, not fortuitous, and that the situation, instead of improving, was according to the usual fate of institutions, daily growing worse and worse. The publication of the Red Book in 1790, demonsrated this truth by figures. Then it was that the Revolution became popularized and inevitable.

The question which we have taken for the text of this study: — *Is there sufficient reason for a revolution in the nineteenth century?* — resolves itself into the following: — *What is the tendency of society in our day?*

Hence, but a few pages will suffice to support the answer which I do not hesitate to point out now. Society, as far as it has been able to develop freely for half a century, under the distractions of '89—'93, the paternalism of the Empire and the guaranties of 1814, 1830, and 1848, is on a road radically and increasingly wrong.

Let us take our point of view at the very beginning of present society, in 1789.

In 1798 the task of the Revolution was to destroy and rebuild at the same time. It had the old rule to abolish but only by producing a new organization, of which the plan and character should be exactly the opposite of the former, according to the revolutionary rule: Every negation implies a subsequent contradictory affirmation.

Of these, the Revolution, with great difficulty, accomplished only the first; the other was entirely forgotten. Hence this impossibility of living, which has oppressed French society for 60 years.

The feudal order having been abolished on the night of the 4th of August, and the principles of liberty and civil equality proclaimed, the consequence was that in future society must be organized, not for politics and war, but for work. What in fact was the feudal organization? It was one entirely military. What is work? The negation of fighting. To abolish feudalism, then, meant to commit ourselves to a perpetual peace, not only foreign but domestic. By this single act, all the old politics between State and State, all the systems of European equilibrium, were abrogated: the same equality, the same independence which the Revolution promised to bring about among individuals, must exist between nation and nation, province and province, city and city ...

What was to be organized after the 4th of August was not the Government, inasmuch as in restoring government nothing but the ancient landmarks would be restored; it was the national economy and the balance of interests. It was evident that the problem of the Revolution lay in erecting everywhere the reign of equality and industry, in place of the feudal order which had been abolished; inasmuch as, by the new principles, birth no longer counted in determining the condition of the citizen, work was all, even property itself was subordinate: inasmuch as, in foreign affairs, the relations of nations among themselves had to be reformed upon the same principles, since civil law, public law and the law of nations are one in principle and sufficient. The progress in agriculture which was exhibited after the division of the national treasure, the industrial impulse which the nation experienced after the fall of the Empire, the growing interest in all countries since 1830 in economic questions, all these go to prove that it was really in the field of political economy that the efforts of the Revolution should be exerted.

This so manifest, so inevitable conclusion from the act of the 4th of August, 1789, was not understood by those who made themselves its interpreters, even up to 1814.

All their ideas were of politics only. The counter= revolutionary forces aiding, the revolutionary party forced for the moment to place itself on the defensive and to organize itself for war, the nation was again delivered into the hands of the warriors and lawyers. One might say that nobility, clergy and monarchy had disappeared, only to make way for another governing set of Anglomaniac constitutionaries, classic republic= ans, militaristic democrats, all infatuated with the Romans and Spartans, and above all, very much so with themselves; on the other hand, caring but very little for the real needs of the country; which, understanding nothing of what was going on, permitted itself to be half destroyed at their leisure, and finally attached itself to the fortune of a soldier.

To put my thought in one word, however little edifying it may seem, the revolutionaries failed in their mission after the fall of the Bastille, as they have failed since the abdication of Louis Philippe, and for the same reasons: the total lack of economic ideas, their prejudice in favor of government, and the dis= trust of the lower classes which they harbored. In '93, the necessity of resistance to invasion demanding an enormous concentration of forces, the error was con= summated. The principle of centralization, widely ap= plied by the Committee of Public Safety, passed into a

dogma with the Jacobins, who transmitted it to the
Empire, and to the governments that followed it. This
is the unfortunate tradition which, in 1848, determined
the retrograde movement of the Provisory Government,
and which still constitutes the whole of the science
which nourishes the politics of the republican party.

Thus the economic organization called for as a
necessary consequence of the complete abolition of
feudalism, left without guidance from the first day,
politics taking the place of industry in the minds of
everybody, Quesnay and Adam Smith giving way to
Rousseau and Montesquieu; it necessarily followed that
the new society, scarcely conceived, should remain in
embryo; that, instead of developing according to econ=
omic laws, it should languish in constitutionalism, that
its life should be a perpetual contradiction, that, in
place of the orderly condition which is characteristic
of it, it should exhibit everywhere systematic corruption
and legal inefficiency; finally, that the power which
is the expression of this society, reproducing with the
most scrupulous fidelity the antinomy of its principles,
should find itself continually in the position of fighting
with the people and the people in continual need of
attacking power.

To sum up: the society which the Revolution of '89
should have created, does not yet exist. That which
for sixty years we have had, is but a superficial,
factitious order, hardly concealing the most frightful
chaos and demoralization.

We are not in the habit of looking so long beforehand
for the causes of social disturbances and revolutions.
Above all, economic questions are repugnant to us. The
people, after the great struggle of '93, has been so
distracted from its real interests, men of brains so
thrown off by the discussions of the legislative
chamber, of public meetings and of the press, that one
may be almost sure, in leaving politics for economics,
to be in turn immediately abandoned by readers, and
to have only the paper for a confidant. Nevertheless
we must understand that outside the sphere of

parliamentarism, as sterile as it is absorbing, there is another field incomparably vaster, in which our destiny is worked out; that beyond these political phantoms, whose forms capture our imagination, there are the phenomena of social economy, which, by their harmony or discord, produce all the good and ill of society. Will the reader deign to follow me for a quarter of an hour among the broad considerations into which I am obliged to enter? That done, I promise to come back to politics.

2. Chaos of economic forces. Tendency of society toward poverty.

I call certain principles of action *economic forces,* such as the Division of Labor, Competition, Collective Force, Exchange, Credit, Property, &c., which are to Labor and to Wealth what the distinction of classes, the representative system, monarchical heredity, administrative centralization, the judical hierarchy, &c., are to the State.

If these forces are held in equilibrium, subject to the laws which are proper to them, and which do not depend in any way upon the arbitrary will of man, Labor can be organized, and comfort for all guaranteed. If, on the other hand, they are left without direction and without counterpoise, Labor is in a condition of chaos; the useful effects of the economic forces is mingled with an equal quantity of injurious effects; the deficit balances the profit; Society, in so far as it is the theatre, the agent, or the subject of production, circulation and consumption, is in a condition of increasing suffering.

Up to now, it does not appear that order in a society can be conceived except under one of these two forms, the political and the industrial; between which, moreover, there is fundamental contradiction.

The chaos of industrial forces, the struggle which they maintain with the governmental system, which is the only obstacle to their organization, and which they cannot reconcile themselves with nor merge themselves

in, is the real, profound cause of the unrest which
disturbs French society, and which was aggravated
during the second half of the reign of Louis Philippe.

Seven years ago, I filled two octavo volumes[13] with
the story of these disturbances, and of the terrible con=
flicts which spring from them. This work, which
remained unanswered by the economists, was received
no more favorably by the Social=Democracy. I permit
myself to make this remark, merely to show by my own
experience how little favor researches in political econ=
omy obtain, how little revolutionary therefore is our
epoch.

I shall limit myself to recalling very briefly some of
the most general facts, in order to give the reader a
glimpse of this order of forces and phenomena, which
has been hidden from all eyes until now, and which
alone can put an end to the governmental drama.

Everybody has heard of the *division of labor.*

It consists of the distribution of the hand work of a
given industry in such a manner that each person
performs always the same operation, or a small number
of operations, so that the product, instead of being the
integral product of one workman, is the joint product
of a large number.

According to Adam Smith, who first demonstrated
this law scientifically, and all the other economists, the
division of labor is the most powerful lever of modern
industry. To it principally must be attributed the
superiority of civilized peoples to savage peoples.
Without division of labor, the use of machines would
not have gone beyond the most ancient and most com=
mon utensils: the miracles of machinery and of steam
would never have been revealed to us; progress would
have been closed to society; the French Revolution itself,
lacking an outlet, would have been but a sterile revolt;
it could have accomplished nothing. But, on the other
hand, by division of labor, the product of labor mounts
to tenfold, a hundredfold, political economy rises to

---

[13] The reference is to *Economical Contradictions.*

the height of a philosophy, the intellectual level of
nations is continually raised. The first thing that
should attract the attention of the legislator is the
separation of industrial functions — the division of
labor — in a society founded upon hatred of the feudal
and warlike order, and destined in consequence to
organize itself for work and peace.

It was not done thus. This economic force was left
to all the overturns caused by chance and by interest.
The division of labor, becoming always more minute,
and remaining without counterpoise, the workman has
been given other to a more and more degrading subjec=
tion to machinery. That is the effect of the division
of labor when it is applied as practised in our
days, not only to make industry incomparably more
productive, but at the same time to deprive the worker,
in mind and body, of all the wealth which it creates
for the capitalist and the speculator. Here is how an
observer, who is not suspected of sympathy with labor,
M. de Tocqueville, sums up on this grave subject:

"In proportion to the more complete application
"of the principle of the division of labor, the work=
"man becomes weaker, more limited and more depen=
"dent."

J. B. Say had already said:

"A man who all his life has performed but one
"operation certainly learns to execute it more
"quickly and more skilfully than another; but at the
"same time he becomes less capable of every other
"operation, whether physical or intellectual; his other
"faculties are extinguished, and degeneration results
"in him, considered as an individual. It is a sad
"account to offer of himself that he has never made
"more than the twenty=sixth part of a pin ... In result,
"it may be said that the division of labor is a skilful
"mode of employing the power of a man; that it
"adds prodigiously to the products of a society; but
"that it subtracts something from the capacity of
"each man taken individually."

All the economists are in accord as to this fact, one of the most serious which the science has to announce; and, if they do not insist upon it with the vehemence which they habitually use in their polemics, it must be said, to the shame of the human mind, that it is because they cannot believe that this perversion of the greatest of economic forces can be avoided.

So the greater the division of labor and the power of machines, the less the intelligence and skill of hand of the worker. But the more the value of the worker falls and the demand for labor diminishes, the lower are wages and the greater is poverty. And it is not a few hundreds of men but millions, who are the victims of this economic perturbation.

In England, through the division of labor and the power of machinery, the number of workmen has been observed to diminish by a third, by a half, by three-quarters, by five-sixths; and the wages decreasing in like proportion, fall from 60 cents a day to 10 cents and 6 cents. Throughout entire provinces the proprietors have driven out useless mouths. Everywhere first women, then children, have taken the place of men in manufacture. Consumption being unable to keep pace with production among an impoverished people, the latter is obliged to wait; and regular out-of-work periods are the result; of six weeks, three months and six months out of each year. Statistics of these periods of idleness by Parisian workmen have recently been published by one of them, Pierre Vincard; the details are heartrending. The smallness of the wages being in proportion to the time of idleness, the conclusion is reached that certain workwomen who earn 20 cents a day, must live on 10, because they are idle for six months. This is the rule to which a population of 320,000 in Paris must submit. And the situation of the class of working women everywhere throughout the Republic may the judged from this sample.

Philanthropic conservatives, admirers of ancient customs, charge the industrial system with this anomaly. They want to go back to the feudal-farming period.

4

I say that it is not industry that is at fault, but
economic chaos: I maintain that the principle has been
distorted, that there is disorganization of forces, and
that to this we must attribute the fatal tendency with
which society is carried away.

Another example.

Competition, next to the division of labor, is one of
the most powerful factors of industry; and at the same
time one of the most valuable guaranties. Partly for the
sake of it, the first revolution was brought about. The
workmen's unions, established at Paris some years since,
have recently given it a new sanction by establishing
among themselves piece work, and abandoning, after
their experience of it, the absurd idea of the equality
of wages. Competition is moreover the law of the
market, the spice of trade, the salt of labor. To sup≉
press competition is to suppress liberty itself; it is to
begin the restoration of the old order from below, in
replacing labor by the rule of favoritism and abuse, of
which '89 rid us.

Yet competition, lacking legal forms and superior
regulating intelligence, has been perverted in turn, like
the division of labor. In it, as in the latter, there is
perversion of principle, chaos and a tendency toward
evil. This will appear beyond doubt if we remember
that of the thirty≉six million souls who compose the
French nation, at least ten millions are wage workers,
to whom competition is forbidden, for whom there is
nothing but to struggle among themselves for their
meagre stipend.

Thus that competition, which, as thought in '89,
should be a general right, is today a matter of excep≉
tional privilege: only they whose capital permits them to
become heads of business concerns may exercise their
competitive rights.

The result is that competition, as Rossi, Blanqui, and
a host of others have recognized, instead of democra≉
tizing industry, aiding the workman, guaranteeing the
honesty of trade, has ended in building up a mercantile
and land aristocracy, a thousand times more rapacious

than the old aristocracy of the nobility. Through com=
petition all the profits of production go to capital; the
consumer, without suspecting the frauds of commerce,
is fleeced by the speculator, and the condition of the
workers is made more and more precarious. Speaking
of this, Eugene Buret says: "I assert that the working
"class is turned over, body and soul, to the sweet will
"of industry." And elsewhere he says: "The most
"trifling speculation may change the price of bread one
"cent a pound, which means $124,100,000 for thirty=six
"million people."

It was recently seen how little free competition could
do for the people, and how illusory it is as a guaranty
with us at present, when the Prefect of Police, yielding
to the general demand, authorized the sale of meat at
auction. Nothing less than all the energy the people
could muster, aided by governmental power, could
overcome the monopoly of the butchers.

Accuse human nature, say the economists, do not ac=
cuse competition. Very well, I will not accuse compe=
tition: I will only remark that human nature does not
remedy one evil by another, and ask how it has
mistaken its path. What? Competition ought to
make us more and more equal and free; and instead it
subordinates us one to the other, and makes the
worker more and more a slave! This is a perversion of
the principle, a forgetfulness of the law. These are
not mere accidents; they are a whole system of
misfortunes.

Pity is expressed for those who work in dangerous
or unwholesome occupations: it is desired that civiliz=
ation should do without their services, out of compas=
sion for their lot. These sad occurrences, inherent in
certain occupations, are nothing in comparison with the
scourge of economic chaos.

Let us cite one more example.

Of all economic forces, the most vital, in a society
reconstructed for industry by revolution, is *credit*. The
proprietary, industrial, trading business world knows
this well: all its efforts since '89 have tended, at the

4*

bottom, toward only these two things, peace and credit, all through the Constituent and Legislative Assemblies, the Convention, the Directory, the Empire, the Restoration, the monarchy of July. What did it not do to win over the unmanageable Louis XVI? What did it not pardon in Louis Philippe?

The peasant also knows it: of the whole of politics, he, like the business man, understands only these two things, taxes and interest. As for the working class, so marvellously fitted for progress, such is the ignorance in which it has been kept as to the true cause of its sufferings, that it is hardly since February that it has begun to stammer the word, credit; and to see in this principle the most powerful of revolutionary forces. In the matter of credit, the workingman knows but two things, his account with the baker and the pawn= broker's shop.

In a nation devoted to labor, credit is what blood is to an animal, the means of nutrition, life itself. It can= not be interrupted without danger to the social body. If there is a single institution which should have ap= pealed before all others to our legislators, after the abolition of feudal privileges and the levelling of clas= ses, assuredly it is credit. Yet not one of our pompous declarations of right, not one of our constitutions, so long drawn out, not one of these has mentioned it at all. Credit, like the division of labor, the use of machinery and competition, has been left to itself; even the FINANCIAL power, far greater than that of the executive, legislative and judicial, has never had the honor of mention in our various charters. Handed over by a decree of the Empire of the 23rd of April, 1803, to a company of revenue farmers, it has remained until now in the condition of a hidden power: hardly anything can be found relating to it, except a law of 1807, fixing the rate of interest at five per cent. After the Revolution as before it, credit got along as best it could; or rather, as it pleased the largest holders of coin. It is only fair to say that the Government, while sacrificing the Country, did not spare itself; it treated itself as it treated others: we have nothing against it on this score.

What has been the result of this incredible negligence?

In the first place, forestalling and usury being practised upon coin by preference, coin being at the same time the tool of industrial transactions and the rarest of merchandise, and consequently the safest and most profitable, dealing in money was rapidly concentrated in the hands of a few monopolists, whose fortress is the Bank.

Thereupon the Country and the State were made the vassals of a coalition of capitalists.

Thanks to the tax imposed by this bankocracy upon all industrial and agricultural industry, property has already been mortgaged for two billion dollars, and the State for more than one billion.

The interest paid by the nation for this double indebtedness, with costs, renewals, commissions and discounts on loans included, amounts to at least 240 million dollars.

This enormous sum of 240 millions does not yet express all that the producers have to pay to the financial exploitation: we should add from 140 to 160 million for discounts, advances, delays in payments, dividends, obligations under private seal, court expenses, &c.

Property, fleeced by the Bank, has been obliged to follow the same course in its relations with industry, to become a usurer in turn toward labor; thus farm rent and house rent have reached a prohibitive rate, which drives the cultivator from the field and the workman from his home.

So much so that today they whose labor has created everything cannot buy their own products, nor obtain furniture, nor own a habitation, nor ever say: This house, this garden, this vine, this field, are mine.

On the contrary, it is an economic necessity, in the present system of credit, and with the growing disorganization of industrial forces, that the poor man, working harder and harder, should be always poorer, and that the rich man, without working, always richer, as one may easily convince himself by the following.

If we may believe the estimate of a skilled economist, M. Chevé, out of two billions of value produced every year, one and one-fifth billions are taken away by parasites; that is to say, by finance, by predaceous property, and by the budget and its satellites: the balance, perhaps four-fifths of a billion, remains for the producers. Another able economist, M. Chevalier, dividing the estimated product of the country by its thirty-six million inhabitants, has found that the income per head per day was an average of 13 cents; and, as from this figure must be deducted enough to pay interest, rent, taxes, and the expenses which they involve, M. de Morogues, yet another learned economist, has concluded that for a large part of the population daily consumption was less than 5 cents. But since rents, the same as taxes, continually increase, while through economic disorganization work and wages diminish, it follows that, according to the aforesaid economists, the material comfort of the working classes follows a decreasing progression, which may be represented by this series of numbers: 65, 60, 55, 50, 45, 40, 35, 30, 25, 20, 15, 10, 5, 0, —5, —10, —15, &c. This law of impoverishment is the corollary of the Malthusian law; its fundamental fact may be found in every book of statistics.

Some utopians attack competition; others refuse to accept the division of labor and the whole industrial order; the workingmen, in their crass ignorance, blame machinery. No one, to this day, has thought of denying the utility and legitimacy of credit; nevertheless it is incontestable that the perversion of credit is the most active cause of the poverty of the masses. Were it not for this, the deplorable effects of the division of labor, of the employment of machinery, of competition, would scarcely be felt at all, would not even exist. Is it not evident that the tendency of society is towards poverty, not through the depravity of men, but through the disorder of its own elementary principles?

It may be said that this is a misuse of logic, that capital, land, houses, cannot be let for nothing, that every service should be paid for, &c. Possibly. I will admit that lending wealth, as much as creating it, is a service that merits recompense. When it is a question of the advantage of others, I would rather exceed justice than stop short of it; but that does not alter the facts. I maintain that credit is too dear; that it is with money as it is with meat, which the prefect of police supplies us with today from 3 to 5 cents cheaper than the market stall keepers; as it is with transportation, which would cost 80 per cent less than present rates, if the railroads could or would permit the country to use their immense resources. I say that it would be possible, yes, easy, to lower the price of credit from 75 to 90 per cent. without wronging the lenders, and that it depends upon the nation and the State that this should be done. Let there be no argument as to a pre= tended legal impossibility. It is with the seignorial rights of the capitalists as it was with those of the nobles and monasteries, nothing easier than to abolish them; and, I repeat, that for the safety of property itself they must be abolished.

Can it be believed that the revolutionaries of '89, '92, '93, '94, who swung the axe with such ardor against the feudal tree, would not have uprooted it to its last fibres, if they had foreseen that, in the shadow of their half=way governmentalism, such sprouts would grow?

Can it be believed that, instead of reestablishing the seignorial courts and the parliaments under other names and other forms, of re=erecting absolutism after bap= tising it with the name of Constitution, of enslaving the provinces as before, under the pretext of unity and centralization, of sacrificing all liberties, by giving them for an inseparable companion a pretended *public order,* which is but confusion, corruption and brute force — can it be believed, I say, that they would not have welcomed the new order, and completed the Revolution, if their sight had penetrated the organism which their instinct sought, but the state of knowledge and the distractions of the moment did not permit them to conceive? . . . . .

It is not only that our present society, through having forsaken its principles, tends continually to impoverish the producer, to subordinate labor to capital — a contradiction in itself — but that it tends also to make of workingmen a race of helots, inferior to the caste of free men as of old; and it tends to erect into a political and social dogma the enslavement of the working class and the necessity of its poverty.

A few facts, selected from among millions, will excmplify this fatal tendency.

From 1806 to 1811, according to Chevalier, the annual consumption of wine in Paris was 170 quarts per head: it is now only 95 quarts. Abolish the duties, which, with the accessory expenses, amount to at least 6 to 7 cents a quart with the retailer, and the consumption will increase from 95 to 200; moreover the vine grower, who does not know what to do with his products, will be able to sell them.

But in order to do this, it would be necessary either to reduce the amount of the budget, or to place the taxes upon the rich; and, as neither the one nor the other seems practicable, and besides as it is not well that the workingman should drink too much, seeing that the use of wine is incompatible with the modesty which is becoming in men of that class, the duties will not be lowered, neither will they be raised.

According to Raudot, a writer whose conservative opinions relieve him from any charge of exaggeration, France is reduced to buying annually in foreign markets nine million head of sheep and cattle for the slaughter house, despite the high tariff. Notwithstanding this importation, the quantity of meat offered for sale does not exceed an average of 40 lbs. per head per annum, a trifle less than 2 ounces a day. But if we recall that 85 cities, towns and capitals of provinces, with a total population of not more than 3 millions, absorb a quarter of this, the conclusion is reached that the majority of Frenchmen never eat meat; which is in fact true.

It is by virtue of this policy that wine and meat are today excluded from the list of articles of first necessity, and that so many people, in France as in Ireland, eat only potatoes, chestnuts, buckwheat or oatmeal.

The effects of this state of affairs are such as might be expected from theory. Everywhere in Europe the constitution of the laborer is weakened. In France, the Council of Revision has established that within fifty years the average stature has diminished by a half an inch, and this reduction bears chiefly upon suffering humanity, the working class. Before '89, the required minimum height for the army was 5 feet 1 inch. Afterwards following the diminution of stature and the weakening of health, as well as the excessive destruction of life, this was reduced to 4 feet 10 inches. As for exemptions from service for deficient height and health, they were, from 1830 to 1839, 45½ per cent., and from 1839 to 1848, 50 ½ per cent.

The average length of life, it is true, has increased, but at the expense of the same laboring class, as is proved, among other proofs, by the tables of mortality of Paris, in which the death rate for the 12th precinct is 1 in 26, while for the 1st precinct it is only 1 in 52.

Can it be doubted that there is a tendency toward ill in existing society, at least among the working people? Does it not seem that society has been made, as Saint Simon says, not for the amelioration of the people, physically, morally and intellectually, but for their impoverishment, depravity and ignorance?

The average number of students received each year by the Polytechnic School is, I believe, 176. According to Chevalier, it would not be exaggeration to say that twenty times as many might be received. But what would our capitalist society do with the 3520 graduates which the School would turn out at the end of each school year? I insist upon this question: What would it do?

When the management ordered that only 176 scholars should be received, in place of the 3520 who could be received, it was because it was not possible for the government, with its still feudal-industrial system, to make proper provision for more than 176 of these young people.

Science is not cultivated for the sake of science: one does not study chemistry, integral calculus, analytical geometry, mechanics, in order to become a mechanic or a laborer. Superabundance of ability, far from being of service to the country and the State, is an inconvenience to them. In order to avoid dangerous upsetting of classes, it is necessary that instruction should be given in proportion to fortune; that is should be slight or none at all for the most numerous and lowest class, moderate for the middle class, superior only for a small number of the well-to-do, destined to represent by their talents the aristocracy whence they sprang..... That is what the Catholic clergy, faithful to its principles, faithful to its feudal traditions, has always understood: the law placing the University and the schools in their hands was only an act of justice.

Thus, instruction cannot be universal, and, most of all, it cannot be free, in a still feudal society: that would be nonsense. It is necessary, in order to maintain the subordination of the masses, to restrain the flowering-forth of ability, to reduce the too numerous and too unmanageable attendance at colleges, to keep in systematic ignorance the millions of workers doomed to repugnant and painful labor, to make use of instruction by not making use of it, that is to say, by turning it toward the brutalization and exploitation of the lower classes.

And, as if evil as well as good must have its sanction, pauperism, thus foreseen, provided for, organized, by the economic chaos, has found its own; it is included in the criminal statistics. Here is the progression for 25 years past, of the number of arrests and of cases prosecuted at the request of the public prosecutor:

Years	Arrests	Cases
1827	47,443	34,908
1846	101,443	80,891
1847	124,159	95,914

In the district courts the progression has increased in the same way:

Years	Arrests	Cases
1829	159,740	108,390
1845	197,913	152,923
1847	239,291	184,922

When the workingman has been brutalized by the division of labor, by attending machines, by teaching that does not teach; when he has been discouraged by small wages, demoralized by being out of work, famished by monopoly; when he has neither bread nor dough, neither cash nor credit, neither fire nor hearth; then he lies, he thieves, he robs, he assassinates. After having passed through the hands of the plunderers, he passes through those of the dealers in justice. Is that clear?

Now I return to politics.

---

3. Anomaly of Government. Tendency toward Tyranny and Corruption.

It is by contrast with error that truth impresses itself upon the understanding. In place of liberty and industrial equality, the Revolution has left us a legacy of authority and political subordination. The State, growing more powerful every day, and endowed with prerogatives and privileges without end, has undertaken to do for our happiness what we might have expected from a very different source. How has it acquitted itself of its task? What part has the government played during the last fifty years, regardless of the particular form of its organization? What has been its tendency? That is now the question.

Up to 1848, statesmen, whether belonging to the ministry or the opposition, whose influence directed

public sentiment and governmental action, did not seem
to have been aware of the mistaken course of society
in what especially concerns the laboring classes. Most
of them indeed made it a merit and a duty to busy
themselves in the amelioration of the workers' lot. One
would cry out for teachers; another would talk against
the premature and immoral employment of children in
manufactories. This one would demand the lowering
of duties upon salt, beverages and meat; that one called
out for the complete abolition of town and custom
house tariffs. In the lofty regions of power there was
a general impulse toward economic and social ques=
tions. Not a soul saw that, in the present state of our
institutions, such reforms were but innocent chimaeras;
that, in order to bring them about, nothing less than a
new creation was necessary; in other words, a revolu=
tion.

Since the abdication of Louis Philippe, on the 24th of
February, the governmental set, participants in privi=
lege, have changed their opinion. The policy of op=
pression and impoverishment which they formerly fol=
lowed without knowing it, I had almost said, in spite
of themselves, has been accepted by many of them,
this time with full knowledge.

The government is the organ of society.

That which goes on in the social body most secretly,
most metaphysically, shows itself in government with a
quite military frankness, a fiscal crudity. A long time
ago a statesman said that a government could not exist
without a public debt and a large budget. This aphor=
ism, to which the opposition was wrong in taking
exception, is the financial expression of the retrograde
and subversive tendency of Power: we may now
measure the depth of it. It means that Government,
instituted for the guidance of society, is but the
reflection of society.

April 1st 1814, the interest on the public debt was $12,661,523
July 31st 1830, „   „   „   „   „   „   „   39,883,541
Jan. 1st 1847, „   „   „   „   „   „   „   47,422,671
Jan. 1st 1851, „   „   „   „   „   „   „   54,200,000

The public debt, for both the State and the towns, which it is fair to regard here as parts of the central authority, is about half of the sum total of mortgages and notes of hand, which weigh down the country: both of these, under the same impulse, have grown along with each other. The tendency is unmistakeable. Whither is it leading us? To bankruptcy.

The first regular budget since the Directory is that of 1802. Dating from this time, the expenses have continually grown, in the same progression as the debt of the country and of the State.

1802	$117,000,000.
1819	172,770,622.
1829	201,982,886.
1840	259,702,889.
1848	338,436,222.

In fifty years, the budget of expenses has almost tripled; the mean annual increase is about five millions. It would be too foolish to attribute this increase to the incapacity of ministers, to their more or less intelligent and liberal policy, as has been done under each succes‑ sive change: the Restoration and the monarchy of July, the dynastic opposition and the republican conspiracy. To explain a phenomenon as constant and regular as is the growth of the budget by the inefficiency of men, especially when it has its correlative in the increase of mortgages and of notes of hand, is as absurd as it would be to explain the Oriental plague and the yellow fever by the incapacity of physicians. It is the hygiene that must be attacked; it is your economic order that calls for reform.

Thus the Government, which is called the instrument of order and the guaranty of our liberties, keeps step with society, falls more and more into difficulties, incurs indebtedness, and tends toward bankruptcy. We are about to see how, as society, given over to the dis‑ organization of its elements, tends to reestablish the former castes; the Government, on its side, tends to unite its efforts with this new aristocracy and to com‑ plete the oppression of the lower classes.

Solely because the powers of society were left unorganized by the Revolution, there results an inequality of conditions, of which the cause is not, as formerly, the natural inequality of ability; but which finds a new pretext in the accidents of society, and adds, among its claims, the injustices of fortune to the caprices of nature. Privilege, abolished by law, is born again through lack of equilibrium: it is no longer a mere result of divine predestination: it has become a necessity of civilization.

Once justified as in the order of nature and of Providence, what does privilege lack in order to assure its triumph definitely? It has only to make laws, institutions, the Government, in harmony with itself: toward this end it is about to direct all its forces.

In the first place, as no law forbids, so far at least as it flows from one of these two sources, nature or accident, privilege may call itself perfectly legal: in this regard it may already claim the respect of citizens and the protection of Government.

What is the principle which rules existing society? *Each by himself, each for himself. God and* LUCK *for all.* Privilege, resulting from luck, from a commercial turn, from any of the gambling methods which the chaotic condition of industry furnishes, is then a providential thing, which everybody must respect.

On the other hand, what is the function of Government? To protect and defend each one in his person, his industry, his property. But if by the necessity of things, property, riches, comfort, all go on one side, poverty on the other, it is clear that Government is made for the defence of the rich against the poor. For the perfecting of this state of affairs, it is necessary that what exists should be defined and consecrated *by law:* that is precisely what Power wants, and what demonstrates from beginning to end our analysis of the budget.

I am talking at random.

The Provisory Government has made known that the increases of salary of Government functionaries from 1830 to 1848 amounted to the sum of 13 million dollars. Supposing that only half of this were used for the salaries of newly created offices, the average salary being assumed at $200, it follows that the Government added 32,500 employees during the reign of Louis Philippe. Today the total number of function= aries, according to Raudot, is 568,365: in every nine men there is one who lives on the Government, either of the Country or of the towns. Whatever outcry may be made against waste, I shall never believe that the creation of 32,500 offices was anything but plunder.

What interest had the king or the ministers, or any of the individuals who already held office, in adding to their number? Is it not true that, the agitation of the working classes becoming more threatening with time, and consequently the danger greater for the privileged class, Power, the force that represses and protects, had to fortify itself in proportion, on pain of being overthrown at the first opportunity?

Examination of the budgets for the army and navy confirms this opinion.

From 1830 to 1848, — I borrow this detail from the periodical *Europe and America* — the united budgets of the navy and of war were gradually raised from $64,796,000 to $107,167,400. The average annual amount was $84,000,000; the average increase $2,400,000. The grand total for eighteen years, $1,501,000,000.

In the same period the budget for public instruction increased from $451,600 to $3,859,600. The grand total was $46,560,400. Difference between this and the war= making budget, $ 1,454,439,000.

Thus while the Government spent an average of 2½ millions for fostering popular ignorance, under the name of public instruction, it spent 84 millions, thirty=two times as much, to restrain this ignorance by steel and fire, if the frenzy of poverty should cause it to burst forth. That is what the politicians of the day have called an *armed peace*. The same tendency is shown in the other budgets: I mean to say that the budgets have always increased in direct proportion to their services to the cause of privilege, and inversely to those which they could render to the producers. But when it is admitted that the lofty financial and administrative capacities which governed France during those eighteen years had no such intentions as are indicated by these comparisons of the budgets, which after all, matter little, it would remain not the less true that the system of impoverishment and repression by the State developed with a spontaneity and certainty that might well dispense with any complicity on the part of statesmen.

Once again, there is here no question of persons.

Above the spirit of men there is the spirit of things; it is with this latter that the philosopher concerns himself, always well disposed towards his fellows.

If the composition of the budget of expenses is curious, that of the account of receipts is no less instructive. I will not enter into details; the general character will suffice. It is in generalization that truth is discovered.

Since 1848 it has been proved by figures that if the existing system of duties were replaced by a single tax on capital of say, one per cent., the tax would be distributed with an almost ideal equality, uniting the advantages of proportionality and progression, without any of their drawbacks. By this system labor would be little if at all affected; capital, on the contrary, would be scientifically reached. Where capital was not protected by the labor of the capitalist, it would be exposed to levy; while the workingman, whose pos÷ sessions did not exceed a taxable amount, would pay nothing. Justice in taxation would be the *ne plus ultra* of fiscal science. But that would be the reverse of government. The proposition, scouted by the prac÷ tical politicians, served only to discredit and almost discourage its authors.

The system of taxation actually folowed is just the opposite of that. It is planned in such a way that the producer pays all, the capitalist nothing. In fact, whenever the latter is put down on the books of the assessor for any amount whatever, or pays the duties established by the fiscal authority on objects of consumption, it is clear that, as his income is composed solely of the interest upon his capital, and not by the exchange of his products, his income remains free from taxation; inasmuch as it is only the producer that pays.

That injustice had to be; and Government was in this in perfect accord with Society. If the inequality of conditions which results from the economic disorganization be taken as an indication of the will of Providence, the Government cannot do better than to follow his will; for that reason, not content with defending privilege, Government comes to its assistance by asking nothing from it. Grant the time, and Government will make privilege an Institution, under the titles of Nobility, Burghers, or otherwise.

There is therefore a compact between Capital and Power to make the worker exclusively pay the taxes; and the secret of this compact is simply, as I have said, to place the taxes on products, instead of on capital.

Through this disguise the capitalist seems to pay on his land, on his house, on his furniture, on his securities, on his travelling, on his food, like the rest of the citizens. Also he says that his income, which without tax would be 600, 1200, 2000 or 4000 dollars, is no more, thanks to the tax, than 500, 900, 1600 or 3000 dollars. And he complains against the amount of the budget with more indignation than his tenants.

A complete mistake. The capitalist pays nothing: the Government divides up with him; that is all. They make common cause. What one of the workers would not esteem himself lucky if he were granted $400 income, upon the sole condition that he should give up a quarter of it in redemption?

There is one chapter in the accounts of receipts that has always seemed to me like a reminiscence of the old system, that of assessment.

It is not enough that the producer pays for the liberty to manufacture, cultivate, sell, buy or transport that

5

the fiscal authority grants him; the assessments forbid him to hold property as far as possible. So much for an inheritance from a father, so much from an uncle, so much for a rental, so much for a purchase. It is as if the legislator of '89 had had the intention of reenacting the inalienability of real estate, in exact correspondence with feudal rights! As if he had wanted to remind the wretch who had been freed by the night of the 4th of August that he was still of servile condition, that he had no right to own the soil, that every cultivator is only a tenant and distrainable by law, unless he has permission from the sovereign! We must take care: there are people who hold these ideas religiously: those people are our masters and the friends of all those who lend to us on mortgage.

The partisans of governmental rule repel, with all the force of conviction, criticism which, instead of finding fault with men, attacks institutions, and endangers and threatens what they consider their hereditary rights.

Is it the fault, they cry, of our representative institutions? Is it the fault of the constitutional principle, or that of incapable, corrupt, wasteful ministers, if a portion of those millions, taken from property, from agriculture and from industry, at the price of so great sacrifices, have served only to support sinecures and to salve consciences? Is it the fault of this magnificent centralization, if the taxes, having become exorbitant, weigh more heavily upon the worker than on the proprietor; if, with a subsidy of 84 millions, our ports are bare of ships, our shops of materials; if, in 1848, after the revolution of February, the army was without provisions, the cavalry without horses, the fortifications in bad condition; if we could not put upon a war footing more than sixty thousand men? On the contrary, is it not a case in which not the system but the mode of carrying it out should be blamed? And then what becomes of your denunciations of the tendencies of society and of government?

Indeed! We may then add corruption to the intrinsic vices and feudal inclinations of the political order. Far from weakening my argument, it strengthens it. Corruption allies itself well with the general tendencies of Power; it forms a part of its methods; it is one of its elements.

What does the system demand?

That the capitalistic feudalism shall be maintained in the enjoyment of its rights; that the preponderance of capital over labor shall be increased; that the parasite class shall be reinforced, if possible, by providing for it everywhere hangers-on, through the aid of public functions, and as recruits if necessary, and that large properties shall be gradually reestablished, and the proprietors ennobled; — did not Louis Philippe, toward the end of his reign, devote himself to conferring titles of nobility? — that thus, by indirect ways, certain services, which the official list of offices cannot satisfy, shall be recompensed; finally, that everything shall be attached to the supreme patronage of the State — charities, recompenses, pensions, awards, concessions, exploitations, authorizations, positions, titles, privileges, ministerial offices, stock companies, municipal administrations, etc., etc.

This is the reason for that venality whereof the scandals under the last reign so surprised us; but at which the public conscience would have been less astonished, if the mystery had been explained. This too is the ulterior aim of that centralization which, under pretext of the general interest, exerts pressure upon local interests, by selling to the last and highest bidder the justice which they claim.

Understand clearly that corruption is the soul of centralization. There is not a monarchy nor a democracy that is free from it. Government is unchangeable in its spirit and essence; if it takes a hand in public economy, it is to establish, by favor or by force, what accident tends to bring about. Let us take the custom house for an example.

5*

Custom house duties, both import and export, but not including those on salt, produce 32 millions for the State. 32 millions to protect national industry! Do you perceive the jugglery? Suppose that the customs did not exist; that Belgian, English, German, American competition surrounded our markets on every side, and that then the State should make the following proposition to French industry: In order to protect your interests, which would you prefer to do, to pay me 32 millions or to receive them yourselves? Do you think that the industries would elect to pay them? That is just what the Government requires them to do. To the regular charges which foreign products and those which we send abroad cost us, the Government adds 32 millions, which serve it as drink-money; that is what the custom house amounts to. And the question today is so entangled, that there is not one person in the whole Republic who would dare to propose to abolish at one blow this absurd tribute.

Moreover this sum of 32 millions, said to be levied for the protection of national industry, is far from expressing all the advantage which the Government draws from the custom house.

The Department of Var is not well supplied with live-stock; it lacks meat, and would ask nothing better than to import cattle from Piedmont, a frontier province. The Government, the protector of the school-boy nation, will not permit it. What does this mean? That the lobbyists of the Camargue have more influence with the ministry than the would-be purchasers of Var: ask for no other reason.

The story of the Department of Var is that of the eighty-five remaining Departments. All have their special interests; are in consequence antagonists, and seek an arbitrator. It is these interests, far more than the army, which form the strength of the Government. Also, observe, the Government has made itself the grantor of mines, of canals, of railroads, in just the same way that the Court, before '89, sold the ranks of colonel and captain, as well as clerical benefices.

I can believe that all the personages who have taken charge of affairs since 1830 remained pure, except one; but is it not evident that if, through the remarkable integrity of French character, peculators are rare, nevertheless peculation is organized: it exists.

Toulon, situated on the sea, has lost its right to fish; do you know how? The city of Marseilles desiring the monopoly of this lucrative industry, the Government pretended that the nets of the Toulon fishermen hampered the movements of national vessels! That is why the inhabitants of Toulon import their fish from Marseilles.

For a long time the shipping trade has asked for the abolition of transportation duties on the canals, which yield an insignificant amount for the customs, but are a disastrous fetter on commerce. The Government objects that it is not free, that it needs a law of redemption, that, moreover, it is engaged upon a project of farming out the duties. The gist of it is that there exist franchises which hope to sell out at a high price; moreover, if the duties on navigation were abolished, the canals would compete with the railroads, and the holders of the railroad franchises, very often members of the ministry, have no interest in reducing the railroad charges. Do you suspect that Messrs. Leon Faucher, Fould, Magne, even the President of the Republic, make money out of their position? I do not. I only say that, if the man in power wants to peculate, he can do so; and that, sooner or later, he will. What am I talking about? Venality will soon be made one of the prerogatives of government. The tiger devours because he is built to devour, and you expect that a government built for corruption will not be corrupt?

Even charitable institutions serve the ends of those in authority marvellously well.

Charity is the strongest chain by which privilege and the Government, bound to protect them, holds down the lower classes. With charity, sweeter to the heart of men, more intelligible to the poor man than the abstruse laws of political economy, one may dispense with justice. Benefactors abound in the catalogue of saints; not one law dispenser is found there. The Government, like the Church, places fraternity far above justice. A good friend of the poor as much as you like, but it hates calculators. In connection with the discussion on pawnbrokers, the *Journal des Debats* recalled that there were already more than eight hundred county hospitals, and gave it to be understood that there would in time be hospitals everywhere. Loan offices, it added, showed the same progress; each town wanted one for itself, and would soon obtain it. I cannot conceive the indignation of the whole list of bourgeois delegates against the two honorable socialists who proposed to establish a loan office in each county immediately. Never was there a proposition more worthy of the favor of the *Debats*. The establishment for loans upon wages, even if the loan were gratuitous, is the antechamber of the hospital. And what is the hospital? The temple of Poverty.

Through these three ministries, that of agriculture and commerce, that of public works, and that of the interior, through the taxes on consumption and through the custom house, the Government keeps its hand on all that comes and goes, all that is produced and consumed, on all the business of individuals, towns and provinces; it maintains the tendency of society toward the impoverishment of the masses, the subordinating of the laborers, and the always growing preponderance of parasite offices. Through the police, it watches the enemies of the system; through the courts, it condemns and represses them; through the army it crushes them; through public instruction it distributes, in such proportions as suit it, knowledge and ignorance; through the Church it puts to sleep any protest in the hearts of men; through the finances it defrays the cost of this vast conspiracy at the expense of the workers.

Under the monarchy of July, I repeat, the men in power did not understand the thought which ruled them, any more than did the masses. Louis Philippe, Guizot and their associates did things with a simplicity

of corruption which was natural to them, making use
of ways and means marvellously well, but not perceiving
the end distinctly. After the lower classes had made
their formidable voice heard in the revolution of
February, the system began to be understood; it was
propounded with the effrontery of dogmatism, it was
called by its surname MALTHUS, and by its given
name, Loyola. At bottom, nothing was changed by the
event of February, any more than by those of 1830,
1814, 1793, from the order of pretended constitutional
things that had been founded in 1791. Louis Bonaparte,
whether he knows it or not, continues the rule of Louis
Philippe, the Bourbons, Napoleon and Robespierre.

Thus, in 1851 as in 1788, and from analogous causes,
there is in society a pronounced tendency towards
poverty. Now, as then, the wrong of which the laboring
class complains is not the effect of a temporary or
accidental cause, it is that of a systematic diversion
of the social forces.

This diversion dates from far back, even before '89.
It has its principle in the profundities of general economy. The first revolution, struggling against the most
manifest abuses, could act only on the surface. After
having destroyed tyranny, it did not know how to
establish order; whereof the principles were hidden
under the feudal ruins that covered the country.
Moreover, that revolution of which the history seems
so complete to us, was only a negation, and will appear
to posterity as only the first act, the dawn of the great
Revolution, which must occupy the nineteenth century.

The crash of '89 — '91 left no organic principle, no
working structure, after having abolished, together with
the monarchy, the last remains of feudalism, proclaimed
equality before the law and for taxation, freedom of the
press and of worship, and interested the people, as
much as it could, by the sale of national property. It
has not redeemed one of its promises. When the
Revolution proclaimed liberty of the people, equality
before the law, the sovereignty of the people, the
subordination of power to the country, it set up two

incompatible things, society and government; and it is
this incompatibility which has been the cause or the
pretext of this overwhelming, liberty⹁destroying
concentration, called CENTRALIZATION, which the
parliamentary democracy admires and praises, because
it is its nature to tend toward despotism.

M.Royer⹁Collard, in his speech upon the liberty of
the press (Chamber of Deputies, Debate of 19—24 Jan.
1822), expressed himself as follows:

"We have seen the old society perish, and with it a
"swarm of democratic institutions and of independent
"magistracies, which it bore within its bosom, a strong
"combination of private rights, veritable republics
"within the monarchy. These institutions, these mag⹁
"istracies, did not share the sovereignty, it is true, but
"everywhere they placed limits to it, which honor
"defended obstinately. Not one has survived, and
"none other has been erected in their place; the Revo⹁
"lution has left only *individuals.* In this respect, the
"dictatorship in which it culminated, completed its
"work. From this society reduced to dust, sprang
"centralization; its origin need not be sought elsewhere.
"Centralization did not come like other doctrines, head
"erect and with the authority of a principle. It crept
"in modestly, as a necessary consequence. In fact,
"where there are only individuals, all business which is
"not theirs is public business, business of the State.
"Where there are no independent magistrates, there
"are only delegates of the central power. Thus we
"have become a bureau⹁ruled people, under the hand of
"responsible functionaries, themselves centralized in the
"power of which they are the ministers. In this condi⹁
"tion, society was bequeathed to the Restoration.

"The charter then had to reestablish Govern⹁
"ment and Society at the same time. Society
"was not forgotten nor neglected, indeed, but left
"out. The Charter reestablished only the Govern⹁
"ment; and did so by the division of sovereignty
"and the multiplicity of powers. But in order that a
"nation may be free, it is not enough that it be govern⹁

"ed by several powers. The division of sovereignty
"brought about by the Charter, is, no doubt, an
"important accomplishment, and one which has mighty
"consequences, relatively to the royal power which
"it modifies; but the Government which results
"from it, although separated into its elements, is one
"in practice; and, if it meets no outside obstacle which
"it must respect, it is absolute: the nation and the
"nation's rights are its property. It was only when
"it established liberty of the press, that the Charter
"restored Society to its own."

What M.Royer=Collard said of the royalty of 1814,
is even more true of the Republic of 1848.

The Republic had Society to establish: it thought
only of establishing Government. Centralization contin=
ually fortifying itself, while Society had no institution
to oppose to it, through the exaggeration of political
ideas and the total absence of social ideas, matters
reached a point where Society and Government could
not live together, the condition of existence of the
latter being to subordinate and subjugate the former.

Therefore, while the problem propounded in '89
seemed to be officially solved, at the bottom there was
change only in governmental metaphysics — what
Napoleon called *ideology*. Liberty, equality, progress,
with all their oratorical consequences, are written in the
text of the constitutions and the laws; there is no
vestige of them in the institutions. The ancient
hierarchy of classes has been replaced by an ignoble
feudalism, based on mercantile and industrial usury; by
a chaos of interests, an antagonism of principles, a
degradation of law: the abuses have changed the face
which they bore before '89, to assume a different form
of organization; they have diminished neither in
number nor gravity. On account of our being
engrossed with politics, we have lost sight of social
economy. It was in this way that the democratic party
itself, the heir of the first Revolution, came to at=
tempting to reform Society by establishing the initiative
of the State, to create institutions by the prolific virtue

of Power, in a word, to correct an abuse by an abuse.

All minds being bewitched with politics, Society turns in a circle of mistakes, driving capital to a still more crushing agglomeration, the State to an extension of its prerogatives that is more and more tyrannical, the laboring class to an irreparable decline, physically, morally and intellectually.

For many people it is to advance a scandalous and paradoxical proposition, filled with difficulty and disaster, to say that the Revolution of '89, having established nothing, has freed us not at all, but only changed our sad lot; to say that, in consequence, a new revolution to organize and reconstruct is necessary, to fill the void left by the former. The more or less pledged partisans of the constitutional monarchy will not agree; the democrats attached to the letter of '93, who are frightened at such a task, are opposed. According to one or the other, nothing is left but accidental grievances, due chiefly to the incapacity of the depositaries of power, which a vigorous democracy could cure. Thence the disturbance, not to say antipathy, with which the Revolution inspires them; and thence too this reactionary policy in which they have engaged since February.

Nevertheless, such is the evidence of facts, so greatly have statistics and investigations elucidated the matter, that it is more than folly or bad faith to argue in favor of a better policy, when everything shows the contradiction and the weakness of Government.

In place of this governmental, feudal and military rule, imitated from that of the former kings, the new edifice of industrial institutions must be built; in place of this materialist centralization which absorbs all the political power, we must create the intellectual and liberal centralization of economic forces. Labor, commerce, credit, education, property, public morals, philosophy, art, everything in fact require it of us.

I conclude:

There is sufficient cause for a revolution in the nineteenth century.

THIRD STUDY.

The Principle of Association.

The Revolution of '89 had the industrial order to build, after having made a clean sweep of the feudal order. By returning to political theories, it plunged us into economic chaos.

In place of a natural order, conceived in accordance with science and labor, we have a factitious order, in the shadow of which have developed parasite interests, abnormal morals, monstrous ambitions, prejudices at variance with common sense, which today all claim to be legitimate, invoking a tradition of sixty years, and, being unwilling either to abdicate or to modify their demands, place themselves in an antagonistic attitude toward one another, and in a reactionary attitude toward progress.

As this state of affairs, of which the principle, the means and the end is WAR, is unable to answer the needs of an entirely industrial civilization, revolution is the necessary result.

But, as everything in the world is material for usury, when the need for a revolution makes itself plain to the masses, at the same time there arise theories, schools, sects, which take possession of the stage, secure the favor of the people by more or less plausible statements, and, under color of ameliorating their lot, of vindicating their rights, of reestablishing them in the exercise of their authority, work earnestly for their own pockets.

Therefore, before seeking a solution of the problem presented to modern society, it is worth while to estimate the value of the theories offered for popular consumption, the unavoidable luggage of all revolutions. In a work of this nature, utopias may not be passed by in silence; on the one hand, because, as an expression of parties and sects, they play a part in the drama; on the other, because, error being most often but a

distortion or counterpart of truth, the criticism of partial
views renders the comprehension of the general idea
easier.

Let us lay down first a rule of criticism with regard
to revolutionary theories, as we laid down a criterion
upon the hypothesis of revolution itself.

To ask whether there was sufficient reason for
revolution in the nineteenth century, we have said was
equivalent to asking what the tendency was of present
society.

And we have answered: Inasmuch as it is the conclusion of all statistics, of all investigations, of all
reports, and is admitted by all political parties, although
for different reasons, that society is upon a downward
and dangerous road, a revolution is inevitable.

Such has been our reasoning as to the utility and
necessity of the Revolution. In insisting upon it further,
we shall learn from it the rule which we need.

As it is the *tendency* of Society which is bad, the
problem of the Revolution is to change this *tendency*,
to straighten society up again, as a young tree is
straightened with the aid of a support, to make it take
a different direction; as a carriage is turned in a
different direction after is has been pulled out of a rut.
The whole task of the Revolution should consist of this
straightening out: there can be no question touching
Society itself, which we must regard as a superior being,
endowed with independent life, and in consequence
remote from any idea on our part to reconstruct it
arbitrarily.

This first datum is entirely in accordance with the
instincts of the people.

The people indeed are not at all utopian, as the
regular events of revolutions show. Enthusiasm and
frenzy take possession of them only at rare and brief
intervals. They seek not the Sovereign Good, like the
ancient philosophers, nor Happiness, like modern
socialists: they have no faith in the Absolute, and they
reject every *a priori* system, as deadly in its nature.
Their profound sense tells them that the absolute cannot

enter into human institutions, any more than the *status quo*. As the people accepts no final formula, but wants to advance continually, it follows that the mission of its teachers is merely to widen the horizon and to clear the way.

This fundamental condition of the revolutionary solution does not seem to have been understood hitherto.

Systems abound; schemes fall like rain. One would organize workshops, another the Government, in which he has more confidence. We know the social hypotheses of the Saint Simonians, of Fourier, Cabet, Louis Blanc, &c. Recently balm has dropped from the lips of Messrs. Considerant, Rittinghausen and E. Girardin, upon the form of sovereignty. But no one that I know of has said that the question for both politics and economy, was of *tendencies*, rather than of con: stitutions; that before all else, it was for us to find out whither we are going, not to dogmatise; in a word, that the solution lay in drawing Society back out of the dangerous path into which it is hastening, and to set it on the high road of common sense and well:being, which is its law.

Not one of the socialistic or governmental theories which has been proposed has seized this capital point of the question. Far from that, they are all the formal denial of it. The spirit of exclusion, of absolutism, of reaction, is the common characteristic of their authors. With them Society does not live: it is on the dissecting table. Not mentioning that the ideas of these gentlemen remedy nothing, guarantee nothing at all, open no prospect, leave the intelligence more empty, the soul more weary than before.

Instead, therefore, of examining systems, which would be an endless labor, and, what is worse, a labor without the possibility of a conclusion, we are about to examine their fundamental principle, with the aid of our criterion. We are to seek, from the point of view of the present revolution, what these principles contain, what they can give; for it is evident that if the prin:

ciples contain nothing, and can yield nothing, it is useless to consider the systems. The worth of these will have been settled: the most beautiful will have been found the most absurd.

I begin with the principle of Association.

If I wanted merely to flatter the lower classes, the recipe would not be difficult. Instead of a criticism of the social principle, I should deliver a panegyric of workingmen's societies, I should exalt their virtues, their constancy, their sacrifices, their spirit of benevolence, their marvellous intelligence; I should herald their triumphs. What could I not say on this subject, dear to all democratic hearts? Do not the workmen's unions at this moment serve as the cradle for the social revolution, as the early Christian communities served as the cradle of Catholicity? Are they not always the open school, both theoretical and practical, where the workman learns the science of the production and distribution of wealth, where he studies, without masters and without books, by his own experience solely, the laws of that industrial organization, which was the ultimate aim of the Revolution of '89, but of which our greatest and most famous revolutionists caught only a glimpse? What a topic for me, for the manifestation of a facile sympathy, which is not the less disinterested, in that it is always sincere! With what pride do I recall that I too wanted to found an association, more than that, the central agency and circulating organ of workmen's associations! And how I cursed that Government, which, with an expenditure of 300 millions, could not find a cent which it could use for the benefit of poor workingmen! . . .

I have better than that to offer to associations. I am convinced that at this moment they would give much for an idea, and it is ideas that I am bringing them. I should decline their approval, if I could obtain it only by flattery. If those of their members who may read these pages will but deign to remember that, in treating of association, it is a principle, even less than that, a hypothesis, that I discuss: it is not this or that enter=

prise, for which, in spite of its name, association is in nowise responsible, and of which the success, in point of fact, does not depend upon association. I speak of Association in general, not of associations, whatever they may be.

I have always regarded Association in general — fraternity — as a doubtful arrangement, which, the same as pleasure, love, and many other things, concealed more evil than good under a most seductive aspect. It is perhaps the effect of the temperament which nature has given me, that I distrust fraternity as much as I do passion. I have seen few men who were proud of either. Especially when Association is presented as a universal institution, the principle, means and end of the Revolution, does it appear to me to hide a secret intention of robbery and despotism. I see in it the inspiration of the governmental system, which was restored in '91, strengthened in '93, perfected in 1804, erected into a dogma and system from 1814 to 1830, and reproduced in these latter days, under the name of *direct government*, with an impulse which shows how far delusion of the mind has gone with us.

Let us apply the criterion.

What does society want today?

That its tendency toward sin and poverty should become a movement toward comfort and virtue.

What is needed to bring about this change?

The reestablishment of the equilibrium of forces.

Is association the equilibrium of forces?

No.

Is association even a force?

No.

What, then, is association?

A dogma.

Association is so much a dogma, in the eyes of those who propose it as a revolutionary expedient, something finished, complete, absolute, unchangeable, that all they who have taken up this Utopia have ended, without exception, in a SYSTEM. In illuminating with their fixed idea the different parts of the social body, they were bound to end, and in fact they did end, by reconstructing society upon an imaginary plan, much like the astronomer who, from respect for his calculations, made over the system of the universe.

Thus the Saint Simonian school, going beyond the idea of its founder, produced a system: Fourier produced a system; Owen, a system; Cabet, a system; Pierre Leroux, a system; Louis Blanc, a system; as Baboeuf, Morelly, Thomas More, Campanella, Plato, and others before them, who, each starting from a single principle, produced systems. And all these systems, antagonistic among themselves, are equally opposed to progress. Let humanity perish sooner than the principle! that is the motto of the Utopians, as of the fanatics of all ages.

Socialism, under such interpreters, became a religion which might have passed, five or six hundred years ago, as an advance upon Catholicism, but which in the nineteenth century is as little revolutionary as possible.

No, Association is not a directing principle, any more than an industrial force. Association, by itself, has no organic nor productive power, nothing which, like the division of labor, competition, &c, makes the worker stronger and quicker, diminishes the cost of production, draws a greater value from materials, or which, like the administrative hierarchy, shows a desire for harmony and order.

To justify this proposition, I must first cite a few facts as examples. Then I shall prove that, on the one hand, Association is not an industrial force, on the other, as a corollary, that it is not a principle of order.

I have proved somewhere in the *Confessions of a Revolutionary*, that commerce, independently of the service rendered by the material fact of transportation, is in itself a direct spur to consumption, and therefore a cause of further production, a principle of the creation of values.

At first this may seem paradoxical, but it has been demonstrated by economic analysis: the metaphysical act of exchange, in addition to labor, but by a different method from labor, is a producer of real value and of wealth. Furthermore, this assertion will astonish nobody who reflects that production or creation signifies only change of form, and that therefore creative forces, labor itself, are immaterial. So that the merchant who has enriched himself by real speculation, without usurious profit, enjoys the fortune which he has acquired by a perfectly just title: his fortune is as legitimate as that which labor has produced. And pagan antiquity, as well as the Church, has unjustly aspersed commerce, upon the pretext that its rewards were not the remuneration of real services. Once again; Exchange, an entirely immaterial operation, which is accomplished by the reciprocal consent of the parties, cost and distance of transportation being allowed for, is not merely a transposition or substitution, it is also a creation.

Commerce, then, being in itself a producer of wealth, men have engaged in it with ardor in all ages; no need for the legislator to preach its advantages and to recommend the practice of it. Let us suppose, what is not an absolutely absurd supposition, that commerce did not exist, that with our vast means of industrial execution, we had no idea of exchange: it is easy to see that if some one should come to teach men to exchange their products and trade among themselves, he would be rendering them an immense service. The history of humanity mentions no revolutionary who could compare with such an one. The remarkable men who invented the plough, the vine, wheat, did not rank above him who first invented commerce.

Another example:

The union of forces, which must not be confounded with association, as we shall shortly see, is, equally with labor and exchange, a producer of wealth. It is an economic power of which I was, I believe, the first to accentuate the importance, in my first memoir upon *Property*. A hundred men, uniting or combining their forces, produce, in certain cases, not a hundred times, but two hundred, three hundred, a thousand, times as

6

much. This is what I have called *collective force*. I even
drew from this an argument, which, like so many
others, remains unanswered, against certain forms of
appropriation; that it is not sufficient to pay merely
the wages of a given number of workmen, in order to
acquire their product legitimately; that they must be
paid twice, thrice or ten times their wages, or an
equivalent service rendered to each one of them.

Collective force, in its bare metaphysical aspect, is
another principle which is not less a producer of wealth.
Moreover its application is found in every case in which
individual effort, no matter how often repeated, would
be ineffective. Nevertheless, no law commands its
application. It is remarkable that the utopian socialists
have never thought of boasting of it. It is because
collective force is an impersonal act, while association
is a voluntary agreement: there may be points wherein
they meet, but they are not identical.

Let us suppose again, as in the preceding case, that a
working society is composed of only isolated workers,
who do not know how to combine and unite their
efforts when occasion requires: the worker who should
impart to then this secret would himself alone do more
for progress than steam and machinery, since he alone
would make their use posible. He would be one of the
great benefactors of humanity, a revolutionary really
out of the ordinary.

I pass over other facts of the same nature which I
might also cite, such as competition, division of labor,
property, &c., which together constitute what I call
economic forces, real productive principles. The
description of these forces may be found at length in
the works of the economists, who, with their absurd
scorn for metaphysics, have demonstrated, without
suspecting it, through the theory of industrial forces,
the fundamental dogma of Christian theology, creation
out of nothing.

The question remains whether Association is one of
these essentially immaterial forces, which by their
action become productive of utility and a source of

prosperity; for it is evident that only on this condition can the principle of association — I make no distinction of schools — be advanced as the solution of the problem of poverty.

In a word, is Association an economic power? For twenty years now it has been heralded and its virtues set forth. How is it that no one has demonstrated its efficacy? Can it be that the efficacy of Association is more difficult to demonstrate than that of commerce, credit, or the division of labor?

For my part, I answer categorically: No, Association is not an economic force. It is in its nature sterile, even injurious, since it places fetters on the liberty of the laborer. The authors who have advocated utopian fraternities, by which so many are still attracted, have attributed, without reason or proof, a virtue and efficacy to the *social contract*, which belongs only to collective force, the division of labor, or to exchange. The public has not perceived the confusion; hence the experiments of societies with constitutions, their varying fortunes, and the uncertainty of opinion.

When an industrial or commercial society aims at setting to work one of the great economic forces, or at carrying on a business, of which the nature requires that it should remain undivided, such as a monopoly, or an established line of trade, the society formed for this object may result successfully, but it does so not by virtue of its principle, but by virtue of its methods. So true is this that whenever the same result can be obtained without it, the preference is to dispense with association. Association is a bond which is naturally opposed to liberty, and to which nobody consents to submit, unless it furnishes sufficient indemnification; so that, to all utopian socialists, one may oppose this practical rule: Never, except in spite of himself, and because he cannot do otherwise, does man associate.

Let us make a distinction between the *principle* of association, and the infinitely variable *methods*, of which a society makes use when affected by external circumstances foreign to its nature; among which I

6*

place in the first rank the economic forces. The *principle* is one which would defeat the enterprise, unless another motive were found: the *methods* are what permit one to merge himself in it, in the hope of obtaining wealth by a sacrifice of independence.

We will explain this principle, and afterwards the methods.

Whoever talks of association, necessarily implies obligation, common responsibility, fusion of rights and duties in relation to outsiders. It is thus that all the fraternal societies understand it, even the Harmonists, notwithstanding their dream of *emulative competition*.

In association, he who does what he can, does what he ought: for the weak or lazy associate, and for him only, it may be said that the association is of service. Hence the equality of wages, the supreme law of association.

In association, all are responsible for all: the smallest is as much as the greatest: the last comer has the same rights as the oldest member. Association wipes out all faults, levels all inequalities, hence the inclusion in the membership of lack of skill as well as of incapacity.

The formula of association then is as follows; it is thus enunciated by Louis Blanc:

> *From each according to his ability.*
> *To each according to his needs.*

The Code, in its different definitions of civil and commercial society, is in accord with the orator of the Luxembourg: any derogation from this principle is a return to individualism.

Thus explained by Socialists and jurists, can Association be generalized and become the universal higher law, the public civil law of a whole nation?

Such is the question proposed by the different social schools, and all unanimously answer it in the affirmative while varying their modes of application.

My answer is: No, the contract of association, under whatever form, can never become a universal rule, because, being by its nature unproductive and harassing, applicable only to quite special conditions, its incon=

veniences growing much more rapidly than its benefits, it is equally opposed to the advantageous use of labor, and to the liberty of the workman. Whence I conclude that a single association can never include all the workmen in one industry, nor all industrial corporations, nor, *a fortiori*, a nation of 36 millions of men; therefore that the principle of association does not offer the required solution.

I may add that association is not only not an economic force, but that it is applicable only under special conditions, depending on the methods. It is easy to verify this second proposition by the facts, and thence to determine the part played by association in the nineteenth century.

The fundamental characteristic of association, as we have said, is binding union.

What reason then could lead workingmen to form a binding union among themselves, to give up their independence, to place themselves under the absolute law of a contract, and, what is worse, of an overseer?

There might be many reasons, differing much, but the reason, whatever it is, must be external to the society.

People associate themselves sometimes to hold a business that has been started by a single promoter, which they would risk losing if they should separate; — sometimes to carry on together an industry, a patent, a privilege, &c., which could not be profitably worked otherwise, or which would yield less to each, if it were carried on competitively; — sometimes on account of the impossibility of obtaining the necessary capital otherwise; — sometimes, finally, to equalize and divide the chances of loss by shipwreck, conflagration, or to equalize obnoxious or painful services, &c.

Go to the bottom of it, and you will find that every society which prospers, owes it to an outside cause which is foreign to it, and has no relation to its nature; without that, I repeat, the society could not exist, however skilfully organized it might be.

Thus in the first of the instances that we have brought forward, the purpose of the society is to develop a

business of established reputation, which alone is the
most important of its assets; in the second, it is founded
upon a monopoly, that is, upon something most
exclusive and anti-social; in the third, the joint-stock
company, the society sets to work some economic force,
whether collective power or division of labor; in the
fourth, the society is confounded with insurance, which
is a gambling contract, invented precisely for the
purpose of supplying the place of the fraternity which
is absent or inactive.

Under any of these conditions, the society is seen not
to exist by virtue of its own principles: it depends upon
its powers, upon an outside cause. But what they
promise, what we need, is a fundamental, vivifying,
active, principle.

People associate also for economy in consumption, in
order to avoid the loss incurred by retail buying. That
is the method M. Rossi advises for small households,
whose resources do not permit them to buy at
wholesale. But this sort of association which is that of
purchasers of meat at auction, bears witness against
association as a principle. Give the producer the power,
by the exchange of his products, to buy his provisions
at wholesale; or, what comes to the same thing, organize
retail trade under conditions that will give it almost the
same advantages of cheapness as buying at wholesale,
and association becomes useless. People who are in easy
circumstances do not need to join such associations:
they are more bother than they are worth.

Notice too that in every society thus founded for a
definite purpose, the obligation of the contract never
extends beyond what is strictly necessary. The members
do indeed answer for each other to outsiders, and to
the law, but beyond that they remain without obligation.
Thus several workmen's working associations in Paris,
which at first wanted, through an excess of devotion,
to do better than usual, and organized on the principle
of equality of wages, were afterwards compelled to
abandon it. At present, in all such associations, the
members do piecework, so that the associated contribu-

tion consists chiefly of labor, each one being remunerated in proportion to his product, in wages and in profits. The working association is just the opposite of the joint stock company: it is a joint stock company in which the subscription, instead of being in money is made in work, which is quite the opposite of fraternity. In a word, in every association, the members, seeking, by the union of their labor and capital, certain advantages which they could not obtain otherwise, arrange to have as little obligation and as much independence as possible.

Is that clear? and is it not time to shout, like St. Thomas, *Conclusum est adversus Manichaeos!*[14]

Association formed without any outside economic consideration, or any leading interest, association for its own sake, as an act of devotion, a family tie, as it were, is an act of pure religion, a supernatural bond, without real value, a myth.

This becomes very striking when we examine the different theories of association brought forward for the acceptation of disciples.

Fourier, for instance, and after him, Pierre Leroux, assure us that if the workers group themselves according to certain organic mental affinities, of which the character is described, by that alone they will grow in energy and capacity; that the spirit of the worker, so sad usually, will become gay and joyous; that the product, both individual and collective, will be greatly augmented; that therein lies the productive power of association, which may hereafter rank as an economic force. *Attractive labor* is the accepted formula for describing this marvellous result of association. This is quite a different matter, it will be seen, from the *devotion*, at which the theories of Louis Blanc and Cabet so pitifully stop.

I dare to say that the two eminent socialists, Fourier and Pierre Leroux, have taken their symbolism for

---

[14] It has been decided against the Manichaeans!

reality. In the first place, no one has ever seen anywhere in practice this social force, analogous to collective force and the division of labor; even the inventors of it and their disciples have yet to make their first experiment. In the second place, the slightest acquaintance with the principles of political economy and of psychology would suffice to show that there can be nothing in common between an exaltation of the soul, such as the cheerfulness of companionship, the synergic song of oarsmen, &c., and an industrial force. Such manifestations would most often be in opposition to the seriousness, the taciturnity, of labor. Labor, along with love, is the most secret, the most sacred, function of man: it is strengthened by solitude, it is dissolved by prostitution.

But such a review of these psychological considera= tions and of the absence of all experimental data, does not take into account that what these two authors believe they have discovered, after so many profound researches, the one in the *Series of Contrasted Groups,* the other in the *Triad,* is nothing but the mystic and apocalyptic expression of what has existed always in industrial practice; the *division of labor, collective force, competition, exchange, credit,* even *property* and *liberty.* Who cannot see that it is with utopians, both ancient and modern, as it is with theologians of all religions? While the latter, in their mysteries, do nothing but rehearse the laws of philosophy and of humanitarian progress the former, in their philanthropic essays, dream, without being aware of it, the great laws of social economy. Most of these laws, these forces of production, which ought to save mankind from poverty and crime, I have above mentioned. These are the true economic forces, the immaterial principles of all wealth, which, without chaining man to man, leave to the producer the most complete liberty, lighten labor, inspire it, double its product, establish among men an obligation which has nothing personal about it, and unite them by bond stronger than all sympathetic unions and all contracts.

The wonders announced by these two prophets have been known for centuries. We can see the influence of that efficacious grace, of which the organizer of the *Series* dreamed; that gift of divine love which the disciple of Saint Simon promised to his followers; corrupt as it was, lawless as the revolutionaries of '89 and '93 have left it to us, we can follow its oscillations at the Stock Exchange and in our markets. Let the Utopians awaken from their sentimental ecstasies, let them deign to look at what is passing about them, let them read, listen, experiment; they will see that what they attribute with so much enthusiasm, one to the *Series*, another to the *Trinity*, another to devotion, is nothing but the product of the economic forces that were analyzed by Adam Smith and his successors.

As it is above all in the interest of the working class that I have entered upon this discussion, I shall not end without saying something more about workmen's associations, of the results which they have obtained, and of the part which they are to play in the Revolution.

The great majority of these societies have been formed by men who were filled with fraternal theories, and convinced, although they may have been unaware of it, of the economic validity of the principle. In general these societies were sympathetically received: they enjoyed the favor of the Republic, which secured them, at the outset, the beginnings of membership: newspaper advertising was not lacking; all the elements of success, which have not been sufficiently taken into account, were there, but quite foreign to the principle.

Now, how do we find them?

Among them a goodly number sustain themselves and promise to develop further: everybody knows why.

Some of them are composed of the most skilful workmen in their trade: it is the monopoly of talent that supports them.

Others have attracted and retain membership by low prices: it is competition which gives them life.

I say nothing of those which have obtained government orders and credit; a purely gratuitous encouragement.

Finally, in general, with all these associations, the workmen, in order to dispense with middlemen, commission dealers, promoters, capitalists, &c., who, in the old order of things, stand between the producer and consumer, have had to work a little more, and get along with less wages. There is nothing in this but what is quite a matter of course in political economy; for the securing of which, as I shall show forthwith, there was no need of association.

Assuredly, the members of these societies are filled with the most fraternal sentiments toward each other and toward the public. But let them tell whether this fraternity, far from being the cause of their success, is not itself caused by the strict justice which rules in their mutual relations: let them tell what would become of them, if they did not find the guaranty of their enterprise elsewhere than in the charity which animates them, and which is but the cement of the edifice, whereof the stones are labor, and the forces which multiply labor?

As for societies which have only the doubtful virtue of association to sustain them, whose industries might be carried on privately, without any meeting of workmen, they are carried on with the greatest difficulty; and they manage to fill the voids in their organization only by devoted effort, by continual sacrifices, and by unlimited patience.

As an example of rapid success, the butchery associations are brought up, which are becoming the fashion everywhere. This example, more than any other, shows how far the inattention of the public and the incorrectness of ideas extend.

The butchery associations have no association about them but the name; they are *competitions* supported at common expense by the citizens of each community against the butchers' monopoly. They are the application, such as it may be, of a new principle, not to say a new economic force, *Reciprocity*[15], which consists in the sellers and buyers guaranteeing each other, irrevocably, their products at cost price.

This principle then, on which is founded all the importance of the butchers' stores, called coöperative, has so little association about it, that in many of them the service is by paid workers, under the direction of a supervisor who represents the stockholders. For this office, the first-come butcher who left the coalition was sufficient; there was no need of going to the expense of new men, as there was for new materials.

The principle of reciprocity, on which are founded the coöperative butcher's and grocer's stores, is tending now to displace that of fraternity, as an organic element, in workmen's associations. This is how *The Republic* of April 20th, 1851, describes a new society, *The Reciprocity*, formed by journeymen tailors: —

"These are workmen who challenge the maxim of "the old economy, 'No capital, no work,' which, if it "were founded on correct principle, would condemn to "hopeless and endless servitude and poverty the in= "numerable class of workers, who, living from hand to "mouth, are without any capital. Unwilling to admit "this desperate conclusion of official science, and "consulting rather the rational laws of the production "and consumption of wealth, these workmen think that "capital, which is said to be an essential element for "the exercise of labor, is really only a conventional "utility; and that the only productive agents are the "intelligence and hands of man. They think that "therefore it is possible to organize production, and to "secure the exchange of products and their normal "consumption, merely by providing *direct communica= "tion between producers and consumers,* who will be "permitted, by the suppression of oppressive go= "betweens, to reap the benefits which at present are

---

[15] Reciprocity is not the same thing as exchange: nevertheless it tends to become more and more the law of exchange, and to become lost therein. The scientific analysis of this law was given for the first time, in a pamphlet, Organization of Credit and Currency (Paris, 1848, Garnier Bros.), and the first application attempted by the People's Bank.

"gathered by capital, that sovereign ruler of labor, and
"of the needs and life of everybody.

"According to this theory, the emancipation of the
"workers is thus made possible by bringing together
"individual powers and needs, in other words, by *the*
"*association of producers and consumers*, who, ceasing
"to have opposite interests, will escape permanently
"from the domination of capital.

"In fact, as the needs of consumption are fixed,
"if the *producers and consumers* enter into direct
"relations, if they associate themselves and give each
"other credit, it is clear that there will no longer be
"any reason for the rise and fall of prices, the
"factitious increase or arbitrary depreciation to which
"speculation forces labor and production to submit.

"This is the ideal of *The Reciprocity*, which its
"founders have already realized to the exent of their
"ability, by the issue of notes, called *notes of*
"*consumption*, which are always redeemable in the
"products of the association. Thus *financed by those*
"*who make use of it*, the association sells its products
"*at cost*, making no addition for the remuneration of
"its own services, but a moderate charge for the actual
"labor. This is the rational solution which the founders
"offer for all the important questions of economics
"which have of late been raised, notably the following:
    "Abolition of exploitation in all its forms.
    "Gradual and peaceful abolition of capital.
    "*Creation of gratuitous credit.*
    "Guaranty and equitable reward of labor.
    "Emancipation of the lower classes."

This association of tailors is the first which has been
founded officially and, so to speak, scientifically, upon
an economic force which has remained to this day
hidden and unused in commercial routine. It is evident
that employment of this force in no way constitutes
a social contract, but at the most a contract of
exchange in which the mutual or reciprocal relation
between merchant and customer is at least understood,

if not formally expressed. And when the author of the article, who is an old communist, makes use of the word *association* to designate the new relations which *The Reciprocity* proposes to develop between *producers* and *consumers*, it is evident that he yields to former preconceptions, or that he is influenced by habit.

Moreover, while granting due honor to the founders of *The Reciprocity* for this great principle, the writer in the *Republic* should have reminded them, for their guidance, of the following fundamental facts relating to their own theory, that is to say, that the obligation on the part of the producer toward the consumer to deliver his products at cost price, which constitutes the new economic power, is essentially mutual and two-sided. That it would not suffice, moreover, as the basis of an association of workers, if the law of reciprocity were universally adopted and put into practice. That a society formed on this basis alone should sustian itself, requires that the majority of the community, despising it, should leave the profit to its members; and that, on the day when reciprocity shall become a law of social economy, by the consent of all citizens, the first-comer who is not a member of the society will be able to offer to the public the same advantages that the society offers, with even greater advantage, in that he has no overhead expenses, that the society then will be objectless.

Another association of the same sort, of which the mechanism approaches even more closely the elementary formula of reciprocity, is *The Housekeeper*, which the same newspaper, the *Republic*, has described in its issue of the 8th of May. Its aim is to assure to consumers all the articles of consumption at reduced prices, of superior quality, and without any fraud. To join, it is sufficient to subscribe the sum of *one dollar*, called social capital, plus 10 cents for general expenses of administration. Observe that the members *accept no responsibility, make no engagement,* have no other obligation except to pay for articles which are delivered at their homes upon their order. The general agent only is responsible.

The principle is the same in both cases. In the coöperative butcher shops, the guaranty of cheapness, good quality and full weight is obtained by a joint stock company, limited, managed by a special agent, discharging the functions of owner and manager toward this express end. In *The Housekeeper*, there is a general manager, representing all possible lines of trade, who takes the responsibility of furnishing all articles of consumption, upon a subscription of one dollar, with ten cents additional for expenses. With the tailors, there is one extra piece of mechanism, of wide range in its possibilities, but at present adding little real advantage, the *note of consumption*. Suppose that all the merchants, manufacturers and dealers of the city should make an engagement among themselves and with the public like that which the coöperative butcher shops, the founder of *The Housekeeper*, and the tailors of *The Reciprocity* make with their members, the association would then become universal. But it is clear that such an association would not be an association at all; commercial customs would be changed, that would be all; reciprocity would have become the rule, yet everybody would be just as free as before.

Therefore, although I am far from suggesting that association will ever disappear entirely from the system of human transactions, inasmuch as I admit that there are circumstances wherein it is indispensable, nevertheless I may assert, without fear of contradiction, that the principle of association is undermined every day by the practice of it; and while, scarcely three years ago, workingmen all tended toward fraternal association, today they are aiming at a system of guaranties, which, once realised, will render association superfluous in a multitude of cases, at the same time, note well, that it will demand association in others. At the bottom, existing associations, in forming an irresistible mass of producers and consumers in direct relation with one another, have no other end than to produce this result.

But if association is not a productive force, if on the contrary it imposes onerous conditions, from which labor naturally seeks to free itself, it is clear that association can no longer be considered an organic law; that, far from assuring equilibrium, it would tend rather to destroy harmony, by imposing upon all general obligation, instead of justice, instead of individual responsibility. Association therefore cannot be maintained from the point of view of right, and as a scientific factor; but only as a sentiment, a mystic principle, a divine institution.

Nevertheless the champions, despite everything, of association, feeling how sterile is their principle, how opposed to liberty, how little therefore it can be accepted as the sovereign formula of the Revolution, are making the most incredible efforts to sustain this will-o'-the-wisp of fraternity. Louis Blanc has gone so far as to reverse the republican motto, as if he wanted to revolutionize the revolution. He no longer says, as everybody else says, and according to tradition, *Liberty, Equality, Fraternity;* he says *Equality, Fraternity, Liberty!* We begin with Equality nowadays; we must take equality for our first term; upon it we must build the new structure of the Revolution. As for Liberty, that is deduced from Fraternity. Louis Blanc promises liberty after association, as the priests promise paradise after death,

I leave you to guess what kind of socialism it will be which plays thus with transpositions of words.

Equality! I had always thought that it was the natural fruit of Liberty, which has no need of theory nor of constraint. I had thought, I say, that from the organization of economic forces, the division of labor, competition, credit, reciprocity, above all, education, that Equality would be born. Louis Blanc has changed all that. A new Sganarelle, he puts Equality on the left, Liberty on the right, Fraternity between them, like Jesus Christ between the two thieves. We cease

to be free, as nature made us, in order to become equal,
which only labor can make us, as a preliminary, by
State order; after which we become more or less free,
according to the convenience of the Government.

From each according to his capacity;

To each according to his needs.

Equality demands this, according to Louis Blanc.

Let us pity those whose revolutionary capacity
reduces itself to this casuistry. But let not that prevent
us from refuting them, for the Kingdom of Innocents is
theirs.

Let us recall the principle once more. Association is
then, as Louis Blanc defines it, a contract which wholly
or partially (General and Special Associations, Civil
Code, Art. 1835) places the contracting parties on a
level, subordinates their liberty to social duty,
depersonalizes them, treats them almost as M. Humann
would treat taxpayers when he laid down this axiom:
Make them pay all the taxes they can! How much
does a man produce? How much does it cost to feed
him? That is the supreme question which springs from
the, what shall I call it? declension formula — From
each . . To each . . . in which Louis Blanc sums up
the rights and duties of an associate.

Who then shall determine his capacity? who shall
be the judge of his needs?

You say that my capacity is 100: I maintain that it
is only 90. You add that my needs are 90: I affirm that
they are 100. There is a difference between us of
twenty upon needs and capacity. It is, in other words,
the well-known debate between *demand* and *supply*.
Who shall judge between the society and me?

If the society persists, despite my protests, I resign
from it, and that is all there is to it. The society comes
to an end from lack of associates.

If, having recourse to force, the society undertakes
to compel me; if it demands from me sacrifice and
devotion, I say to it: Hyprocrite! You promised to
deliver me from being plundered by capital and power;
and now, in the name of equality and fraternity, in your

turn you plunder me. Formerly, in order to rob me, they exaggerated my capacity and minimized my needs. They said that products cost me so little, that I needed so little to live! You are doing the same thing. What difference is there then between fraternity and the wage system?

It is one of two things: either association is compulsory, and in that case it is slavery; or it is voluntary, and then we ask what guaranty the society will have that the member will work according to his capacity and what guaranty the member will have that the association will reward him according to his needs? Is it not evident that such a discussion can have but one solution — that the product and the need be regarded as correlated expressions, which leads us to the rule of liberty, pure and simple?

Reflect a moment. Association is not an economic force; it is only a bond of conscience, obligatory before that inward tribunal, and of no effect, or rather of an injurious effect, in relation to labor and wealth. And it is not by the aid of a more or less skilful argument that I prove it: it is the result of industrial practice since the origin of associations. Posterity will not understand how, in a century of innovation, writers, reputed to be the first in understanding social matters, should have made so much noise about a principle which is entirely subjective, and which has been explored to its foundations by all the generations of the globe.

In a population of 36 millions, there are 24 millions occupied with agriculture. These you can never associate. What use would it be? To work the soil requires no social mapping-out; and the soul of the peasant is averse to association. The peasant, remember, applauded the repression of June, 1848, because he saw in it an act of liberty against communism.

Out of the 12 millions remaining, at least 6 millions, composed of mechanics, artisans, employers, function= aries, for whom association is without object, without profit, without attraction, would prefer to remain free.

7

There are then 6 million souls, composing in part the wage-working class, whom their present condition might interest in workmen's associations, without closer examination, and upon the strength of promises. I venture to say in advance to these six million persons, fathers, mothers, children, old men, that they will hasten to free themselves from their voluntary yoke, if the Revolution should fail to furnish them with more serious, more real reasons for associating themselves, than those which they fancy they perceive, of which I have demonstrated the emptiness.

Association has indeed its use in the economy of nations. The workmen's associations are indeed called upon to play an important part in the near future; and are full of hope both as a protest against the wage system, and as an affirmation of *reciprocity*. This part will consist chiefly in the management of large instruments of labor, and in the carying out of certain large undertakings, which require at once minute division of functions, together with great united efficiency; and which would be so many schools for the laboring class if association, or better, participation, were introduced. Such undertakings, among others, are railroads.

But Association, by itself, does not solve the revolutionary problem. Far from that, it presents itself as a problem, the solution of which implies that the associates enjoy all their independence, while preserving all the advantages of union; which means that the best association is one into which, thanks to a better organization, liberty enters most and devotion least.

It is for this reason that workmen's associations, which have now almost changed their character as to the principles which guide them, should be judged, not by the more or less successful results which they obtain, but only according to their silent tendency to assert and establish the social republic.

Whether the workingmen know it or not, the importance of their work lies, not in their petty union interests, but in their denial of the rule of capitalists, money lenders and governments, which the first revolution left undisturbed. Afterwards, when they have conquered the political lie, the mercantile chaos, the financial feudality, the bodies of workers, abandoning the article of Paris and such toys, should take over the great departments of industry, which are their natural inheritance.

But, as remarked a great revolutionary, St. Paul, error must have its day, *Heresies must come.* It is to be feared that we have not yet done with the utopian Socialists. Association will be a pretext for agitation and an instrument for charlatanism for a long while yet, for a certain class of preachers and chatterers. With the ambitions which it arouses, the envy which disguises itself as devotion, the instincts of domination which it reawakens, it will be for a long time yet one of the regrettable prepossessions which delay the understanding of the Revolution among the people. The workmen's associations themselves, justly proud of their first successes, carried away by their competition with their former employers, intoxicated by the testimony which already salutes in them a new power, zealous, like all fraternities, to establish their power-seeking predominance, will have difficulty to refrain from overdoing, and to remain within the bounds of their part. Exorbitant pretensions, gigantic, irrational coalitions, disastrous fluctuations, may occur; which a better acquaintance with the laws of social economy would have prevented.

In this respect, a grave responsibility will rest upon Louis Blanc in history. It was he who, at the Luxembourg, with his riddle, Equality, Fraternity, Liberty, with his incantation, From each . . . To each . . . began the wretched opposition of ideology to ideas, and aroused common sense against Socialism. He thought himself the bee of the revolution: he has been only the grasshopper. After having infected the workmen with his absurd formulas, may he grant the boon of silence to the cause of the working classes, which have fallen into his hands for one day of error.

7*

FOURTH STUDY.

The Principle of Authority.

I beg that the reader will pardon me, if in the course of this study an expression should escape me which might betray any feeling of self-esteem. I have the double regret, in this great question of authority, of being, on the one hand, as yet alone in asserting the Revolution categorically; on the other, in having perverse ideas attributed to me, which I, more than anybody, abhor. It is not my fault if, in supporting so lofty a thesis, I seem to plead my own personal cause. At least I shall do so, even if I may not defend myself with some vivacity, that the intelligence of the reader may lose nothing. Moreover our mind is so constructed that it sees the light never better than when it springs from the clash of opposing ideas. Man, says Hobbes, is a fighting animal. It was God himself who, when placing us in this world, gave us this precept: *Increase, multiply, labor and fight.*

Some twelve years ago, well I may recall it, while busying myself with researches into the foundations of society, having in view not at all political eventualities, impossible then to have foreseen, but solely for the greater glory of philosophy, I was the first to cast into the world a denial which has since obtained great renown, the denial of Government and of Property. Others before myself, to seem original, humorous, or seeking a paradox, had denied those two principles; not one had made this denial the subject of a serious, earnest criticism. One of our most good-natured journalists, M. Pelletan, undertaking my defence one day, *motu proprio*, made this singular statement to his readers, that, in attacking sometimes property, sometimes power, sometimes something else, I was firing a gun into the air, to attract toward myself the attention of empty-heads. M. Pelletan was too good indeed, and I cannot be too much obliged to him for his kindness: he must have taken me for a literary person.

It is time that the public should know that, in philosophy, in politics, in theology, in history, negation is the preliminary requirement to affirmation. All progress begins by abolishing something; every reform rests upon denunciation of some abuse; each new idea is based upon the proved insufficiency of the old idea. Thus Christianity, in denying the plurality of gods, in becoming atheistic, from the pagan point of view, asserted the unity of God, and from this unity deduced its whole theology. Thus Luther, in denying the authority of the Church, asserted the authority of reason, and laid the first stone of modern philosophy. Thus our fathers, the revolutionaries of '89, in denying the sufficiency of feudal rule, asserted, without understanding it, the necessity of some different system, which it is the mission of our age to explain. Thus, finally, I myself, having demonstrated afresh, under the eyes of my readers, the illegitimacy and powerlessness of government as a principle of order, will cause to arise from this negation a productive, affirmative idea, which must lead to a new form of civilization.

The better to explain my position in this examina‹ tion, I will make another comparison.

It is with ideas as with machines. No one knows the inventor of the first tools, the hoe, the rake, the axe, the wagon, the plough. These are found among all the nations of the globe from the earliest antiquity. But this spontaneity is not found with perfected instruments, the locomotive, the daguerreotype, the art of ballooning, the electric telegraph. The finger of God, if I may venture to say so, is no longer there: the names of the inventors, the dates of their first experiments, are known: the aid of science, together with prolonged practical skill, has been required.

Thus are born and thus develop the ideas which serve to guide the human race. The earliest are furnished by spontaneous, immediate intuition, in which priority cannot be claimed by anybody. But the day comes when these gifts of common sense no longer suffice for collective life: it is then that reason, which alone can show this insufficiency, can alone supply that which is lacking. All nations have produced and organized by themselves, without the aid of teachers, the ideas of authority, of property, of government, of justice, of worship. Now that these ideas are growing weaker, that a methodical analysis, an official inquiry, if I may say so, has established their insufficiency, at the bar of reason and of society, the question is for us to discover, through science, what substitute we can find for ideas which, according to the verdict of science, are condemned as false and injurious.

Whoever then openly, in the face of the people, by a sort of extra≠judicial act, has been the first to propound a view directed against government and established property, is bound to explain further his ideas for a new social organization. I will attempt the solution, as I attempted before the criticism of it: I mean that after having given to my contemporaries consciousness of their own deficiencies, I will try to explain to them the secret of their own aspirations. God forbid that I should set myself up as prophet, or that I should pretend to have ever *invented an idea!* I see, I observe, I write. I may say, with the Psalmist: I have believed because I have spoken.

Why is it that with the simplest question some ambiguity must mingle?

Priority in philosophical conceptions is not less an object of emulation than priority in industrial inventions, with lofty minds which know their value and seek the glory of their discovery, although they can be neither sold nor patented. In the domain of pure thought, as well as in that of mechanical improvement applied to the arts, there are rivalries, imitations, I had almost said counterfeits, were it not that I fear, by the use of so strong a term, to asperse an honorable ambition, which attests the superiority of the present generation. The idea of *Anarchy* had this fortune. The denial of government having been renewed since the revolution of February with new ardor and some success, certain men of note in the democratic and socialistic party, whom the idea of *Anarchy* filled with disquietude, thought that they might appropriate the arguments directed against government, and upon these arguments, which were essentially negative, might restore the very principle which was at stake, under a new name, and with a few modifica= tions. Without intending it, without suspecting it, these honorable citizens took the position of counter= revolutionaries, since a counterfeit, for after all this word expresses my idea better than any other, a counterfeit, in political and social affairs, is really counter=revolution. I shall prove it immediately. That is what these restorations of authority really are, that have been undertaken recently in competition with *anarchy*, and that have occupied public attention under the names of *Direct Legislation, Direct Government*, of which the authors or editors are, in the first place, Messrs. Rittinghausen and Considerant, and afterwards, M. Ledru Rollin.

According to Messrs. Considerant and Rittinghausen, the first idea of direct government came from Germany; as for M. Ledru=Rollin, he only claims it, and with reservations, for our first revolution; this idea being found at length in the Constitution of '93, and in the Social Contract.

It must be understood, that if I intervene in my turn in the discussion, it is not to claim a priority which I reject with all my power in the terms in which the question has been put. *Direct Government* and *Direct Legislation* seem to me the two biggest blunders in the annals of politics and of philosophy. How is it that M. Rittinghausen, who understands German philosophy to the bottom; how is it that M. Considerant, who ten or fifteen years ago wrote a pamphlet, under the title, *Breaking-up of Politics in France;* how is it that M. Ledru-Rollin, who, when he subscribed to the Constitution of '93, made such generous and futile efforts to make direct government practicable, and to reduce it within the bounds of common sense; how is it, I ask, that these gentlemen have not understood that the very arguments which they use against *indirect* government, have no force that does not apply equally against *direct* government; that their criticism is admissible only when made absolute; and that, in stopping half-way, they have fallen into the most pitiful inconsequence? Above all, how is it that they have not seen that their pretended direct government is nothing but the reduction to absurdity of the governmental idea; to the extent that, if through the progress of ideas and the complexity of interests, society is forced to abjure every kind of government, it will be just because direct government, the only form of government that seems to be rational, liberal, equal, is nevertheless impossible?

Meanwhile comes along M. de Girardin, aspiring, no doubt, to have a share in the invention, or at least, in the completion, who proposed this formula: *Abolition of Authority through the Simplification of Government.* What was M. de Girardin doing with this foolish business? Such a mind, so resourceful, can never be restrained! You are too quick, M. de Girardin, to accomplish anything. Authority is to Government what the thought is to the word, the idea to the fact, the soul to the body. Authority is government in principle, as government is authority in practice. To abolish either, if it is a real abolition, is to abolish both. By the same token, to preserve one or the other, if the preservation is effective, is to keep both.

Moreover, M. de Girardin's simplification has long been known to the public. It is a combination of personages borrowed from what merchants call their Journal. There are three clerks: the first named *Debts,* the second named *Assets*, the third named *Balance*. Nothing is lacking but the Chief, who orders them about and directs them. Among the thousands of ideas which M. de Girardin's brain throws off every day, without any of them taking root, no doubt he will not fail to find one to fulfil this indispensable function of his government.

Justice must be done to the public. What the public has seen most clearly is that among all these fine governmental inventions, *Direct Government, Simplified Government, Direct Legislation, Constitution of '93*, the Government, whatever it may be, is very sick, and tending more and more toward *Anarchy*. My readers may give this word any meaning they choose. Let Messrs. Considerant and Rittenhausen pursue their researches; let M. Ledru=Rollin dig deeper into the Constitution of '93; let M. de Girardin have more con=fidence in his inspirations, and we shall arrive forthwith at pure negation. That accomplished, it will only remain, by opposing the negation to itself, as the Germans say, to discover the affirmation. Onward, innovators! less haste and more boldness! Follow the light which has appeared to you from afar: you are at the boundary between the old world and the new.

In March and April, 1850, the Revolution put the following question to the vote: *Monarchy or Republic?* The voters declared themselves for the Republic: the Revolution won the victory.

I take upon myself today to show that the dilemma of 1850 had no other meaning than this: *Government or No=government?* If you can refute this dilemma, reactionaries, you will have struck the heart of the Revolution.

As for *Direct Legislation, Direct Government* and *Simplified Government*, I think that their authors will do well to hand in their resignations, as soon as possible, if they have the slightest regard for their standing as revolutionaries, or for the esteem of liberal thinkers.

I shall be brief. I know that volumes would be needed to explain so grave a question, with due form and including all useful implications. But the mind of the people is quick in our time: they understand everything, guess everything, know everything. Their daily experience, their intuitive spontaneity, take the place of dialectic and erudition: they can grasp in a few pages, what, not more than four years ago, would have demanded a folio from the professional publicists.

I. TRADITIONAL DENIAL OF GOVERNMENT.

Emergence of the Idea which Succeeds it.

The form under which men first conceived of Order in Society is the patriarchal or hierarchical; that is to say, in principle, Authority; in action, Government. Justice, which afterwards was divided into distributive and commutative justice, appeared at first under the former heading only: a *SUPERIOR* granting to *Inferiors* what is coming to each one.

The governmental idea sprang from family customs and domestic experience: no protest arose then: Government seemed as natural to Society as the subordination of children to their father. That is why M. de Bonald was able to say, and rightly, that the family is the embryo of the State, of which it reproduces the essential classes: the king in the father, the minister in the mother, the subject in the child. That is also the reason that all the fraternity socialists, who take the family as the rudiments of Society, arrive at a dictatorship, which is the most exaggerated form of government. The administration of M. Cabet in his estate of Nauvoo is a good example. How much longer will it take us to understand this connection of ideas?

The primitive conception of order through Government is found among all peoples; and if, from the very beginning, the efforts that were made to organize, modify and limit the action of Power, to devote it to general needs and to special circumstances, show that the denial of government was implied in its affirmation, it is certain that no rival hypothesis arose; the spirit always remained the same. As the nations emerged from a state of savagery and barbarism, they are observed to have immediately entered upon the governmental path, and to traverse a circle of institu= tions which are always the same, and which historians and publicists arrange in classes succeeding one another, Monarchy, Aristocracy, Democracy.

But there is something more serious.

The prejudice in favor of government having sunk into our deepest consciousness, stamping even reason in its mould, every other conception has been for a long time rendered impossible, and the boldest thinkers could but say that Government was no doubt a scourge, a chastisement for humanity; but that it was a neces= sary evil!

That is why, up to our own days, the most emanci= pating revolutions and all the eruptions of liberty have always ended in a reiteration of faith in and sub= mission to power; why all revolutions have served only to re=establish tyranny: I make no exception of the Constitution of '93, any more than of that of 1848, the two most advanced expressions nevertheless of French democracy.

What has maintained this mental predisposition and made its fascination invincible for so long a time, is that, through the supposed analogy between Society and the family, the Government has always presented itself to the mind as the natural organ of justice, the protector of the weak, the preserver of the peace. By the attribution to it of provident care and of full guaranty, the Government took root in the hearts, as well as in the minds of men; it formed a part of the universal soul, it was the faith, the intimate, invincible superstition of the citizens! If this confidence weakened, they said of Government, as they said of Religion and Property, it is not the institution which is bad, but the abuse of it; it is not the king who is wicked but his ministers; Ah, if the king knew!

Thus to the hierarchical and absolutist view of a governing authority, is added an ideal which appeals to the soul, and conspires incessantly against the desire for equality and independence. The people at each revolution think to reform the faults of their government according to the inspiration of their hearts; but they are deceived by their own ideas. While they think that they will secure Power in their own interest, they really have it always against them: in place of a protector, they give themselves a tyrant.

Experience, in fact, shows that everywhere and always the Government, however much it may have been for the people at its origin, has placed itself on the side of the richest and most educated class against the more numerous and poorer class; it has little by little become narow and exclusive; and, instead of maintaining liberty and equality among all, it works persistently to destroy them, by virtue of its natural inclination towards privilege.

We, have shown in a previous study how since 1789, the revolution having founded nothing, society, as M. Collard expressed it, having been reduced to dust, the distribution of wealth left to chance, the Government, whose task it is to protect property as well as person, found itself in fact established for the rich against the poor. Who does not see now that this anomaly, which then it was thought proper to embody in the political constitution of our country, is common to all governments? At no epoch is property found to depend on labor exclusively: at no epoch has work been guaranteed by the equilibrium of economic forces: in this matter, the civilization of the nineteenth century is not any more advanced than that of the Middle Ages. Authority, in defending rights, however estabilished, in protecting interests, however acquired, has always been for riches against misfortune: the history of governments is the martyrology of the proletariat.

Most of all in a democracy, which is the last phase of governmental evolution, it is necessary to study this inevitable desertion by Power of the cause of the people.

What do the people do when they proclaim their own sovereignty, that is, the authority of their own votes, after they are tired of their aristocrats, and indignant at the corruption of their princes?

They say to themselves:

Before everything else, order is necessary in society.

The guardian of this order, which should mean liberty and equality for us, is the Government.

Therefore let us take the Goverment into our own hands. Let the Constitution and the laws become the expression of our own will; let the office holders and magistrates, who are our servants elected by us, and always subject to recall, never be permitted to do anything but what the good pleasure of the people has determined upon. Then we shall be sure, if our watchfulness never relaxes, that the Government will be devoted to our interests, that it will no longer be the tool of the rich, nor the prey of ambitious politicians; that affairs will be conducted as we wish and to our advantage.

Thus reasons the multitude, at each epoch of oppres= sion. Simple reasoning, logic that cannot be more straightforward, and which never fails in its effect. Even if the multitude went so far as to say, with Messrs. Considerant and Rittinghausen: Our deputies are our enemies; let us govern ourselves and we shall be free; — there would be no change in the argument. The principle, that is to say, Government, remaining the same, there would still be the same conclusion.

For several thousand years this theory has diverted the oppressed classes and the orators who defend them. Direct government dates neither from Frankfort, nor from the Convention, nor from Rousseau; it is as old as indirect: it dates from the foundation of societies.

"No more hereditary royalty,

"No more presidency,

"No more representation,
"No more delegation,
"No more alienation of power,
"Direct government,
"THE PEOPLE! in the permanent exercise of their sovereignty."

What is there at the end of this refrain which can be taken as a new and revolutionary proposition, and which has not been known and practised long before our time, by Athenians, Boeotians, Lacedemonians, Romans, &c.? Is it not always the same vicious circle, always the same drop to absurdity, which, after having sucked dry and eliminated successively absolute monarchies, aristocratic or representative monarchies, and democracies, comes to the turning point of direct government, only to begin again with a dictatorship for life and hereditary royalty? Direct government, among all nations, has been an epoch of renewed life for destroyed aristocracies and broken-down thrones: it could not maintain itself among peoples which, like Athens and Sparta, had the advantage of a very small population and the service of slaves. It would be for us the prelude to Caesarism, despite our post office, our railroads, our telegraphs, despite the simplification of laws, the recall of officials, the imperative mandate. It would hurl us so much the more quickly toward imperial tyranny, in that our lower classes are no longer willing to be wage-workers, our proprietors would not suffer themselves to be expropriated, and the partisans of direct government, doing everything through politics, seem to have no notion of economic organization. One step more on this road, and the era of Caesars will have dawned: to an unworkable democracy will succeed, without any step of transition, the empire, with or without Napoleon.

We must get out of this vicious circle. The political idea, the ancient notion of distributive justice, must be contradicted through and through; and that of commutative justice must be reached, which, in the logic of history as well as of law, succeeds it. Blind men by choice, seeking in the clouds for what is under your nose, read again your authors, look about you, analyze your own formulas, and you will find the solution, which has dragged from immemorial time through the centuries, and which neither you nor any one of your satellites have deigned to notice.

All ideas are co-eternal in the mind: they seem to be successive only in history, in which they come in their turn to assume direction of affairs and to occupy the first rank. The operation by which one idea is driven from power is called in logic, *negation;* that by which another is established is called *affirmation.*

Every revolutionary negation therefore implies a subsequent affirmation: this principle, which the practice in revolutions proves, is about to receive a wonderful confirmation.

The first authentic negation of the idea of authority which has been made is that of Luther. This negation, nevertheless, did not go beyond the sphere of religion: Luther, like Leibnitz, Kant, Hegel, was a thoroughly governmental mind. This negation was called *free criticism.*

What does free criticism deny? The authority of the Church.

What does it imply? The authority of reason.

What is reason? An agreement between intuition and experience.

The authority of reason; that is the eternal, positive idea, substituted by the Reformation for the authority of faith. As philosophy formerly sprang from revelation, revelation hereafter will be subordinated to philosophy. Their parts are changed: the government of society is not what is was: morality is changed: destiny itself seems to be modified. We can already in our time catch a glimpse of all that this renewal of reign contained, in which the words of man took the place of the voice of God.

A like movement is about to take place in the sphere of political ideas.

Following Luther, the principle of free criticism was carried, notably by Jurieu, from the spiritual to the temporal. To the sovereignty of divine right, the adversary of Bossuet opposed the sovereignty of the people, which he expressed with infinitely more precision, force and profoundness by the words *Social Contract* or *Pact*, of which the contradiction is manifest to such words as power, authority, government, *imperium*, αρχη.

What really is the *Social Contract?* An agreement of the citizen with the government? No, that would mean but the continuation of the same idea. The social contract is an agreement of man with man; an agreement from which must result what we call society. In this, the notion of *commutative justice*, first brought forward by the primitive fact of exchange, and defined by the Roman law, is substituted for that of *distributive justice*, dismissed without appeal by republican criticism. Translate these words, *contract, commutative justice*, which are the language of the law, into the language of business, and you have *Commerce*, that is to say, in its highest significance, the act by which man and man declare themselves essentially producers, and abdicate all pretension to govern each other.

Commutative justice, the *reign of contract*, the *industrial* or *economic system*, such are the different synonyms for the idea which by its accession must do away with the old systems of *distributive justice*, the *reign of law*, or in more concrete terms, *feudal, governmental* or *military* rule. The future hope of humanity lies in this substitution.

But before this revolution of doctrine can be formulated, before it can be comprehended, before it can take possession of the peoples who alone can put it into practice, what fruitless debates! what weary inactivity of ideas! what a time for agitators and sophists! From the controversy of Jurieu with Bossuet, to the publication of Rousseau's *Social Contract* almost a century elapsed; and when the latter appeared, it was not to assert the idea, but to stifle it.

Rousseau, whose authority has ruled us for almost a century, understood nothing of the social contract. To him, most of all, must be ascribed the great relapse of '93, expiated already by fifty-seven years of fruitless disorder, and which certain minds more ardent than wise wish us still to regard as a sacred tradition.

The idea of contract excludes that of government: M. Ledru-Rollin, who is a lawyer, and whose attention I call to this point, ought to know it. What characterizes the contract is the agreement for equal exchange; and it is by virtue of this agreement that liberty and well being increase; while by the establishment of authority, both of these necessarily diminish. This will be evident if we reflect that contract is the act whereby two or several individuals agree to organize among themselves, for a definite purpose and time, that industrial power which we have called *exchange;* and in consequence have obligated themselves to each other, and reciprocally guaranteed a certain amount of services, products, advantages, duties, &c., which they are in a position to obtain and give to each other; recognizing that they are otherwise perfectly independent, whether for consumption or production.

Between contracting parties there is necessarily for each one a real personal interest; it implies that a man bargains with the aim of securing his liberty and his revenue at the same time, without any possible loss.[16] Between governing and governed, on the contrary, no matter how the system of representation or of delegation of the governmental function is arranged, there is *necessarily* alienation of a part of the liberty and of the means of the citizen; in return for what advantage we have explained above.

The contract therefore is essentially reciprocal: it imposes no obligation upon the parties, except that

---

[16] I have taken the liberty to change two words in this passage, as a literal rendering would make nonsense of it. There must be some error in the text. Trans.

which results from their personal promise of reciprocal delivery: it is not subject to any external authority: it alone forms the law between the parties: it awaits their initiative for its execution.

But if such is the contract in its most general acceptation, and in daily practice; what will be the Social Contract, which is relied upon to bind together all the members of a nation into one and the same interest?

The Social Contract is the supreme act by which each citizen pledges to the association his love, his intelligence, his work, his services, his goods, in return for the affection, ideas, labor, products, services and goods of his fellows; the measure of the right of each being determined by the importance of his contributions, and the recovery that can be demanded in proportion to his deliveries.

Thus the social contract should include all citizens, with their interests and relations. — If a single man were excluded from the contract, if a single one of the interests upon which the members of the nation, intelligent, industrious, and sensible beings, are called upon to bargain, were omitted, the contract would be more or less relative or special, it would not be social.

The social contract should increase the well-being and liberty of every citizen. — If any one-sided conditions should slip in; if one part of the citizens should find themselves, by the contract, subordinated and exploited by the others, it would no longer be a contract; it would be a fraud, against which annulment might at any time be invoked justly.

The social contract should be freely discussed, individually accepted, signed with their own hands, by all the participants. If the discussion of it were forbidden, cut short or juggled, if consent were obtained by fraud; if signature were made in blank, by proxy, or without reading the document and the preliminary explanation; or even if, like the military oath, consent were a matter of course and compulsory; the social contract would then be no more than a conspiracy against the liberty and well-being of the most ignorant, the weakest and the most numerous, a systematic spoliation, against which every means of resistance, and even of reprisal, would be a right and a duty.

We may add that the social contract of which we are now speaking has nothing in common with the contract of association by which, as we have shown in a previous study, the contracting party gives up a portion of his liberty, and submits to an annoying, often dangerous, obligation, in the more or less well-founded hope of a benefit. The social contract is of the nature of a contract of exchange: not only does it leave the party free, it adds to his liberty; not only does it leave him all his goods, it adds to his property; it prescribes no labor; it bears only upon exchange: all these being points which are not found in the contract of association, which is even antagonistic to it.

Such should be the social contract, according to the definitions of the law and universal practice. Is it necessary now to say that, out of the multitude of relations which the social pact is called upon to define and regulate, Rousseau saw only the political relations; that is to say, he suppressed the fundamental points of the contract, and dwelt only upon those that are secondary? Is it necessary to say that Rousseau understood and respected not one of these essential, indispensable conditions, — the absolute liberty of the party, his personal, direct part, his signature given with full understanding, and the share of liberty and prosperity which he should experience?

For him, the social contract is neither an act of reciprocity, nor an act of association. Rousseau takes care not to enter into such considerations. It is an act of appointment of arbiters, chosen by the citizens, without any preliminary agreement, for all cases of contest, quarrel, fraud or violence, which can happen in the relations which they may subsequently form among themselves, the said arbiters being clothed with sufficient force to put their decisions into execution, and to collect their salaries.

8*

Of a real, true contract, on whatsoever subject, there is no vestige in Rousseau's book. To give an exact idea of his theory, I cannot do better than compare it with a commercial agreement, in which the names of the parties, the nature and value of the goods, products and services involved, the conditions of quality, delivery, price, reimbursement, everything in fact which constitutes the material of contracts, is omitted, and nothing is mentioned but penalties and jurisdictions.

Indeed, Citizen of Geneva, you talk well. But before holding forth about the sovereign and the prince, about the policeman and the judge, tell me first what is my share of the bargain? What? You expect me to sign an agreement in virtue of which I may be prosecuted for a thousand transgressions, by municipal, rural, river and forest police, handed over to tribunals, judged, condemned for damage, cheating, swindling, theft, bankruptcy, robbery, disobedience to the laws of the State, offence to public morals, vagabondage, — and in this agreement I find not a word of either my rights or my obligations, I find only penalties!

But every penalty no doubt presupposes a duty, and every duty corresponds to a right. Where then in your agreement are my rights and my duties? What have I promised to my fellow citizens? What have they promised to me? Show it to me, for without that, your penalties are but excesses of power, your law-controlled State a flagrant usurpation, your police, your judgment and your executions so many abuses. You who have so well denied property, who have impeached so eloquently the inequality of conditions among men, what dignity, what heritage, have you for me in your republic, that you should claim the right to judge me, to imprison me, to take my life and honor? Perfidious declaimer, have you inveighed so loudly against exploiters and tyrants, only to deliver me to them without defence?

Rousseau defined the social contract thus:

"To find a form of association which defends and "protects, with the whole power of the community, the

"person and goods of each associate; and by which each
"one, uniting himself to all, obeys only himself and
"remains as free as before."

Yes, these are indeed the conditions of the social
pact, as far as concerns *the protection and defence of
goods and persons*. But as for the mode of acquisition
and transmission, as to labor, exchange, value and price
of products, as to education, as to the multitude of
relations which, whether he wishes it or not, places man
in perpetual association with his fellows, Rousseau says
not a word; his theory is perfectly meaningless. Who
does not see that without some definition of rights and
duties, the sanction which follows is absolutely null;
who does not see that where there are no stipulations,
there can be no infractions, nor, in consequence, any
criminals; and, to conclude with philosophical rigor,
that a society which after having provoked revolt,
punishes and kills by virtue of such authority, itself
commits assassination with premeditation and by
treachery.

Rousseau is so far from desiring that any mention
should be made in the social contract of the principles
and laws which rule the fortunes of nations and of
individuals, that, in his demagogue's programme, as well
as in his Treatise on Education, he starts with the false,
thievish, murderous supposition that only the individual
is good, that society depraves him, that man
therefore should refrain as much as possible from all
relations with his fellows; and that all we have to do in
this world below, while remaining in complete isolation,
is to form among ourselves a mutual insurance society,
for the protection of our persons and property; that all
the rest, that is to say, economic matters, really the only
matters of importance, should be left to the chance of
birth or speculation, and submitted, in case of litigation,
to the arbitration of elected officers, who should
determine according to rules laid down by themselves,
or by the light of natural equity. In a word, the social
contract, according to Rousseau, is nothing but the
offensive and defensive alliance of those who possess,

against those who do not possess; and the only part played by the citizen is to pay the police, for which he is assessed in proportion to his fortune, and the risk to which he is exposed from general pauperism.

It is this contract of hatred, this monument of incurable misanthropy, this coalition of the barons of property, commerce and industry against the disinherited lower class, this oath of social war indeed, which Rousseau calls *Social Contract*, with a presumption which I should call that of a scoundrel, if I believed in the genius of the man.

But if the *virtuous and sensitive* Jean=Jacques had taken for his aim the perpetuation of the discord among men, could he have done better than to offer them, as their contract of union, this charter of their eternal antagonism? Watch him at work: you will find in his theory of government the same spirit that inspired his theory of education. As the tutor, so the statesman. The pedagogue preaches isolation, the publicist sows dissension.

After having laid down as a principle that the people are the only sovereign, that they can be represented only by themselves, that the law should be the expression of the will of all, and other magnificent commonplaces, after the way of demagogues Rousseau quietly abandons and discards this principle. In the first place, he substitutes the will of the majority for the general, collective, indivisible will; then, under pretext that it is not possible for a whole nation to be occupied from morning till night with public affairs, he gets back, by the way of elections, to the nomination of representatives or proxies, who shall do the law= making in the name of the people, and whose decrees shall have the force of laws. Instead of a direct, personal transaction where his interests are involved, the citizen has nothing left but the power of choosing his rulers by a plurality vote. That done, Rousseau rests easy. Tyranny, claiming divine right, had become odious; he reorganizes it and makes it respectable, by making it proceed from the people, so he says. Instead

of a universal, complete agreement, which would assure
the rights of all, provide for the needs of all, and guard
against all difficulties, which all must understand,
consent to and sign, he gives us, what? That which today
we call *direct government,* a recipe by which, even in
the absence of all royalty, aristocracy, priesthood, the
abstract *collectivity* of the people can still be used for
maintaining the parasitism of the minority and the
oppression of the greater number. It is, in a word, the
legalization of social chaos by a clever fraud, the
consecration of poverty, based on the sovereignty of
the people. Moreover there is not a word about labor,
nor property, nor the industrial forces; all of which it
is the very object of a Social Contract to organize.
Rousseau does not know what economics means. His
programme speaks of political rights only; it does not
mention economic rights.

It is Rousseau who teaches us that the people, a
collective being, has no unitary existence; that it is an
abstract personality, a moral individuality, incapable by
itself of thinking, acting or moving; which means that
general reason is not superior to individual reason, and,
in consequence, that he who has the most developed
individual reason best represents general reason. A
false proposition, which leads directly to despotism.

It is Rousseau who teaches us by aphorisms the
whole of this liberty-destroying theory, making his
deductions from this first error.

That popular or direct government results essentially
from the *yielding up* of liberty that each one must make
for the advantage of all.

That *the separation of powers is the first condition
of government.*

That in a well-ordered Republic no association or
special meeting of citizens can be permitted, because it
would be a State within a State, a government within a
government.

That a sovereign is one thing, a prince is another.

That the first by no means excludes the second; so
that the most direct government may well exist with a

hereditary monarchy, as was seen under Louis Philippe, and as some people would like to see again.

That as the sovereign, that is to say, the People, is a fictitious being, an ideal person, a mere conception of the mind, it has, as its natural and visible representative, the prince, who is the more valuable because he is one.

That the Government is not within a society, but *outside* of it.

That according to all these considerations, which are linked together in Rousseau like the theorems of geometry, a real democracy has never existed, and never will exist, seeing that in a democracy it is the greater number that should lay down the law and exercise the power, while it is contrary to the order of nature that the greater number should govern and the less be governed.

That direct government is impracticable, above all in a country like France, because, before everything else, it would be necessary to equalize fortunes, and equality of fortunes is impossible.

That besides, on account of the impossibility of maintaining equal conditions, direct government is of all the most unstable, the most perilous, the most fruitful of catastrophes and civil wars.

That as the ancient democracies could not maintain themselves, despite the powerful aid of slavery, it would be vain to attempt to establish this form of government among ourselves.

That democracy is made for gods, not for men.

After having trifled with his readers thus for a long time, after having drawn up the Code of Capitalist and Mercantile Tyranny, under the deceptive title of *Social Contract*, the Genevese charlatan deduces the necessity of a lower class, of the subordination of labor, of a dictatorship and of the Inquisition.

It appears to be the privilege of literary people that style should take the place of reason and morality.

Never man united to such an extent intellectual pride, aridity of soul, lowness of tastes, depravity of habits, ingratitude of heart; never did the warmth of eloquence, the pretence of sensitiveness, the effrontery of paradox, arouse to such infatuation. Since the time of Rousseau, and following his example, there has been founded among us a sentimental and philantrophic school, I should say, industry, which is able to gather in the honor due to charity and devotion, while really practising the most complete selfishness. Distrust this philosophy, this politics, this socialism of Rousseau. His philosophy is all phrases and covers only emptiness, his politics is full of domination; as for his ideas about society, they scarcely conceal their profound hypocrisy. They who read Rousseau and admire him, are simply dupes, and I pardon them: as for those who follow and copy him, I warn them to look to their own reputation. The time is not far away when a quotation from Rousseau will suffice to cast suspicion upon a writer.

Let me say, in conclusion, that, to the shame of the eighteenth century and of our own, the *Social Contract* of Rousseau, a masterpiece of oratorical jugglery, has been admired, praised to the skies, regarded as the record of public liberties; that Constituents, Girondins, Jacobins, Cordeliers, have all taken it for an oracle; that it served for the text of the Constitution of '93, which was declared absurd by its own authors; and that it is still by this book that the most zealous reformers of political and social science are inspired. The corpse of the author, which the people will drag to Montfaucon, on the day when they shall have learned the meaning of these words: Liberty, Justice, Morality, Reason, lies glorious and venerated in the catacombs of the Pantheon, where never one will enter of these honest laborers who nourish with their blood their poor families; while the profound geniuses set up for their adoration send, in lubricious frenzy, their bastards to the almshouse.

Each aberration of the public conscience carries its punishment with it. The vogue of Rousseau has cost France more gold, more blood, more shame, than the hateful reign of the three famous courtesans, Cotillon I, Cotillon II, Cotillon III, (Chateauroux, Pompadour,

Dubarry) ever caused her to sacrifice. Our country, which never suffers but from the influence of foreigners, owes to Rousseau the bloody struggles and failures of '93.

Thus, while the revolutionary tradition of the sixteenth century gave us the idea of the Social Contract as an antithesis to that of Government, an idea which the Gallic genius, so judicial in its character, had not failed to penetrate; the tricks of a rhetorician sufficed to divert us from the true road, and to cause delay in the interpretation of it. The negation of government, which is at the foundation of the Utopia of Morelly, which cast a gleam, soon extinguished, over the sinister manifestations of the *Enragés* and *Hébertists*, and which would have emerged from the doctrines of Baboeuf, if Baboeuf had known how to reason and deduce his own principles: — this great and decisive negation remained not understood, all through the eighteenth century.

But an idea cannot perish. It is born again, always from its contradictory. Let Rousseau triumph: his glory of a moment will be but the more detested. While waiting for the theoretical and practical deduction of the Contractual Idea, complete trial of the principle of authority will serve for the education of Humanity. From the fulness of this political evolution will finally arise the opposite hypothesis: Government, exhausting itself, will give birth to Socialism as its historic sequel.

It was Saint Simon who first took up the thread again, in timid language, and with a still dim consciousness.

"The human race," he wrote in the year 1818, "has "been called upon to live at first under governmental "and feudal rule. It is destined to pass from the "*governmental* or *military* rule to *administrative* or "*industrial* rule, after it has made sufficient progress "in the physical sciences and in industry.

"Finally, it has been subjected through its organi≈
"zation to endure a long and violent crisis in its
"passage from a military to a pacific system.

"The present period is one of transition.

"The transitional crisis began by the preaching of
"Luther; since that time the tendency of thought has
"been fundamentally critical and revolutionary."

Saint Simon then cites in support of his ideas, as
having had a more or less vague apprehension of this
great metamorphosis, among statesmen, Sully, Colbert,
Turgot, Necker, even Villèle; among philosophers,
Bacon, Montesquieu, Condorcet, A. Comte, B. Con≈
stant, Cousin, A. de Laborde, Fièvée, Dunoyer, &c.

All Saint Simon is in these few lines, written in the
style of the prophets; but too hard of assimilation for
the age when they were written, and too condensed in
meaning for the youthful spirits who first attached
themselves to the noble innovator. Note well, that
therein is found neither community of goods nor of
women, nor purification of the flesh, nor androgyny,
nor a Supreme Father, nor *Circulus*, nor Triad. Nothing
of all that has been disseminated by his disciples
really belongs to the master; on the contrary, the dis≈
ciples have quite misunderstood the meaning of Saint
Simon.

What did Saint Simon mean?

From the moment when, on the one hand, philosophy
succeeds to faith, and replaces the ancient conception
of government by that of contract; or, on the other,
when after a Revolution which has abolished feudalism,
society requires the development and harmonization of
its economic powers; from this moment it becomes
inevitable that government, already denied in theory,
should fall to pieces in practice. And when Saint Simon,
to designate this new order of things, conforms to the
old style and uses the word government, joined with
the epithet *administrative* or *industrial*, it is evident
that this word, from his pen, acquires a metaphorical,
or rather analogical, meaning, which could not but
mislead the uninitiated. How is it possible to misunder≈

stand the thought of Saint Simon, in reading the still more explicit passage which I here cite:

"If we observe the course which is followed in the "education of individuals, we notice that in the "primary schools government has the most import= "ance; and in schools of a higher grade, the govern= "ment of the children continually diminishes in "intensity, while instruction plays a more important "part. *It has been the same in the education of* "*society.* Military activity, that is to say, feudal or "governmental, had to be strongest at the origin of "society; it always had to diminish, while adminis= "trative activity had to acquire greater importance; "and the administrative power must end by entirely "overshadowing military power."

To these extracts from Saint Simon must be added his famous *Parable,* which in 1819 fell like an axe upon the official world; and for which the author was tried in the Court of Assizes, on the 20th of February, 1820, and acquitted. The length of this work, which is moreover well known, forbids us from quoting it here.

Saint Simon's negation of government, as is easily seen, is not deduced from the idea of contract, which for eighty years Rousseau and his votaries had corrup= ted and dishonored. It flows out of a different kind of insight, entirely experimental and *a posteriori,* such as is suited to an observer of facts. The end of govern= ments, which the providentially inspired theory of contract had, since the time of Jurieu, foreshadowed in the future of society, Saint Simon establishes from the law of the evolution of humanity, appearing at his strongest in the heat of discussion. Thus the theory of the Law and the philosophy of history, like two surveyor's poles planted one in front of the other, direct the mind toward an unknown revolution; one step more and we shall reach the issue.

All roads lead to Rome, says the proverb. All inves= tigations also conduct to the truth.

I think that I have over=abundantly established that the eighteenth century would have reached the negation

of government by the development of the idea of
contract, that is to say, by the judicial road, if it had
not been turned from the path by the classic, retro=
spective and declamatory republicanism of Rousseau.

This negation of government Saint Simon deduced
from observation of history, and of the progress of
humanity.

In my turn I have completed the analysis of econo=
mic functions, and of the theory of credit and ex=
change, if I may speak of myself at this time, when I
alone represent the revolutionary point of view. To
establish this discovery, I have no need, I fancy, to
mention the different works and articles in which it
is recorded: they have obtained enough notoriety in
the past three years.

Thus the Idea, the incorruptible seed, passes along
the ages, illuminating from time to time a man of
willing mind, to the day when an intellect that nothing
can intimidate receives it, broods upon it, then hurls
it like a meteor among the astonished crowds.

The idea of contract, in opposition to that of govern=
ment, which was the outcome of the Reformation,
passed through the seventeenth and eighteenth
centuries, without being noticed by a single publicist,
nor observed by a single revolutionary. On the other
hand, all that was most illustrious in the Church, in
philosophy, in politics, conspired to oppose it. Rousseau,
Siéyès, Robespierre, M. Guizot, all that school of
parliamentarians, bore the banner of the opposition.
At last one man, perceiving the disregard of the leading
principle, brought again to the light the new and
fruitful idea: unfortunately the practical side of his
doctrines deceived his own disciples: they could not
see that the producer is the negation of the ruler, that
organization is incompatible with authority; and thus
for thirty years the principle was lost to sight. Finally,
it took hold of public opinion, through the loudness of
protest; but then, *O vanas hominum mentes, o pectora
coeca!*[17] opposition brings about revolution! The idea

---

[17] Oh, dim minds! Oh, dull hearts of men!

of Anarchy had hardly been implanted in the mind of the people when it found so-called gardeners who watered it with their calumnies, fertilized it with their misrepresentations, warmed it in the hothouse of their hatred, supported it by their stupid opposition. Today, thanks to them, it has borne the anti-governmental idea, the idea of Labor, the idea of Contract, which is growing, mounting, seizing with its tendrils the workingmen's societies, and soon, like the grain of mustard seed of the Gospel, it will form a great tree, with branches which cover the earth.

The sovereignty of Reason having been substituted for that of Revolution,

The notion of Contract succeeding that of Government,

Historic evolution leading Humanity inevitably to a new system,

Economic criticism having shown that political institutions must be lost in industrial organization,

We may conclude without fear that the revolutionary formula cannot be *Direct Legislation,* nor *Direct Government,* nor *Simplified Government,* that it is NO GOVERNMENT.

Neither monarchy, nor aristocracy, nor even democracy itself, in so far as it may imply any government at all, even though acting in the name of the people, and calling itself the people. No authority, no government, not even popular, that is the Revolution.

Direct legislation, direct government, simplified government, are ancient lies, which they try in vain to rejuvenate. Direct or indirect, simple or complex, governing the people will always be swindling the people. It is always man giving orders to man, the fiction which makes an end of liberty; brute force which cuts questions short, in the place of justice, which alone can answer them; obstinate ambition, which makes a stepping stone of devotion and credulity.

No, the old serpent shall not prevail: it has strangled itself by involving itself in this question of direct government. Now that we grasp, as a clear antithesis, the political idea and the economic idea, Production and Government; now that we can deduce them reciprocally one from the other, test them and compare them, the opposition of Neo-Jacobinism is no longer to be feared.

They who are still fascinated by the schism of Robespierre will tomorrow be the orthodox of the Revolution.

II. GENERAL CRITICISM OF THE IDEA OF AUTHORITY.

I have demonstrated two things in the first part of this study:

1. That the principle of authority and government has its source in the dominating attitude of the family.

2. That it has been used by the unanimous consent of all peoples, as a condition of social order.

3. That at a certain period of history this principle began to be denied spontaneously, and to be replaced by another idea, which until then had seemed subordinate, the idea of Contract, which implies a quite different social order.

In this second part, I shall recall briefly the causes, or rather the grounds, as much of fact as of right, which led society to deny Power, and which exhibit the reason for its condemnation. The criticism which you are about to read is not mine, it is that of the people themselves, a criticism entered upon often, and always from a different point of view; but the conclusion is always the same at the end of each experiment, and promises in 'our days to become operative. It is not my thought which I give: it is the thought of the centuries, the thought of the human race. I but report it.

1. Thesis. — Absolute Authority.

Every idea is established or refuted by a series of terms which are, as it were, its organism; of which the last term demonstrates infallibly its truth or error. If the development, instead of being merely in the mind and in theory, is carried out at the same time in facts and institutions, it constitutes history. This is the case with the principle of authority or government.

The first form under which this principle is manifested is that of absolute power. This is the purest, the most rational, the most efficient, the most straightforward, and taken altogether, the least immoral and the least disagreeable form of government.

But absolute power, in its simplest expression, is odious to reason and to liberty: the feeling of the people is always aroused against it: following feeling, revolt makes its protest heard. Then the principle of authority is forced to retire: it retires step by step, by a series of concessions, each one more insufficient than the other, of which the last, pure democracy, or direct government, ends in the impossible and the absurd. The first term of the series then being *ABSOLUTISM*, the last fateful term is *ANARCHY*, in every sense.

We are about to pass in review, one after the other, the principal terms of this great evolution.

Humanity asks its masters: Whence these pretensions of yours to reign over me and govern me?

They answer: Because society cannot dispense with order: because in a society it is necessary that there should be some who obey and labor, while others give orders and directions: because, individual faculties being unequal, interests opposite, passions antagonistic, the advantage of one opposed to the general advantage, some authority is needed which shall assign the boundaries of rights and duties, some arbiter who will cut short conflicts, some public force which will put into execution the judgments of the sovereign. The power of the State is just this discretionary authority, this arbiter who renders to each what is his, this force which assures that the peace shall be respected. Government, in a word, is the principle and guaranty of social order: that is what both nature and common sense tell us.

This explanation has been repeated since the origin of societies. It is the same at all epochs, and in the mouth of all powers. You will find the identical statement, invariably, in the books of Malthusian economists, in Opposition newspapers, and in the professions of faith of Republicans. There is no difference among them, except in the proportion of the concessions to liberty that they propose to make, in derogation of the principle of authority: — illusory con= cessions, which add to the forms of government called moderate, constitutional, democratic, &c., a flavoring of hypocrisy, of which the taste renders them only the more contemptible.

Thus Government, in its unmodified nature, presents itself as the absolute, necessary, *sine qua non* condition of order. For that reason it always aspires toward absolutism, under all disguises; in fact, according to the principle, the stronger the Government, the nearer order approaches perfection. These two notions then, government and order, are in the relation to each other of cause and effect: the cause is *GOVERNMENT*, the effect is *Order*. It is thus that primitive societies have reasoned. We have already remarked upon this subject, that, from what such societies could conceive of human destiny, it was impossible that they should have reasoned otherwise.

But this reasoning is none the less false, and the conclusion is quite inadmissible, because, according to the logical classification of ideas, the relation of government to order is not that of cause to effect, as the statesmen pretend, it is that of a particular to a general. *ORDER* is the genus: *Government* is the species. In other words, there are many ways of conceiving order; but who has proved to us that order in a society is what its masters choose to call it?

On the one hand is alleged the natural inequality of faculties, whence is deduced that of conditions; on the other, the impossibility of uniting the divergence of interests and of harmonizing opinions.

9

But in this antagonism there is at most but a problem to be solved, it should not be a pretext for tyranny. Inequality of faculties! divergence of interests! Well, sovereigns, with your crowns, robes and fasces, that is precisely what is meant by the social question; and you think to solve it with club and bayonet! Saint Simon was quite right in regarding the words *govern= mental* and *military* as synonyms. Government cause order in society? It is like Alexander untying the Gordian knot with his sword!

Who then, shepherds of the people, authorizes you to think that the problem of opposition of interests and inequality of faculties cannot be solved; that the distinction of classes necessarily springs from it; and that, in order to maintain this natural and providential distinction, force is necessary and legitimate? I affirm, on the contrary, and all they whom the world calls Utopians, because they oppose your tyranny, affirm, with me, that the solution can be found. Some believe that they have found it in the community, others in association, yet others in the industrial series. For my part, I say that it is found in the *organization of economic forces*, under the supreme law of *CONTRACT*. Who can assure you that none of these hypotheses is true?

The advance of labor and of ideas sets this liberal theory, through my lips, against your governmental theory, which has no basis but your ignorance, no principle but a sophism, no method but force, no object but the robbery of humanity.

To find a form of transaction which, in drawing together the divergence of interests, in identifying individual advantage, in effacing the inequality of nature by that of education, solves all political and economical contra= dictions; under which each individual will be both producer and consumer as synonymous, both citizen and prince, ruler and ruled; under which his liberty steadily increases, with no need of giving up any part of it; under which his material prosperity grows indefinitely, without his experiencing any loss through the act either of society or of his fellow citizens, either in his property, or in his work, or in his recompense, or in his relations of interest, of opinion, or of attachment among his fellows.

What, do these conditions seem to you impossible to satisfy? Does it seem to you impossible to imagine anything more inextricable than the social contract, when you think of the frightful number of relations that it must regulate — something like squaring the circle, or finding perpetual motion? That is the reason why, wearied of the struggle, you fall back upon absolutism and force.

Consider, moreover, that if the social contract can be solved between two producers, — and who doubts that it can be solved, when reduced to these simple terms? — it can as well be solved among millions, as it relates always to a similar engagement; and that the number of signatures adds nothing to it, while making it more and more effective. Your plea of inability then does not exist, it is ridiculous, and you are left without excuse.

However that may be, listen, men of power, to the words of the Producer, the proletarian, the slave, of him whom you expect to force to work for you: I demand neither the goods nor the money of anybody; and I am not disposed to allow the fruit of my labor to become the prey of another. I, also, want order, as much as they who are continually upsetting it by their alleged government; but I want it as the result of my free choice, a condition for my labor, a law of my reason. I will not submit to it coming from the will of another, and imposing sacrifice and servitude upon me as preliminary conditions.

2. Laws.

What with the impatience of the people, and the imminence of revolt, the Government must yield. It has promised *institutions* and *laws;* it has declared that its most fervent desire was that each one should enjoy the fruit of his labor under his own vine and

9*

fig tree. This was a necessity of its position. From the time that the Government presented itself as the judge of what was right, as the sovereign arbiter of destinies, it could not pretend to drive men at its own good pleasure. King, President, Directory, Committee, Popular Assembly, it matters not: power must have rules of conduct: how can it establish discipline among its subjects without them? How can citizens conform to orders, if they are not notified of what the orders are; or if the orders are revoked when scarcely announced; if they change from day to day, from hour to hour?

So the Government must make laws; that is to say, place limits for itself; for whatever is a rule for the citizen is a limit for the ruler. It must make as many laws as it finds interests; and, as interests are innumerable, relations arising from one another multiply to infinity, and antagonism is endless, law=making must go on without stopping. Laws, decrees, edicts, ordinances, resolutions, will fall like hail upon the unfortunate people. After a time the political ground will be covered with a layer of paper, which the geologists will put down among the vicissitudes of the earth as the *papyraceous formation*. The Convention in three years one month and four days passed eleven thousand six hundred laws and decrees: the Constituent and Legislative Assemblies passed as many: the Empire and the Governments that followed continued the work. At present, the *Bulletin of Laws* contains, it is said, more than fifty thousand: if our representatives do their duty, this enormous figure will soon be doubled. Do you suppose that the people, or even the Government itself, can keep their reason in this labyrinth?

Certainly we are already far from the primitive institution. It is said that the Government fills the part of father in Society; but what father ever made an agreement with his family, or granted a charter to his children, or arranged a balance of power between himself and their mother? The head of a family is inspired by his heart in his government: he does not rob his children; he supports them by his labor: guided by his love, he thinks only of their interests and circumstances: his will is their law, and all, mother and children, have confidence in it. The little State would be doomed if paternal action encountered the least opposition, if it were limited in its prerogatives or determined in advance in its effects. What! can it be true that the Government is not a father to the people, since it submits to regulations, compromises with its subjects, and makes itself the slave of a rule, which, whether divine or popular, is not its own?

If this is so, I do not see why I myself should submit to this law. Who guarantees to me its justice, its sincerity? Whence comes it? Who made it? Rousseau teaches in unmistakeable terms, that in a government really democratic and free the citizen, in obeying the law, obeys only his own will. But the law has been made without my participation, despite my absolute disapproval, despite the injury which it inflicts upon me. The State does not bargain with me: it gives me nothing in exchange: it simply practises extortion upon me. Where then is the bond of conscience, reason, passion or interest which binds me?

But what do I say? Laws for one who thinks for himself, and who ought to answer only for his own actions; laws for one who wants to be free, and feels himself worthy of liberty? I am ready to bargain, but I want no laws. I recognize none of them: I protest against every order which it may please some power, from pretended necessity, to impose upon my free will. Laws! We know what they are, and what they are worth! Spider webs for the rich and powerful, steel chains for the weak and poor, fishing nets in the hands of the Government.

You say that you will make but few laws; that you will make them *simple* and *good*. That is indeed an admission. The Government is indeed culpable, if it avows thus its faults. No doubt the Government will have engraved on the front of the legislative hall, for

the instruction of the legislator and the edification of
the people, this Latin verse, which a priest of Boulogne
had written over the door to his cellar, as a warning to
his Bacchic zeal:

"Pastor, ne noceant, bibe pauca sed optima vina."[18]

Few laws! Excellent laws! It is impossible. Must not
the Government regulate all interests, and judge all
disputes; and are not interests, by the nature of society,
innumerable; are not relations infinitely variable and
changeable? How then is it possible to make few laws?
How can they be simple? How can the best law be
anything but detestable?

You talk of simplification. But if you can simplify in
one point, you can simplify in all. Instead of a million
laws, a single law will suffice. What shall this law be?
*Do not to others what you would not they should do to
you: do to others as you would they should do to you.*
That is the law and the prophets.

But it is evident that this is not a law; it is the
elementary formula of justice, the rule of all transactions.
Legislative simplification then leads us to the idea of
contract, and consequently to the denial of authority.
In fact, if there is but a single law, if it solves all the
contradictions of society, if it is admitted and accepted
by everybody, it is sufficient for the social contract. In
promulgating it, you announce the end of government.
What prevents you then from making this simplification
at once?

3. The Constitutional Monarchy.

Before '89, the Government in France was what it is
still in Austria, in Prussia, in Russia, and in several
other countries of Europe, an uncontrolled Power, with
certain institutions that had the force of law for all.
It was, as Montesquieu said, a *qualified, monarchy.*
This Government disappeared, together with the
feudal and ecclesiastical privileges which it had consen=
ted to defend, inadvisedly, although quite conscien=
tiously. It was replaced, after violent shocks and

---

[18] Pastor, for your health, drink but little wine, but of the best.

many oscillations, by the so-called representative
Government, or *Constitutional Monarchy*.   It would
be too much to say that the liberty and prosperity of
the people thereupon increased, except for the relief
from the feudal rights which were abolished, and the
sale of national property which was seized.   Nevertheless it is certain and it must be admitted that this
new retreat of the governmental principle caused the
revolutionary denial of government to advance by just
so much. That is the real, decisive reason that makes,
for us who consider only the right, the constitutional
monarchy preferable to the qualified monarchy; in the
same way that representative democracy, or the rule
of universal suffrage, seems to us preferable to constitutionalism, and direct government preferable to
representation.

But it may already be foreseen that when we arrive
at this last term, direct government, confusion will be
at its height; and there will be nothing for it but one
of these two things, either to continue the development
of government, or to proceed to the abolition of it.

Let us resume our criticism.

Sovereignty, say the Constitutionalists, is in the
People. Government emanates from them. Therefore
let the most enlightened part of the Nation be called
upon to elect citizens who are the most notable,
through their fortune, their wisdom, their talents or
their virtues, who are the most directly interested in
the justice of the laws and the good administration of
the State, and who are the most capable of taking their
part therein. Let these men, periodically assembled and
regularly consulted, enter into the councils of the
prince, and participate in the exercise of his authority.
We shall then have done all that it is possible to expect
from the imperfection of our nature, for the liberty
and prosperity of men. Then the Government will
present no danger, as it will always be in contact with
the People.

Surely these are great words, but words that would
indicate some notable swindle, if, since '89, and thanks

chiefly to Rousseau, we had not learned to believe in the good faith of all who mingle with public affairs.

We must first understand the constitutional system, the interpretation of the new dogma, the sovereignty of the People. Some other time we shall seek to comprehend what this sovereignty is.

Until the Reformation, Government had been regarded as of divine right: *Omnis potestas a Deo.*[19] After Luther, it began to be considered a human institution: Rousseau, who was one of the first to grasp this view, deduced his theory from it. Government had been from on high: he made it come from below, through the machinery of the suffrage, more or less universal. He took no care to understand that if the Government in his time had become corrupt and weak, it was because the principle of authority applied to nations is false and mischievous; that, in consequence, it was not the form nor the origin of Power that it was necessary to change, but rather to deny its application.

Rousseau did not see that authority, of which the proper sphere is the family, is a mystical principle, anterior and superior to the will of the parties interested, of the father and mother, as well as of the children; that what is true of authority in the family would be equally true of authority in Society, if Society contained in itself the principle and reason of any authority whatsoever; that, once the theory of a social authority is admitted, it cannot in any case depend upon an agreement; that it is contradictory that they who must obey authority should begin by decreeing it. On the other hand, that if Government ought to exist, it exists by the necessity of things; that, as in the family, it is part of the divine or natural order, which for us is the same thing; that it is not proper for anybody to discuss it, or to pass judgment upon it; that therefore, far from power submitting itself to the control of representatives, to the jurisdiction of popular

---

[19] All power is from God.

assemblies, it belongs to government alone to preserve, develop, renew, and perpetuate itself, by inviolable method, which no one has the right to touch, and which leaves to its subjects only permission to offer their very humble opinions, information and condol= ence, to enlighten the justice of the prince.

There are not two kinds of government, just as there are not two kinds of religion. Government is by divine right, or it is nothing, just as religion is from heaven or it is nothing. *Democratic Government* and *Natural Religion* are two contradictions, unless you prefer to see in them two mystifications. The People have no more voice in the State than they have in the Church: their part is to believe and obey.

Moreover, as principles cannot be mistaken, as only men have the right to be illogical, Government, as well that of Rousseau as that of the Constitution of '89, and all that have followed it, is always, despite the form of elections, only a Government by divine right, a mystical and supernatural authority, which imposes itself upon liberty and conscience, while assuming the air of asking their support.

Follow this series:

In the family, in which authority is closely bound up with human feelings, authority imposes itself by *generation.*

Among savage or barbarous peoples, it imposes itself by the *patriarchate,* which is included in the previous category, or by *force.*

Among sacerdotal peoples, it imposes itself by *faith.*

In aristocracies, it imposes itself by *primogeniture,* or *caste.*

In Rousseau's system, it imposes itself by *lot,* or by *number.*

Generation, force, faith, primogeniture, lot, number, all things equally unintelligible and impenetrable, upon which one must not reason, only submit; such are, I will not say the principles, — Authority, like Liberty, recognizes only itself as a principle, — but the different modes through which is accomplished, in human societies, the investiture of Power. For a primitive, superior, anterior, undebateable principle, popular in stinct has always sought an expression which should be equally primitive, superior, anterior and undebateable. As far as concerns the production of Power, force, faith, heredity, or number, are the variable forms which clothe this ordeal; they are the judgments of God.

Does number offer to your mind something more rational, more authentic, more moral, than faith or force? Does the ballot seem to you more trustworthy than tradition or heredity? Rousseau declaims against the right of the strongest, as if force, rather than number, constituted usurpation. But what is number? What does it prove? What is it worth? What relation is there between the opinion of the voters, more or less sincere and unanimous, and that which rules all opinion, all voting, — truth and right?

What! the question is as to all that is dearest to me, my liberty, my labor, food for my wife and children; and when I am expecting to make an agreement with you, you send the whole business to an assembly, selected by the accident of drawing lots! When I present myself to make a contract, you tell me that it is necessary to elect arbiters, who, without knowing me, without understanding me, will pronounce my acquittal or condemnation! What relation is there, I ask, between this assembly and me? what guaranty can it offer me? why should I make this enormous, irreparable, sacrifice to its authority, to accept whatever it may be pleased to resolve, as the expression of my will, as the just measure of my rights? And when this assembly, after debates of which I understand nothing, proceeds to impose its decision upon me as law, at the point of the bayonet, I ask, if it is true that I am a sovereign, what becomes of my dignity? if I am to consider myself as party to a contract, where is the contract?

They pretend that the representatives will be the most capable, the most honest, the most independent men of the country, selected as such by citizens chosen as most interested in order, in liberty, in the prosperity of the laborers, and in progress. A plan wisely conceived, which answers for the good intentions of the candidates!

But why do the honorable bourgeois who compose the middle class understand my true interests better than I myself? The question is as to my labor, and the exchange of my labor, the thing which, next to love, least bears authority, as the poet says:

"Non bene conveniunt, nec in una sede morantur Majestas et amor! . . ."[20]

And you are going to dispose of my labor, my love, by proxy, without my consent! Who can assure me that your proxies will not use their privilege to make the Power that it gives them an instrument for plunder? Who will guarantee me that the smallness of their number will not deliver them to corruption, hands, feet and consciences bound? And if they will not permit themselves to be corrupted, if they fail to make authority listen to reason, who can assure me that authority will submit?

From 1815 to 1830, the country, as legally constituted, was continually at war with authority: the struggle ended in a revolution. From 1830 to 1848, the electoral class, duly strengthened after the unfortunate experiment of the Restoration, was exposed to the seductions of Power; the majority had already been corrupted when the 24th of February burst: the betrayal ended once more in a revolution. Proof has been made: it will not be tried again. Now then, partisans of representative rule, you will do us a real service if you can preserve for us forced marriages, ministerial corruption, popular insurrections: *A spiritu fornicationis, ab incursu et daemonio meridiano.*[21]

4. Universal Suffrage.

The solution is found, cry the courageous. Let all the citizens take part in the voting: there will be no power

---

[20] Authority and love do not fit well together, nor stay long together.
[21] From the spirit of fornication: from the attack of the noonday fiend.

that can resist them, no seduction that can corrupt them. That is what the founders of the Republic thought, the day after the 24th of February.

Some added: Let the mandate be imperative, the representative always subject to recall, and the integrity of the law will be guaranteed, the fidelity of the legislator assured.

We proceed to take a hand in the discussion.

I have no belief at all, and with good reason, in this divinatory instinct of the multitude, which enables it to discern at a glance the merit and worth of the candidates. Examples abound of persons elected by acclamation, who, on the very platform on which they presented themselves to the view of the people, were already preparing the net for their betrayal. Hardly could the people at election pick out one honest man from a dozen scamps.

But, once more, what do all these elections matter to me? What need have I of proxies, any more than of representatives? And, since it is necessary that I specify what I want, can I not explain it without the aid of anybody? Will it cost me any more? Am I not more sure of myself than of my attorney?

It is said that it is necessary to do something; that it is impossible that I should attend to so many different interests; that after all, a council of arbitrators, whose members have been appointed by the votes of all the people, promises an approximation to truth and right, far superior to the justice of an irresponsible monarch, represented by insolent ministers, and by magistrates whose irremoveability places them as much out of my reach as the prince himself.

In the first place, I do not see the necessity of doing anything at such a price: I do not see moreover that anything is accomplished. Neither election nor voting, even if unanimous, solves anything. During the sixty years that we have used all sorts of methods of electing, what have we accomplished? What have we even outlined? What light have the people obtained from their assemblies? What guaranties have they obtained?

Does it add a cent to their income that they have to repeat their commands ten times a year, and to reëlect every month their municipal officers and judges? Are they any more sure when they go to bed at night, that they will have something to eat, something wherewith to feed their children, on the morrow? Can they even be sure that they will not be arrested and dragged to prison?

I understand that one may submit to an arbitrary decision upon questions that are not susceptible of a regular solution, for unimportant interests, for ordinary affairs. Such transactions have this moral, this consolation, that they prove the existence in the soul of something superior even to justice, the fraternal sentiment. But upon principles, on the essence of rights, on the direction to impress upon society, on the organization of industrial forces, upon my labor, my subsistence, my life, upon this very hypothesis of Government that we are discussing, I reject all presumptive authority, all indirect solutions; I recognize no star-chamber; I desire to negotiate directly individually, for myself; universal suffrage is in my eyes nothing but a lottery.

On the 25th of February, 1848, a handful of Democrats, after having driven out the monarchy, proclaimed the Republic at Paris. They took counsel with themselves only for this step: they did not wait until the people had pronounced upon it, in their primary meetings. The support of the citizens was boldly presumed by them. I believe upon my soul and conscience, that they did well: I believe that they acted in the fulness of their right, although they were to the rest of the people as 1 to 1000. And, because I was convinced of the justice of their work, I did not hesitate to associate myself therewith: the Republic, in my opinion, being but the cancellation of a lease between the People and the Government. *Adversus hostem aeterna auctoritas esto* [22]

---

[22] Against the enemy the right of defence is inalienable.

says the Law of the Twelve Tables. Against Power the right to reclaim cannot lapse; usurpation is meaningless.

Nevertheless, from the point of view of the sovereignty of numbers, of the imperative mandate, and of universal suffrage, which are more or less accepted by us, these citizens committed an act of usurpation, a criminal attack against public faith and the law of nations. By what right did they without a mandate, they, whom the People had not elected, they who were only an imperceptible minority in the mass of citizens; by what right, I ask, did they rush upon the Tuileries like a band of pirates, abolish the Monarchy and proclaim the Republic?

The Republic is above universal suffrage! we said in the elections of 1850; and this was repeated afterwards from the tribune, amid acclamations, by a man not suspected of anarchical opinions, General Cavaignac. If this is true the morality of the revolution of February is vindicated; but what can we say of those who, while proclaiming the Republic, saw in it nothing but the exercise of universal suffrage, the establish= ment of a new form of government? The governmental principle admitted, it was for the People to pronounce upon the form; and who can say that the People would have voted in favor of the Republic, if they had been appealed to?

On the 10th of December, 1848, the People were consulted upon the choice of their first magistrate, and they named Louis Bonaparte, by a majority of five and a half millions, out of seven and a half million voters. In choosing this candidate, the People, in their turn, took counsel only with their own inclinations: they took no account of the predictions and opinions of Republicans. For my part, I disapproved this election for the same reasons that led me to support the proclamation of the Republic. And, because I disapproved of it, I have since opposed, as far as in me lay, the government of the People's Choice.

Nevertheless from the point of view of universal suffrage, of the imperative mandate, and of the sovereignty of numbers, I ought to believe that Louis Bonaparte expresses the ideas, the needs and the tendencies of the nation: I ought to accept his policy as the policy of the People. Even if it were opposed to the Constitution, the mere fact that the Constitution did not emanate directly from the People, while the President was the personification of the majority of votes, his policy should be held as approved, inspired and encouraged by the sovereign People. They who went to the Conservatory on the 13th of June, 1848, were but factionaries. Who gave them the right to suppose that the People, at the end of six months, would discard their President? Louis Bonaparte presented himself under the auspices of his uncle;[23] everybody knows what that means.

Do you still talk about the People? I mean the People as it show itself in mass meetings, at the ballot box; the People, which they did not dare to consult about the Republic in February; the People, which on the 16th of April and in the days of June, declared itself by an immense majority against Socialism; the People, which elected Louis Bonaparte, because it adored Napoleon Bonaparte; the People, which elected the Constituent Assembly, and afterwards the Legislative Assembly; the People, which did not rise on the 13th of June; the People, which did not protest on the 31st of May; the People which signed petitions for revision and petitions against revision. Is this the People which will be enlightened from above. its representatives, inspired by its wisdom, be rendered thereby infallible, when it comes to picking out the most virtuous and most capable, and of deciding upon the organization of Labor, of Credit, of Property and of Power itself?

Neither M. Rittinghausen, who discovered the principle of *Direct Legislation* in Germany, nor M. Considerant, who asked pardon of God and man for having so long rejected this sublime idea, nor M. Ledru=

---

[23] Louis Egalité, Duke of Orleans.

Rollin, who refers them both to the Constitution of '93 and to Jean Jacques Rousseau, nor M. Louis Blanc, who, placing himself between Robespierre and M. Guizot, summons all three back to pure Jacobinism. nor M. Girardin, who, having no more confidence in direct legislation than in universal suffrage or representative monarchy, believes it to be more expeditious, more useful, more easily accomplished, to simplify the Government; — not one of these men, the most advanced of the age, knows what is necessary to be done in order to bring about security of labor, justice in property, honesty in commerce, morality in competition, productiveness in credit, equality in taxation, &c.; or, if any of them knows, he dares not tell.

Yet ten million citizens, who have not studied, analysed, referred to their causes, compared in their affinities, the principles of social organization, as have these professional thinkers; ten million, feebly minded, who have sworn by all the idols, have applauded all programmes, have been the dupes of all political schemes, — these ten millions, drawing up their platforms, and naming their proxies for the purpose, will infallibly solve the problem of the Revolution! Ah, sirs, you do not really think so, you do not really hope so. What you do believe, what you are almost sure of is that you will all be elected by some portion of the people, as men of well-known ability, M. Ledru-Rollin as President of the Republic, M. Louis Blanc as Minister of Progress, M. de Girardin as Minister of Finance, M. Considérant as Minister of Agriculture and Public Works, M. Rittinghausen as Minister of Justice and Public Instruction; after which the problem of the Revolution may solve itself as it will. Enough, let us be frank, universal suffrage, the imperative mandate, the responsibility of representatives, in fact, the whole elective system, is but child's play; I will not trust them with my labor, my peace of mind, my fortune; I will not risk a hair of my head to defend them.

5. Direct Legislation.

Direct legislation! Willy-nilly, we have got to take it up. Robespierre, quoted by Louis Blanc, cries in vain: "Do you not see that this project (the appeal to "the people) tends only to destroy the Convention "itself; that the primary assemblies, once convened, "would be forced by political intrigue and agitation "to deliberate upon *ALL THE PROPOSITIONS* which "might serve their perfidious purposes; that they "would question even the proclamation of the "Republic?... I can see in your system nothing but a "project to destroy the work of the People, and to "rally the enemies that have been overcome by it. If "you have such a scrupulous regard for its sovereign "will, learn to respect it; fulfil the duties which it has "confided to you. It is trifling with the majesty of a "sovereign to refer to him business which he has "ordered you to attend to. *If the People had the time* "*to assemble to judge in trials, and to decide questions* "*of State,* they would not have entrusted to you the "care of their interests. The only way of showing your "fidelity is by making just laws, not by arousing civil "war."

Robespierre does not convince me at all. I perceive his despotism too plainly. *If the primary assemblies,* says he, *were summoned to judge questions of State, the Convention would be destroyed.* True, clearly. If the People become the legislators, what need for representatives? If the People themselves govern, what need for ministers? If we give them the control, what becomes of our authority?... Robespierre was one of those who by preaching respect for the Convention, withdrew the people from the habit of taking part in public affairs, and paved the way for the reaction of Thermidor.[24] To make himself head of this reaction, he had only to guillotine his competitors, instead of foolishly allowing himself to be guillotined by them. Then, while awaiting the invincible Emperor, he might

---

[24] 27 th of July, 1794, by which Robespierre himself was overthrown.

10

have taken his place as one of a Triumvirate or Direc‑
tory. There would have been no difference in the
fate of the Republic; there would have been only one
more recantation.

Finally he says, the people have not time!... Pos‑
sibly. But that is no reason why I should trust to
Robespierre. I wish to do my own bargaining, I repeat,
and, if there must be legislation, to be my own legis‑
lator. Let us begin then by discarding this intolerant
sovereignty of the Arras lawyer; then, when we have
duly buried his theory, we come to that of M. Ritting‑
hausen.

And what is that?

That we should bargain with each other, in
proportion to our needs, directly and without inter‑
meddling? Not at all. M. Rittinghausen is not an
enemy of power to that extent. He only wishes
instead of using universal suffrage for the election of
legislators, to use it for the direct enactment of
uniform and impersonal laws. So it remains still a
contest, a mystification.

I will not repeat, in relation to the application of
universal suffrage to legislation, the objections that
have always been made to deliberative assemblies; for
example, that, as a single vote may make a majority,
by a single vote the law may be passed. If this vote
goes one way, the legislator says: Yes; if it goes the
other way, he says: No. This parliamentary absurdity,
which is the mainspring of the political machine, car‑
ried into the field of universal suffrage, would
undoubtedly bring terrible conflicts, along with
monstrous scandals. The People, as a legislator, would
soon become discredited, and odious to itself. I leave
such objections to petty critics, and insist only upon
the fundamental error, and the unavoidable deception
attending this so‑called direct legislation.

What M. Rittinghausen is in search of, although he
may not always say so, is the general, collective,
synthetic, indivisible Thought; in a word, the Thought
of the People, considered, not as a multitude, nor, on

the other hand, as a creature of the imagination, but as a superior living being. The theory of Rousseau him‹ self led to this view. What did he intend; what do his disciples intend, by this talk of universal suffrage and of the law of the majority? They intend to ap‹ proximate, as far as possible, the general, instinctive feeling, regarding the opinion of the greater number as an adequate expression of that feeling. M. Ritting‹ hausen supposes that a vote upon a law by all the people will give a closer approximation than the mere vote of a majority of representatives: all the originality, all the morality of his theory lies in this hypothesis.

But this supposition necessarily implies another, to wit, that there is in the collectivity of the People some special kind of thought, capable of representing at once collective and individual interests; which can be reached, with more or less exactitude, by some sort of balloting process; consequently that the People is not only a *creature of the mind, a personification of thought*, as Rousseau said, but a true personality, which has its own reality, its own individuality, its own essence, its own life, its own reasoning power. If it were not so; if it were not true that the vote, or universal suffrage, were regarded by their partisans as giving an approximate opinion superior to truth, on what, I ask, would rest the obligation of the minority to submit to the majority? The idea of the *reality* and *personality* of the Collective Being, an idea which Rousseau's theory negatives from the beginning, in the most express manner, is then at the foundation of this theory; all the more must it be of those whose aim is to cause the People to take part in the making of the law more completely and immediately.

For the present, I shall not dwell on the reality and personality of the Collective Being, an idea which has not occurred, in its fulness, to any philosopher, until the present day; and which would require a book as big as this one to explain. I confine myself to observing that this idea, which only expresses concretely the sovereignty of the human race, identical with the
10*

sovereignty of the individual, is the secret, although unadmitted, principle of all systems that consult the People.

Returning to M. Rittinghausen, I say to him: How can you believe that an expression of opinion at once particular and general, collective and individual, in a word, synthetic, can be obtained by balloting, which is the official expression of diversity? A hundred thousand voices singing IN UNISON would hardly give you the vague feeling of the Popular Being. But a hundred thousand voices that were consulted individually, each one answering according to his own opinion, — a hundred thousand voices singing separately, in different keys, could only give a frightful uproar; and the greater the number of voices, the greater the confusion. All you have to do then, in order to approximate the collective opinion, which is the essence of the People, is, after having gathered the *real* opinions of every citizen, to form an abstract of all their opinions, to compare their motives, and then reduce them, by a more or less exact induction, to form the synthesis, which is the general opinion, superior to individual opinions, which alone can be attributed to the people. But how long would be needed for such an operation? Who would undertake to execute it? Who would answer for the fidelity of the work, and for the certainty of the result? What logician would undertake to draw from this ballot box, which contains only dead ashes, the living and life-giving germ, the Popular Idea?

Evidently such a problem is inextricable, insoluble. Moreover, M. Rittinghausen, after bringing forward the finest maxims upon the inalienable right of the people to legislate their own laws, ends, like all political operations, by juggling the question. The people are not to *propose* the questions: the government is to do that. Only to questions *proposed* by the government, the people may answer *Yes* or *No*, like a child in the catechism. The people will not even have a chance to make amendments.

Thus it must be in this system of *discordant legislation* if anything is to be obtained from the multitude. M. Rittinghausen recognizes this frankly. He admits that if the people, assembled in meeting, had the power of *amending* questions, or, what is still more important, of *proposing* them, direct legislation would be only a Utopia. To make this kind of legislation practicable, it is necessary that the sovereign should have to decide on but one alternative, which therefore should embrace in one of its terms, all the truth, nothing but the truth; in the other, all error, nothing but error. If one or the other of the two terms contained more or less than truth, more or less than error, the sovereign, deceived by his minister's question, would inevitably answer foolishly.

But it is impossible in universal questions, embracing the interests of a whole people, ever to arrive at a rigorous dilemma, which means that, no matter how the question is put to the people, they are almost sure to vote wrongly.

Let me give some examples.

Suppose that the question is: *Shall the government be direct or indirect?*

After the success which the ideas of Messrs. Rittinghausen and Considerant will have obtained in the democracy, it may be presumed, almost with certainty, that the answer, by an immense majority, will be, DIRECT. But whether the government be direct or indirect, it remains at the bottom, the same; one is as bad as the other. If the people answer, indirect, they abdicate; if they answer, direct, they strangle themselves. What do you say of this result?

Another question.

Shall there be two powers in the government, or shall there be only one? In clearer terms, *Shall a President be elected?*

In the present state of mind, no one doubts that the answer, inspired by a republicanism that deems itself *advanced*, would be negative. But, as everybody knows who is engaged in governmental organization, in thus concentrating all power in a single assembly, the people would be falling out of the frying pan into the fire. The question nevertheless seemed so simple. *Shall taxation be proportional or progressive?*

At some other period, the proportional would appear to be the natural thing: today, the preference has changed, and it would be a hundred to one that the people would choose the progressive tax. In either case, the sovereign people would commit an injustice. If the tax is proportional, labor is sacrificed; if progressive, talent. In either case, public interest is injured, and individual interest suffers. Economic science, superior to all ballots, teaches this. Yet the question seemed one of the most elementary.

I might multiply examples to infinity; I prefer to cite two given by M. Rittinghausen, who naturally thought them sufficiently explicit and convincing.

Shall there be a railroad from Lyons to Avignon?

The people surely will not say, no; since their greatest desire is to place France on a par with Belgium and England, by shortening distances and by fostering the transportation of men and goods as far as possible. They will then vote, yes, as M. Rittinghausen foresaw. This yes may involve a serious mistake; in any case, local rights are infringed .

There is between Chalons and Avignon a navigable route which offers transportation 70 per cent. below railroad rates. This charge can be further lowered, I happen to know, to 90 per cent. below. Instead of building a railroad, at a cost of 40 million dollars, why not use this water route, costing almost nothing? ... But it is not thus understood at the Legislative Chamber, where there is no commissioner; and as the people of France, with the exception of those who live along the Rhone and the Saone, know no more than their representatives, what goes on upon the two rivers, they will decide, it is easy to foresee, not according to their own opinion, but according to the wishes of their deputies. Eighty-two departments will sentence to ruin the four others. Such is direct legislation.

Who shall build the railroad, the State or a stock company?

In 1849, companies were in favor. The people subscribed their savings: M. Arago, a true republican, voted for them. They did not know then what companies were. The State is the choice nowadays: the people, always well instructed, would undoubtedly give it the preference. Whichever course the sovereign legislator takes, he is the puppet of the ambitious of one kind or another. With a company, low price is sacrificed; commerce is under toll; with the State, labor is no longer free. It is the system of Mehemet= Ali applied to transportation. What difference does it make to the Country, whether the railroads fatten certain contractors, or furnish sinecures for the friends of M. Rittinghausen? What is really needed would be to make of the railroads a new kind of property, to perfect the law of 1810 relating to mines, and make it applicable to railroads, granting the privilege of run= ning them, under fixed conditions, to responsible companies, not of capitalists, but of WORKMEN. But direct legislation will never go so far as to emancipate a man: its formula is general; it enslaves everybody.

How shall the State build the railroad? Shall it raise the money needed by taxation? Shall it borrow from the bankers at 8 or 10 per cent., or shall it issue circulating notes, secured by the railroad itself?

Answer: Let it issue circulating notes.

I ask pardon of M. Rittinghausen; the solution which he gives here in the name of the people, is not worth as much as it would seem. It may very well happen, and indeed is very likely, that the circulating notes will lose 5, 10, 15 and more per cent. discount; so that this method may prove more burdensome for the people than either taxation or loans. Again, what difference does it make to the people, whether they pay usurious interest to the bankers, or profits to government agents, who come in on the ground floor?

Shall the State furnish gratuitous transportation, or shall it derive a revenue from the railroad?

If the people demand gratuitous transportation, they deceive themselves, for all services must be paid for. If the people decide that the State shall derive a revenue, they neglect their own interests, since public service should be without profits. The question is not properly phrased. It should be: *Shall the charge for transport= ation be equal to the cost or not?* But as the cost continually varies, and as special investigation and legislation would be necessary in order to follow it, it is clear that on this point, as on all the rest, the people's answer would be not a law but a blunder.

Is it clear that direct legislation can be nothing but continual trickery? Of a hundred questions proposed to the People by the Government, ninety=nine will be in like case with the foregoing; and the reason is, M. Rittinghausen, as a logician, cannot ignore it, that the questions proposed to the people will usually be *special* questions, while universal suffrage can give only *general* replies. The routine legislator, forced to yield to the dilemma, is unable to modify his formula, according to the requirements of place, time and circumstances; the answer, calculated beforehand from the fancies of the public, will be known in advance, and, whatever it may be, will always be a mistake.

6. Direct Government or the Constitution of '93.
Reduction to Absurdity of the Governmental Idea.

The position which M. Ledru=Rollin has taken in this controversy is remarkable. If I understand his thought, he wanted, first, to restore the original idea of direct government of the authors of the Constitution of '93, and in the second place, to show, at the same time, that this Constitution, which was the culmination of democratic progress, reaches, if it does not pass, the limits of possibility; finally, to distract attention from the empty curiosities of utopias, and to fix it again upon the authentic line of the Revolution.

It costs me nothing to recognize that in this M. Ledru= Rollin has shown himself more liberal than M. Louis Blanc, who is an inflexible follower of Robespierre's governmentalism; and more intelligent in political matters than Messrs. Considerant and Rittinghausen, whose theory, entrenched in the impossible, has not even the merit of frank and irreproachable logic.

M. Ledru=Rollin, personifying the Constitution of '93, seems to be a living problem, which says to the People: You may not stop short of it, but you must not go beyond it. And it must be admitted, this estimate of the Constitution of '93 is correct.

But I conclude that the Constitution of '93, compiled by the most liberal spirits of the Convention, is a monument raised by our fathers as a witness against political rule; that we should see in it a lesson, not a programme, and take it for a point of departure, not as an aim to be reached. M. Ledru=Rollin is a man of progress; he cannot refuse to admit a conclusion which takes the Constitution of '93 as the latest expression of governmental practice; and from this as a starting point, rises into a higher sphere, and completely changes the revolutionary field.

From this point of view I shall try to show unmistake= ably, by a final proof, the absolute incompatibility of Power with Liberty, summing up, in a single proposition, all my remarks upon the Constitution of '93, and upon the comments on it recently added by M. Ledru=Rollin.

M. Ledru=Rollin has perceived very clearly that with the enormous restriction placed upon the popular prerogative, by reserving to the Government the right of *proposing* questions which the people may only answer, direct legislation is but a puerile and immoral mystification. Referring again to the Constitution of '93, he said, in accordance with the good sense of ages: The People should pass upon only the most general questions: matters of detail should be left to the ministers and to the Assembly.

"The distinction," said he, "has been justly made "between *Laws* and *Decrees:* the line of demarcation is "easy to preserve, whatever may be said to the "contrary."

No doubt in practice, and when fundamental points of public right are in question, the people can always decide; and it was thus understood by the authors of the Constitution of '93. But in theory, where precise distinctions are wanted, it is quite otherwise; in such matters the Constitution of '93 seems to consecrate a usurpation. "For," as Louis Blanc observes, "when your "37,000 townships can vote upon the *law*, by what right "do you take from them the power to determine what is "a *law*. By what right do you impose upon them *decrees* "which they would not recognize as such, which might "very well allow the old tyranny to continue to exist "under another name?"

The *Pacific Democracy*, the organ of M. Considerant, is even more explicit. "Enough primordial principles "are found formulated in all constitutions, in all the "fundamental laws of Europe. They are fixed, as a "whole, by the laws, but they are upset, ruined in detail "by what you call *decrees*. To introduce your system "is to have liberty of the press proclaimed by the people, "in order to have it destroyed by parliamentary decrees "upon the sale of newspapers, upon stamps, upon "printers' licenses, upon all the apparatus of repression "that is forged in legislative assemblies. It is to have "universal suffrage acclaimed by the People, in order "thereupon to have the *vile multitude* excluded by a "mandatory decree: it is to have the rights of man "published by the People, in order shortly afterwards "to have a *state of siege* established by a decision of the "Chamber; and that too under a pretext of saving the "country and civilization. . . . How, too, will you "prevent a conflict of jurisdiction between your two "legislative powers, a conflict of jurisdiction which the "natural antagonism of your representatives (and the "instinct of resistance which is natural to the masses) "will not fail to arouse every moment? . . ."

These considerations have their merit; nevertheless, with a Constitution like that of '93, I do not believe, I repeat, that they are worth much except in theory.

Here is something that seems to me to bear upon the facts more directly.

The distinction between *laws* and *decrees*, followed by the Constitution of '93 and by M. Ledru-Rollin, is essentially that between the *Legislative* and *Executive Powers*, after the rule laid down by Rousseau.

"The law being but the declaration of the general will, "it is clear that the People cannot be represented in the "legislative power, but they can and should be "represented in the executive power, which is only force "applied to the law."

Through this principle of Rousseau's, under the Charters of 1814 and 1830, while the legislative power resided in the King and the two Chambers, the executive power belonged to the King alone, who thus became, by Rousseau's rule, the single, true representative of the Country.

But before making any distinction between *laws* and *decrees*, and before assigning the former to the People, the latter to the Government, it is necessary, in the opinion of all democratic minds, to put the following preliminary question to the People:

Shall the separation of powers be a condition of Government?

That is to say:

Shall the People be represented in the Executive branch of the Government, seeing that it cannot be represented in the Legislative branch?

In other terms:

Shall there be a President or not?

I defy anybody in the whole democracy to answer affirmatively. So if you want neither a President, nor a Consul, nor Triumvirs, nor Directors, nor a King, nor, despite the oracle of Rousseau, any Representative for the Executive Power, of what use is your distinction between laws and decrees? The People must vote on everything, laws and decrees both included, as M. Rittinghausen wishes. But this is what we have shown is impossible. *Direct Legislation* is buried. We need not return to it.

M. Ledru-Rollin, or rather the Constitution of '93, thought to get around the difficulty by saying, with Condorcet, that the Executive Power should be chosen, not by the People, who are incapable of choosing, but by the Assembly.

I ask pardon of Condorcet. What! you begin by saying that the People can and must be represented in the Executive branch, but when the question comes up of selecting this *Representative* of the People, instead of having him elected directly by the citizens, you want to have him named by their *deputies?* This is taking away from the People the best half of the Government; for the Executive is more than half the Government; it is, indeed, the whole Government. After relieving the People of all legislative duties, you would place upon them the responsibility for every act of Power, pretending that it is but the application of their own laws. You seem to say to the People, the Sovereign, Legislator and Judge: Talk, decide, legislate, vote, command! We, your deputies, charge ourselves with the interpretation and afterwards with the execution of your orders. But whatever we do, you are responsible. *Quidquid dixeris, argumentabimur.*[25]

If M. Ledru-Rollin made a mistake, it was in calling this *Direct Government*, after the example of M. Considerant.

In the first place, if the People, instead of answering, *yes* or *no*, on all affairs of State, as M. Rittinghausen wished, can pronounce upon the laws only, nine-tenths of all questions are removed from their initiative, under the name of *decrees.*

In the second place, the whole *Executive* power is snatched from them: not only may they not make any appointments, they may not even elect their *Representative*, who makes appointments for them.

As the climax of this contradiction, the said Representative is elected by the People's deputies, so that the People who ought not to have any representative, nor

---

[25] Whatever you say, we will bring proof.

delegate any power, whose direct sovereignty, on the contrary, should remain in permanent exercise, the People would find that they have less authority than their deputies, and be forced to recognize, as their *Representative* in the executive power, one or more individuals, whose title had been decreed by their deputies in the legislative branch! . . . .

I say no more, but I ask all honest men, whether the Constitution of '93, which promises everything to the People and gives them nothing, standing at the extreme limit of the rational and real, does not seem to them a beacon, erected by our fathers at the entrance of a new world, rather than a plan for the future, whereof they confided the execution to their descendants?

I dismiss the *more advanced* systems, which cannot fail to arise, following those of Messrs.Rittinghausen and Ledru-Rollin; it would be too tedious to begin a like criticism on each of these; I pass to the final hypothesis.

This is one in which the People, returning to absolute power, and taking themselves, as a whole, as their own Despot, in consequence deal with themselves: in which therefore they would, as is proper, hold all privileges, unite in their own person all powers, legislative, executive, judicial, and others, if there are any others; in which they would make all laws, pronounce all decrees, ordinances, resolutions, sentences, judgments, send out all orders, take charge themselves of all their agents and functionaries, from the highest to the lowest of the hierarchy, transmit to them their will, directly and without intermediaries, supervise and secure their execution, laying on each his share of responsibility, themselves award all endowments, civil lists, pensions, rewards; in fact, would enjoy, as king in fact and of right, all the honors and advantages of sovereignty, power, money, pleasure, leisure, etc.

I try as much as I can, to infuse a little logic into this system, which is our last hope, and which, in clearness, simplicity, rigor of principles, severity in their application, and for democratic and liberal radicalism leaves far behind it the timid, entangled, half-way projects of

Héraut, Séchelles, Considérant, Rittinghausen, Louis Blanc, Robespierre and their consorts.

Unfortunately, this system, irreproachable, I venture to say, as a whole and in detail, meets with an insurmountable difficulty in practice.

It is that Government implies as a correlative somebody to be governed; and if the whole People, claiming sovereignty, assumes Government, one seeks in vain where the governed will be. Renember, the aim of government is not to harmonize antagonistic inter= ests, it admits that it is quite incompetent to do this; but to keep order in society, despite the conflict of interests. In other words, the object of government is to supply the defects of the economic order and the lack of industrial harmony. Therefore if the people, in the interest of their liberty and sovereignty, take charge of government, they can no longer busy themselves with production, since by the nature of things production and government are incompatible functions, and to endeavor to unite them would be to spread division everywhere. Once more then, where will the producers be, where the governed, where the subjects, where the criminals, where the con= demned?

When we were a monarchy, absolute or modified, the Government being the King, the correlative was the NATION. — We did not like this government; we accused it, not without reason, of corruption and licentiousness.

When we were a constitutional monarchy, the Gov= ernment being composed of the King and the two Chambers, both of them formed after some fashion, by heredity, by the choice of the King, or from a certain class of the nation, the correlative was all that took no part in the operation of the government; these were, in differing degrees, an immense majority of the nation. — We have changed all that, not without reason, the Government having become a cancer on the people.

At present we are a quasi=democratic Republic: all the citizens are permitted, every third or fourth year, to elect, first, the Legislative Power, second, the Executive Power, The duration of this participation in the Government for the popular collectivity is brief; forty-eight hours at the most for each election. For this reason the correlative of the Government remains nearly the same as before, almost the whole Country. The President and the Representatives, once elected, are the masters; all the rest obey. They are *subjects*, to be *governed* and to be taxed, without surcease.

When, in this same system, the President and the Representatives were elected every year, and subject to recall at all times, the correlation was felt to be but little different. Some days more for the mass, some days less for the governing minority: the thing was not worth talking about.

That system is worn out: there is no longer anybody, either in the Government or among the people, that wants it.

In despair of their case, they are offering other schemes, under the names of *Direct Legislation, Direct* Government, etc.; as, for instance, to have the legislative work done by all the People, 10 million citizens, or at least a part of them; or to have some of the agents and functionaries of the Executive Power, who are now appointed by the President, selected by these same 10 million men. The tendency of these different systems is to give the Government at least a half plus one of the citizens, the reverse of what Rousseau taught, *that it is against the natural order that the smaller number should be governed by the greater.*

We have just proved that these schemes, which are distinguished from each other only by more or less inconsistency, encounter insurmountable difficulties in practice; that moreover they are all discredited in advance, marked by tyranny and brute force, since the Law of the People, obtained by means of the ballot, is necessarily the law of chance; and the *Power* of the People, based upon numbers, is necessarily the power of brute force.

It is impossible then to stop in this descent. We must come to the last hypothesis, that wherein the People enters into Government in the mass, and wields all the branches of Power; in which they are always unanimous, and have above them neither president, nor representatives, nor deputies, nor law-made country, nor majority; in a word, they are, in their collectivity, the sole legislator and the sole functionary.

But if the People, thus organized for Power, have nothing *above* them, what, I ask, have they *below?* In other words, where is the correlative of government; where are the laborers, the mechanics, the merchants, the soldiers, where are the workers and the citizens?

Will you answer that the People are everything at once, that they produce and legislate at the same time, that Labor and Government are united in them? It is impossible, because, as, on the one hand, the reason for the existence of government is the divergence of interests, as, on the other, no separation of authority nor of majority is possible, the People alone as a whole having the power to make laws; consequently the legislative debate would be prolonged with the number of legislators, the affairs of State growing in direct proportion to the multitude of statesmen, there is no longer time nor leisure for citizens to attend to their industrial occupations, all their daytime is not too much to dispose of the business of Government. There is no middle course: either work or rule: it is the law of the People as of the Prince; ask Rousseau.

Thus it was that affairs were conducted at Athens, where, during several centuries, the whole People were in the public place of gathering, discussing questions from morning till night. But the twenty thousand citizens of Athens, who constituted the sovereign power, had four hundred thousand slaves working for them; while the French People have no one to slave for them, and a thousand times as much business to transact as the Athenians had. I repeat my question: When the People have become both legislator and ruler, upon what will they legislate, for what interests, to

what end? And while they are governing, who will
support them? *Sublata causa, tollitur effectus,*[26] says
the School. When the mass of the People becomes the
State, the State has no longer any reason to exist, since
there is no longer any People, the governmental
equation reduces to zero.

Thus the principle of authority, carried from the
family to the nation, tends unavoidably to do away
with both the Government and the People, through the
successive concessions which it is compelled to make
against itself, concessions of definite laws, concessions
of constitutional charters, concessions of universal suf‹
frage, concessions of direct legislation, etc., etc. And
since the elimination of Government and People is
impossible, at least for the latter, the movement, after
a short period, is interrupted by a conflict; then begins
again by a restoration. Such is the course which France
has followed since 1789, which will continue for ever,
if the public common sense does not end by under‹
standing that a false hypothesis causes the swing back
and forth. The publicists who recall to us the tradition
of '93 cannot ignore that, for our fathers, direct govern‹
ment was but the step to dictatorship, which itself was
the entrance to despotism.

When the Convention, of lamentable memory, had
passed, on the 24th of June, 1793, the famous act by
which the People were summoned to govern themselves
directly, the Jacobins and the Mountain, all‹powerful
since the fall of the Girondins, understood perfectly
what the Utopia of Héraut‹Séchelles was worth: they
had a decree passed by their humble servant, the
Convention, that direct government should be
postponed until peace. Until peace, as you know,
meant twenty‹five years at the start. The organizers of
Direct Government wisely thought that the People, as
legislators, laborers and soldiers, could not fulfil these
noble functions while working with one hand and
fighting with the other, that first the country must be

---

[26] The cause removed, the effect ceases.

11

saved, and afterwards, when the People had nothing to
fear, they could enter upon their sovereignty.

This was the reason that was given to the People at
the time of the postponement of the Constitution
of '93.

Three months, six months, a year, passed, and neither
the Mountain nor the Plain demanded that this un=
constitutional provision, which attacked the sovereignty
of the People, should be repealed. The *Committee of
Public Safety* was reconciled to the revolutionary
Government; as for the People, they seemed to care
little for Direct Government.

Finally Danton, who had spoken upon the neces=
sity of putting an end to the dictation of committees,
was the first to be delivered to the revolutionary
tribunal, accused of moderation and sent to the scaf=
fold. Unlucky man! he was perhaps the first, with
Desmoulins, Héraut=Séchelles and Lacroix, who
believed in the Constitution of '93, or who at least
wanted to try the experiment of it: he was guillotined.
Direct Government, in the eyes of the experienced,
was pure quackery: Robespierre was not willing to
permit the discovery of this piece of trickery. A firm
disciple of Rousseau himself, he had always expressed
himself clearly, strongly, as Louis Blanc recently
showed, in favor of indirect government, which is no
other than that of 1814, or that of 1830, representative
government.

I am not a republican, said Robespierre in '91, after
the treason of Varennes, but I am not a royalist either.
He meant to say: I am neither for *direct* government,
nor am I for absolutism: I am for the middle course.
In fact, it is doubtful whether there was in this
assembly a single republican, except some Girondists,
artists, sacrificed after the 31st of May, and some
Mountainists, of simple faith, whom the Convention
immolated following the days of Prairial. The greater
part shared the ideas of Robespierre, with insensible
variations, which were the ideas of '91, and served in

the Constitution of the Directory. That was what appeared above all at the 9th of Thermidor.

No historian that I know of has given a satisfactory explanation of this day, which made an apostate from democracy into a martyr of the Revolution. Nevertheless the affair is plain enough.

Robespierre, having relieved himself successively by the guillotine of the factions then deemed *anarchic,* the Enragés, the Hébertists, the Dantonists, of all those whom he suspected of taking the Constitution of '93 in earnest, thought that the moment had arrived to strike a last blow, and to reëstablish indirect government upon a normal basis. These were those views of governmental restoration, today condemned by experience, but which in the time of Robespierre were still esteemed by the coalition of powers. What the demanded then from the Convention on the 9th of Thermidor, was, after preliminary purification, always by the guillotine, Committees of Public Safety and of General Security, *a greater concentration of power,* a unifying tendency in the Government, something, in fact, resembling the presidency of Louis=Bonaparte. That is proved by the sequel of his speech, which is recognized by his apologists, notably by Messrs. Buchez and Lebas, and was later made a part of history.

Robespierre knew perfectly well that he was responding to the secret desires of the majority of the Convention. He felt that he was in accordance with them upon principles: no doubt he was not unaware that foreign diplomacy began to look upon him as a statesman with whom it might be possible to come to an understanding. He could not doubt that the *honest men* of the Convention, to whom he had always truckled, would be delighted to reinstate constitutionalism, the object of all their desires, and at the same time to see themselves relieved of a certain number of democrats, whose sanguinary energy terrified their middle=course tendencies. The stroke was well prepared, the plan skilfully conceived, the occasion

11*

could not have been more favorable. What happened immediately after Thermidor, the trials of the revolutionaries, the Constitution of the year V., the policy of the Directory and of Brumaire, were but a continuation of the application of Robespierre's ideas. The place of this man should have been alongside of the Sieyès, the Cambacérès, and others, who, knowing perfectly what to hold upon direct government, wished to return to indirect as soon as possible, that the reaction which they were about to begin against democracy might carry them even to empire.

Unfortunately for himself, Robespierre had few friends in the Convention: his project was not clear: in men who saw him near at hand, his genius inspired little confidence; he opposed them too violently; and then there was the danger for him that the constitutional, middleclass majority in the Convention, to whom he addressed himself, and whom he made thereby masters of the situation, might seize the idea that he suggested, and turn it against the author and his rivals at the same time.

That was precisely what happened.

The leaders of the majority, who had been wheedled by Robespierre, thought that they might kill two birds with one stone; as in 1848 the honest and moderate majority found itself in a position to turn out both the *National* and the *Reform* parties. At the decisive moment they abandoned the *dictator*, who became the first victim of his own reaction. As Robespierre had struck down Danton; as he intended to strike down Cambon, Billaut, Varennes and others; so the moderates of the Convention, upon whom he had counted, and who in fact did not fail him in his expectations, struck him down in turn; the others came afterwards. Indirect government, delivered from its fiercest enemy, Danton, and from its most surly competitor, Robespierre, might again appear.

Some have said that Robespierre aspired to the dictatorship; others that he wished to reëstablish the monarchy. These accusations refute each other.

Robespierre, who did not abandon his convictions any
more than he renounced his popularity, aspired to
be the chief of the executive power in a constitutional
government. He would have accepted a place under
the Directory or under the Consulate: he would have
been of the opposition to the dynasty after 1830: we
should have seen him approving the Provisional
Government after February: his hatred for atheists,
his instinctive love for priests, would have caused him
to vote for the expedition to Rome.

Let those who, with more honesty than prudence,
following the footsteps of Danton, revive today the
proposition for direct government; who, again like
Danton, remind the People of their imprescriptible
rights, and cry: *No more dictators! No more doc-
trinaires!* let them not forget that the Dictatorship is at
the end of their theory, and this *Doctrine*, of which
they are so much afraid, is that of the justly punished
traitor of Thermidor. Direct Government is nothing
but the long known transition, through which the
People, tired of political schemes, bring themselves to
rest in absolute government, where the ambitions of
the reactionaries await them. Has not the thought of
a dictatorship already, as I write these lines, been cast
among the people, and accepted by the impatient and
the timid? The very same men whom we see combatting both direct government and chaos at the same
time, sometimes invoking the reputation of Robespierre,
sometimes hating his name, have we not seen them all,
the day after the revolution of February, putting a stop
to the assertion of liberty, giving a different outlet to
the aspirations of the People, voting for the recall of
candidates, and always, everywhere, paying in talk and
slander, where the People demanded acts and ideas.

I have more than one friend among men who follow,
or think that they follow, even now, the Jacobin
tradition: it is for them chiefly that I write these lines.
May the resemblance of our times to those at last
discover to them, what until now it has been difficult
for them to suspect, the true signification of the 9th

of Thermidor, and the real intention of Robespierre.

Just as in '93, they who boasted most loudly of the
title of revolutionaries desired that questions of
property and social economy should not be agitated,
sending to the scaffold the *Anarchists* who demanded
for the people guaranties of work and living wages;
so to=day, in the midst of a revolution, the successors,
open or secret, of Jacobinism, take their stand solely
on questions of politics, and avoid expressing them=
selves on economic reforms; or, if they touch upon them,
it is only to murmur some innocent precepts of frater=
nity, coming down to us from the love=feasts at Jerusa=
lem.   All the popularity hunters, mountebanks of the
Revolution, have taken for their oracle Robespierre,
the eternal denouncer, with an empty head and a viper's
tongue, who, when summoned to formulate his plans,
to describe his ways and means, did nothing but beat
a   retreat   before   difficulties,   while   accusing   his
opponents of making the difficulties.   This cowardly
rhetorician, who in '90, for fear of embroiling himself
with the Court, disavowed a pleasantry that fell from
his lips and was reported by Desmoulins; who, in '91,
opposed the declaration of abdication of Louis XVI,
and found fault with the petition of the Champ de Mars;
who, in '92, opposed the declaration of war, because it
would give too much reputation to the Girondists;
who, in '93, antagonized the rising in mass; who, in '94,
always and everywhere, advised the people to take no
part in it; who always thwarted, without understanding
them, the plans of Cambon, of Carnot, of all those
whom he disdainfully called *expedition=people;* this
indefatigable calumniator of all the notable men whom
he envied and plagiarized, fifty years later serves as
patron saint to all the dazed revolutionaries, helping
their cause as much as a lame led=horse helps draw the
carriage.   Tell us, for once, all you disciples of the
great Robespierre, what you mean by the Revolution?
What are your *ways and means?*

Alas! one is never betrayed but by his friends.   In
1848, as in 1793, the Revolution had for leaders men

who represented it. Our republicanism, like the old
Jacobinism, is now only a bourgeois fancy, without
principle and without plan, which wants and doesn't
want, which always scolds, suspects, and none the
less is duped; which sees everywhere, outside its set,
nothing but factions and Anarchists; which, searching
the police records, can find only the real or fancied
weaknesses of patriots; which forbids the worship of
Chatel, and has masses sung by the archbishop of
Paris; which, on all questions, avoids the proper
answer, for fear of compromising itself, reserves decision on everything, settles nothing, distrusts plain
reasons and clear positions. Once again, is not all this
Robespierre, the talker without initiative; who found
in Danton too much virility; blamed his generous boldness, because he had none himself; held back from the
10th of August; neither approved nor disapproved the
massacres of September; voted for the Constitution of
'93 and for its postponement until peace; condemned
the Feast of Reason, and established that of the
Supreme Being; prosecuted Carrier and supported
Fouquier-Tinville; gave the kiss of peace to Camille
Desmoulins in the morning, and had him arrested that
night; proposed the abolition of the death penalty, and
drew up the law of Prairial; outbid, in turn, Sieyès,
Mirabeau, Barnave, Pétion, Danton, Marat, Hébert, and
then had guillotined and proscribed, one after the
other, Hébert, Danton, Pétion, Barnave, the first as an
Anarchist, the second as too lenient, the third as a
federalist, the fourth as a constitutionalist; held in
esteem only the governmental bourgeois and the
refractory clergy; cast discredit upon the Revolution,
sometimes about the ecclesiastical oath, sometimes on
the occasion of the assignats; spared only those to
whom silence or death offered a refuge, and at last
succumbed, on the day when, remaining almost alone
among the middle-course men, he endeavored, by con-
nivance with them, and for his own profit, to bind in
chains the Revolution. Ah! I know this reptile too well;
I have felt too often the waving of his tail that I

should spare in him the secret vice of democrats, the ferment that corrupts every republic, Envy. It was Robespierre who, in '94, opening the door to those who were called after the Thermidorians, lost the Revolution; it was upon the example and through the authority of Robespierre that Socialism was proscribed in 1797 and 1848; it is Robespierre who today would bring back a new Brumaire, if his hypocritical and detestable influence had not been finally annihilated.

A revolution is always split by parties and sects, which work to pervert it, while its natural enemies fight it.   Christianity had, from the beginning, its heresies, and later its great schism. The Reformation had its divisions and sects; the French Revolution, to mention the most famous names, its Constitutionalists, Jacobins and Girondists.

The Revolution of the nineteenth century has also its Utopians, its Schools, its parties, all more or less retrograde reflections of reactionary types. You find among revolutionaries, as well as in the ranks of reaction, *friends of order*, who declare themselves ready to march against anarchy, when the stillness of despair reigns among the persecuted radicals; you find *saviors of society*, for whom society means all that the Revolution opposes; you find *middle-course men,* whose policy is to take the part of the Revolution as one takes the part of a conflagration; you find *radicals*, for whom revolutionary phrases take the place of ideas; you find *terrorists*, who, as they cannot be Mirabeaus or Dantons, are willing to accept the immortality of Carriers or Jourdan Headchoppers. To some the Constitution of 1848; to others, direct government; to these the Dictatorship; to those the Revolutionary Tribunal or the Council of War, serve as banner and bass drum. Moreover all these have taken their stand upon the governmental idea. Power is the only idea they can conceive, when Power is breaking down everywhere; the last trace that warns them of their fate, and exhibits them to us as the precursors and victims of the last exterminator, Robespierre.

On the 10th of August, 1792, Royalty fell beneath the bullets of the suburbs; while Robespierre and his Jacobins were still at the Constitution of '91, soaked with the blood of the soldiers of Nancy, and of the patriots of the Champ de Mars.

They kept firing from the heights of their parliamen= tary citadel, and distrusted those who talked of des= troying both Royalty and Constitution. They never pardoned bold revolutionaries like Danton, who had dragged them, like skulking dogs, to hunt down con= stitutional monarchy, of which they hoped to become in their turn the rulers and masters. *The Constitution,* said Robespierre, *suffices for the Revolution.*

The hatred of this party, which has drunk the blood of the best citizens, pursues us still. I can reconcile myself to men, because, like them, I may make a mis= take; but to parties, never! Let them continue to hate us, for alas! it not so soon that the Revolution can be released from the bridle. We will gladly sacrifice our initiative to those who are less advanced, provided that by their hands the Revolution is accomplished. We say to Robespierre, as Themistocles said to Eurybiades: *Strike, hanger=on of Government; strike, sycophant of the Revolution; strike, degenerate follower of Loyola, hypocritical worshipper of the Supreme Being; strike, but hear me.*

FIFTH STUDY.

Social Liquidation.

THE preceding studies, as much upon contemporaneous society as upon the reforms which it suggests, have taught us several things which it is well to recount here summarily.

1. The fall of the monarchy of July and the proclamation of the Republic were the signal for a social revolution.

2. This Revolution, at first not understood, little by little became defined, determined and settled, under the influence of the very same Reaction which was displayed against it, from the first days of the Provisional Government.

3. This Revolution consists in substituting the economic, or industrial, system, for the governmental, feudal and military system, in the same way that the present system was substituted, by a previous revolution, for a theocratic or sacerdotal system.

4. By an industrial system, we understand, not a form of government, in which men devoted to agriculture and industry, promoters, proprietors, workmen, become in their turn a dominant caste, as were formerly the nobility and clergy, but a constitution of society having for its basis the organization of economic forces, in place of the hierarchy of political powers.

5. And to explain that this organization must result from the nature of things, that there is nothing arbitrary about it, that it finds its law in established practice, we have said that, in order to bring it about, the question was of one thing only: To change the course of things, the tendency of society.

Passing then to the examination of the chief ideas that offer themselves as principles for guidance, and that serve as banners to parties, we have recognized:

6. That the principle of association, invoked by most *Schools,* is an essentially sterile principle; that it is neither an industrial force nor an economic law; that it would involve both government and obedience, two words which the Revolution bars.

7. That the political principle revived recently, under the names of *direct legislation, direct government,* etc., is but a false application of the principle of authority, whereof the sphere is in the family, but which cannot legitimately be extended to the city or the nation.

At the same time we have established:

8. That in place of the idea of association, there was a tendency to substitute in the workmen's societies a new idea, reciprocity, in which we have seen both an economic force and a law.

9. That to the idea of government there was opposed, even in the political tradition itself, the idea of *contract,* the only moral bond which free and equal beings can accept.

Thus we come to recognize the essential factors of the Revolution.

Its cause: the economic chaos which the Revolution of 1789 left after it.

Its occasion: a progressive, systematic poverty, of which the government finds itself, willy-nilly, the promoter and supporter.

Its organic principle: reciprocity; in law terms, contract.

Its aim: the guaranty of work and wages, and thence the indefinite increase of wealth and of liberty.

Its parties, which we divide into two groups: the Socialist schools, which invoke the principle of Association; and the democratic factions, which are still devoted to the principles of centralization and of the State.

Finally, its adversaries, the capitalistic, theological, usurious, governmental, partisans of the *statu quo,* all those indeed who live less by labor than by prejudice and privilege.

To deduce the organizing principle of the Revolution, the idea at once economic and legal of *reciprocity* and of *contract*, taking account of the difficulties and opposition which this deduction must encounter, whether on the part of revolutionary sects, parties or societies, or from the reactionaries and defenders of the *statu quo; to* expound the totality of those reforms and new institu= tions, wherein labor finds its guaranty, property its limit, commerce its balance, and government its farewell; that is to tell, from the intellectual point of view, the story of the Revolution.

What I am about to say, as what I have said, is therefore neither prophecy, nor agitation, nor alarm. Everybody to=day knows well enough that I belong to no party and reject all schools, and therefore have no following to which I could give instructions and orders of the day. I tell what is; consequently what will be: I have no reason to write anything but the truth as it strikes me, and the desire to enlighten my compatriots and contemporaries upon their situation.

How and in what order will these questions arise? How long will the working out of the revolution last? Will it be completed in one night, like that of the 4th of August, or by a series of victories of the revolution over the counter=revolution? What compromises will be made? What delays and postponements granted? What modifications in principles will parties, sects, and self= conceit permit to prevail? What parliamentary, administrative, electoral, military, episodes will occur, to enliven and adorn this epic? I do not know: I am absolutely ignorant of these things. Once again, I am no more a fortune=teller than I am a man of party or sect. I deduce the general consequences of the future from the facts of the present; some leaves from the book of Destiny that I throw to the winds. THIS IS TO BE, that is all that I can say, because *it is written,* and we cannot prevent it. But in what manner it will come to pass, I cannot foresee, since we are entirely masters of our fate, and on this point, our free choice is the judge of last resort.

I therefore beg my readers not to judge my sentiments as a man entirely according to my convictions as a historian. More often than once it will fall to me to sustain, from the point of view of the necessity of things, such and such a measure, upon which, if I should listen to my heart, I should perhaps change my mind; a painful wrench for me, but for which the public will forgive me, if it prefers an inflexible logician who instructs it, to the elegant and sentimental writer who flatters it.

After these preliminaries, we have now three things to do:

1st. To cut short the disorganizing *tendency* which the old revolution bequeathed to us, and to proceed, with the aid of the new principle, to the dissolution of established interests. — Thus the Constituent Assembly proceeded on the night of the 4th of August 1789.

2nd. To organize, always with the aid of the new principle, the economic forces, and to lay down the law of property.

3rd. To dissolve, submerge, and cause to disappear the political or governmental system in the economic system, by reducing, simplifying, decentralizing and suppressing, one after another, all the wheels of this great machine, which is called the Government or the State.

Such are the questions that we are about to treat in this study, and in the two succeeding. In another work, taking up again revolutionary practice from a higher standpoint, we shall endeavor to separate from it a loftier view, notably in what concerns religious ideas, morality, philosophy, literature and the arts; and we shall say the last word about the present revolution.

Suppose that in 1852, when they were summoned to elect their representatives, the People, before going to the ballot boxes, had taken counsel with themselves, revised, as in '89, the list of their desires, and ordered their deputies to put them into execution; that they had said to them:

We desire a peaceful revolution, but we want it to be prompt, decisive, complete. We desire that to this system of oppression and poverty should succeed a system of comfort and liberty; that for a constitution of political powers should be substituted an organization of economic forces; that the man and the citizen, instead of being attached to society by any bond of subordina= tion and obedience, should be held only by free contract. Finally we desire that for the realization of our wishes, you should make use of the very institutions which we charge you to abolish, and the principles of law which you will have to complete, in such a way that the new society may appear as the spontaneous, natural and necessary development of the old, and that the Revolution, while abrogating the old order, should nevertheless be derived from it.

Suppose, I say, that the People, once enlightened as to their true interests, declare their will, not to reform government, but to revolutionize society: in that case, without prejudice to a better plan, without pretending that the steps herein pointed out are at all absolute, or incapable of all sorts of modifications, this is how I conceive the Representatives of the People might carry out their mandate.

I take for my starting point a question which may be deemed tiresome, the Bank of Discount: I shall try to present it in a new and more interesting light, by suppressing all technical details, and all discussion of theory.

———

1. National Bank.

Two producers have the right to promise each other, and to guarantee reciprocally for, the sale or exchange of their respective products, agreeing upon the articles and the prices. (Art. 1589 and 1703 of the Civil Code.)

The same promise of reciprocal sale or exchange, under the same legal conditions, may exist among an unlimited number of producers: it will be the same contract, repeated an unlimited number of times.

French citizens have the right to agree, and, if desired, to club together for the establishment of bakeries, butcher shops, grocer stores, &c., which will guarantee them the sale and exchange, at a reduced price, and of good quality, of bread, meat, and all articles of consumption, which the present mercantile chaos gives them of light weight, adulterated, and at an exorbitant price. For this purpose the *Housekeeper* was founded, a society for the mutual insurance of a just price and honest exchange of products.

By the same rule, citizens have the right to found, for their common advantage, a Bank, with such capital as they choose, for the purpose of obtaining at a low price the currency that is indispensable in their trans⸗ actions, and to compete with individual privileged banks. In agreeing among themselves with this object, they will only be making use of the right which is guaranteed to them by the principle of the freedom of commerce, and the articles 1589 and 1703 of the Civil Code, which are the interpretation of it.

Thus a Bank of Discount may be a public establishment, and to found it there is needed neither association, nor fraternity, nor obligation, nor State intervention; only a reciprocal promise for sale or exchange is needed; in a word, a simple contract.

This settled, I say that not only may a Bank of Discount be a public establishment, but that such a bank is needed. Here is the proof:

1. The Bank of France was founded, *with Govern⸗ mental privilege,* by a company of stockholders, with a capital of $18,000,000. The specie at present buried in its vaults amounts to about $120,000,000. Thus five⸗ sixths of this specie which has accumulated in the vaults of the Bank, by the substitution of paper for metal in general circulation, is the property of citizens. Therefore the Bank, by the nature of its mechanism, which consists in using capital which does not belong to it, ought to be a public institution.

2. Another cause of this accumulation of specie is the GRATUITOUS privilege which the Bank of France has obtained from the State of issuing notes against the specie of which it is the depositary. So, as every privilege is public property, the Bank of France, by its privilege alone, tends to become a public institution.

3. The privilege of issuing bank notes, and of gradually displacing coin by paper in the circulation, has for its immediate result, on the one hand, to give to the stockholders of the Bank an amount of interest far in excess of that due to their capital; on the other, to maintain the price of money at a high rate, to the great profit of the class of bankers and money-lenders, but to the great detriment of producers, manufacturers, merchants, consumers of every kind who make use of currency. This excess of interest paid to stockholders, and the rise in the rates for money, both the result of the desire which Power has always had to make itself agreeable to the rich, capitalistic class, are unjust, they cannot last forever; therefore the Bank, by the illegitimacy of its privileges, is doomed to become a public establishment.

I propose therefore, in the first place, in conformity with the indications furnished by financial practice, that the Representatives of the people, who hold the portfolios of their departments, shall make use of the power granted to them by the Constitution of 1848, and promulgate a decree declaring the Bank of France, not the property of the State, I shall shortly tell why, but an institution of public utility, and ordering the dissolution of the company.

That is not all.

The Bank of France, having become an institution of public utility, and having its capital furnished by its own customers, will no longer have to serve any outside interests. In the first place, the axiom of the law, *Res sua nulli servit*, is contrary to it. Moreover, the general good, which requires that money, like meat, wine and other merchandise, shall be sold at the lowest price possible, is opposed to it. All merchants and manufac=

turers recognize this: it is the dearness of money and capital which keeps up poverty in our country, and causes our inferiority to England.

The present rate of interest on money at the Bank is 4 per cent; which means 5, 6, 7, 8 and 9 per cent. at other bankers, who almost alone have the privilege of discounting at the Bank.

Well, as this interest belongs to the public, the public will be able to reduce it at will to 3, 2, 1, ½ and ¼ per cent., according to whether it is found to be of greater advantage to draw a large revenue from the Bank, or to carry on business at lower cost.

Let this course of reduction, for however small an amount, once be entered upon, and continued as slowly as you like, faster or more slowly makes no difference; then, I assert, the social tendency in all that concerns the price of money and discount, throughout the whole territory of the Republic, will be immediately changed, ipso facto, and that this simple change will cause the Country to pass from the present capitalistic and governmental system to a revolutionary system.

Ah! is anything so terrible as a revolution?

If you ask me now how far I for my part think this reduction of interest should be carried, I do not hesitate to answer: to the figure that is rigorously necessary to cover the expenses of administration and wear of metals, perhaps ½ or ¼ per cent.; and I propose to add to the decree a second clause to that effect.

I will not discuss here my reasons for that opinion, which for a long time were personal to me. I have given them elsewhere. For the present I have nothing to do with political economy, nor finances, nor morals; I am talking of revolution pure and simple. That is why I insist chiefly upon the principle, while taking the liberty of expressing my opinion in advance upon what relates to practice. On the day upon which you shall have decreed the democratization of the Bank, and the reduction of interest, on that day you will have entered upon the path to revolution.

12

Nevertheless I must not fail to touch in passing upon one essential consideration. If I desire to pay no interest to the Bank, it is because interest is in my eyes a governmental, feudal practice, from which we shall never be able to escape if the Bank of the Country becomes a Bank of the State. For a long time Socialism has dreamed of a State Bank, State Credit, revenues and profits of the State; all which means the democratic and social consecration of the spoliation principle, robbery of the worker, in the name, with the example, and under the patronage of the Republic. Place the Bank of the People in the hands of the Government, and, under the pretext of saving for the State the profits of discount in place of new taxes, new sinecures, huge pickings, unheard of waste will be created at the expense of the People: usury, parasitism and privilege will again be favored. No, no, I want no State, not even for a servant; I reject government, even direct government; I see in all these inventions only pretexts for parasitism and refuges for idlers.

Such would be my first revolutionary act; that by which I should begin the dissolution of society.

What do you find in this of injustice or violence? Does it seem to you to bear the imprint of despotism, or to be marked by liberty? Do you not recognize the expression of the organic principle, reciprocity, contract? Will the merchants, manufacturers, agriculturists, have anything to complain of? Once the decree is passed by the National Assembly, — for why should I not use things as they are, to change things as they are? — the institution founded, the council of administration elected, what can the Bank of the People have in common with government? And, as for this famous centralization, of which you are so proud, would not that which would reduce the rate of interest in all towns, industries and corporations to 3, 2, 1, or ½ per cent. seem superior to that which would result from the absolute control of all agriculture and industry by a Central Bank, presided over by the Minister of Finance? Understand, routine politicians, that true centralization is not a hierarchy of functionaries, but the equality of wealth and security.

2. The State Debt.

In criticising government generally, I have said that if contract could solve a single question in the relations between two individuals, it could as easily solve all questions that might arise among millions; whence it follows that the problem of order in society is millions of times easier to attack by way of a bargain than by way of authority. That is what I hope to bring home, by the fullest evidence, in this study and the succeeding. The first problem, that of exchange and currency, being solved, all the others will easily follow.

The public debt, floating and funded, is about $1,200,000,000. The interest, according to the budget of 1851, is $54,000,000.

To this charge of $54,000,000 is added another charge, which, under the name of redemption, is intended to extinguish every year, by repurchase, a part of the permanent charge. This redemption charge amounts to $14,800,000.

It is no part of my design to tell how this redemption charge, always carried in the budget, always furnished by the taxpayer, never redeems anything; how the whole of it is charged to excess over expenditure; how the debt unceasingly increases. All that I seek at present is some means of paying off the debt.

Finally, to these $68,800,000 of interest and redemption, add $11,000,000 of pensions and annuities which occasionally the Government presents to its functionaries, after twenty-five or thirty years of service, and you will have the total of $79,800,000 due by the State, outside of all that it pays for service.

From the fact alone that the State, when becoming a borrower, creates a redemption fund, with the avowed intention of freeing itself from debt, it follows that there is both the desire and the intention on the part of the State to pay it off. I say more: the State has the right, a natural right, inherent in its position as a debtor, to achieve its relief by means of reimbursement.

The interest on the debt is fixed at 5, 4½, 4 and 3 per cent. That again shows that, like all borrowers, the

12*

State submits to more or less onerous conditions, ac=
cording to circumstances, and that if it were possible
to borrow at a lower rate, it would have the right to
do so.

In fact, he who talks of permanent interest implies
that the debt cannot be demanded by the creditor, but
may be repaid at will by the debtor: such is recognized
by financiers as the relation of the State to bondholders.

Therefore if, by the first decree that we have sup=
posed the Representatives of 1852 to make, credit were
democratically organized throughout the Republic, and
the interest on money at the National Bank reduced
from 4 to 3 per cent., as a result of competition among
bankers, there would be a flow of capital to the Stock
Exchange, and a demand for bonds of the Government,
which then would be able to replace a part of its
securities at 5, 4½ and 4 per cent. by 3 per cents.; what
is called a conversion. If the interest at the Bank were
reduced to ⅓ or ¼ per cent., the ease of refunding would
increase for the State in like proportion. At the end of
a certain time, the whole debt would have been con=
verted, and the annual interest charge reduced six=
sevenths, or rather, the interest having become
insignificant, the demand for reimbursement would come
from the bondholders themselves, and the State would
no longer have to pay interest but annuities. The force
of circumstances would bring this about, without
solicitation by the State.

Instead of awaiting this movement, the thing to be
done now is to anticipate it, to provoke it, to use, for
the rapid and complete discharge of all State in=
debtness, all the powers secured to it by law, all the
strength furnished by such an institution as a National
Bank.

First, I observe, as I have just done, that whichever
side may be chosen, whether resignedly to await the
effects of the reduction of discount rates, offers of
capital, demands for bonds, etc., or to take an active
part in conversions, the tendency of the budget, and
consequently that of the Country, · will have been

changed, in all that concerns this part of the political
organism, and, once in the way of paying our debts
instead of continually increasing them, we shall be on
the revolutionary road. Whether we move fast or slowly,
the proportionate amount of reduction to be gained
does not touch the principle; and it is the principle, the
tendency, that it is most important to consider.

Do you want to increase your debts? That is Con=
servatism. In that case, no National Bank, no reduction
of interest, entire liberty for usury, permanent grant of
privilege to the Bank of France, periodical funding of the
floating debt, State loans at 25, 30, 40, below par, etc.

Do you, on the contrary, want to diminish your debts?
That is Revolution. You have but one means of doing
this. It is to take away from individual capital the
business of discount; and to fix commercial interest
everywhere at from ½ to ¼ per cent. Thus capital will
flow to the Treasury, and you can convert and redeem
until the debt is extinguished.

That is the whole difference between Conservatism
and Revolution.

Since I have begun to give my views, I will say that,
in my opinion, the wisest course to follow, the surest,
the most just, would be to do with the Debt the same
as with the Bank, to abolish interest at one blow. I mean
that from the day of the decrée, the interest, which
would continue to be paid as before to the bondholders,
would be counted as annuities, and deducted from the
principal, the latter fixed *at par*, whatever the state of
the market, and the difference between the market price
and par taking the place of a premium for the delay in
reimbursement.

Oh, I know well that the bondholders, the stock
gamblers, all the financial gang, will cry spoliation if
the State should lower the rate of interest, instead of
lowering the market value of the principal, as is done
every day on the Stock Exchange. Admire the banco=
cratic morality! Usurious speculation, which raises or
lowers the nominal capital, the only real value, while
keeping the interest the same, is legitimate; but the

decree of the Sovereign People which annuls interest, although restoring the whole capital, is robbery! And these people call themselves economists, moralists, jurisconsults, statesmen! There are even some who pass for Christians! So be it. I have too long disputed with this rabble; I ask pardon of Humanity. They are the strongest! Have patience, things may take a turn.

I address myself to intelligent and sincere people. If in the natural course of affairs, through market fluctu= ations, the rate of interest generally in France should fall to 3 per cent., there is no one who would not regard a refunding of government bonds, from 5, 4½ and 4 per cents. into 3 per cents., as perfectly legitimate. Why should it be less so if, by an act of the sovereign will, by an advance in public intelligence, and a bargain among all interests, the principle, *Trust one another*, which is now but a saying, should become the first article of the social compact; if, by virtue of this law of the Nation, of which the first light is already dawning in coöperative associations, the price of money should decline to the cost of carrying on the Bank? All business being controlled by the rate of discount, what iniquity would there be in demanding reciprocity from creditors of the State? And because the debt might have been contracted before the law was passed, does it follow that the capital lent should be freed from its operation? Would it not suffice, in order that non=retroactivity might be preserved, that the law should affect only loans that expire afterward, and not those that expire before?

What Society does for all, it has a right to expect from each: the same reduction of interest that it grants to each citizen on his discounted notes, it should profit by on the interest which it pays. The former is the measure of the latter: such is the law of Recipro= city, the law of Contract, outside of which there is nothing but poverty and servitude for the producer.

Tell me, is it necessary to revise our political con= stitution a dozen times more, to exhaust us by fifty years more of parliamentary orgies, to begin over again the tragicomedy of '92, '93, '95, '99, 1804, to end by 1814, 1830 and 1848; to wear out even the Nation with such nonsense as Direct Legislation, Direct Government, and the rest, which the sick brains of leaders of parties and schools bring forth daily, in order to accomplish this important reform, to pay off the debts of the State, to forbid all ministers from contracting any further loan in the name of the Country, seeing that under the new system this prac= tice of the old finance will be entirely abandoned; to suppress all pensions, annuities, &c., because it is for counties, towns, corporations, associations, &c., to take care of their invalids, and to recompense and honor their employees; in a word, to discharge the Central Administration from this enormous burden of bond issues, of redemption of the floating debt, of savings banks, of the distribution of crosses, ribbons, annuities and pensions?

An immense majority of the people do not know that there is a debt. They have no idea of what is meant by redemption, consolidation, conversion, an= nuities: they would be terribly scandalized to hear of a loan at 75, 70 or 55. Perhaps half a century will pass before they will be in a position to understand this fact of elementary history, that from 1789 to 1852 matters were so arranged by the Government that, at the second of these dates, after having swept away the debts of the monarchy, the People still had to pay every year a sum exceeding $80,000,000 for replacing the ancient feudal claims which they believed had been abolished, under the names of Public Debt, Refunding, Loans, Pensions, Annuities!

And it is to this people, ignorant of all that is important to it, to which you talk of sovereignty, of legislation, of government! To amuse it, and to dis= tract its thoughts from the Revolution, you talk to it about politics and fraternity! Queer revolutionists you are, who always take the white bean instead of the red, as one of the ancients said, and busy yourselves only with evading, dissimulating, burying really essen=

tial questions! In truth, if such as you had lived in
1789, they would have saved the monarchy and the
feudal system by their prudence. They would not
have permitted anybody to speak to the people about
the *Deficit*, or the *Red Book*, or the *Starvation Pact*, or
the *Tithes*, or *Feudal Rights*, or the *Income of the
Clergy*, or the millions of abuses which made the
Revolution necessary. They would have preached about
Association and the Servant State! Is not that what
they have been doing since February? Who in the
Provisory Government did anything to aid the Revolu=
tion? who worried about a settlement at the Hotel de
Ville? who thought of it at the Luxembourg? who
among the Mountainists dared to mention the
word? . . . .

Let us reckon no longer on these men: the Revolution
in the nineteenth century will be the work of fate.
Fate! have pity on us!

———

3. Debts secured by Mortgage. Simple Obligations.

The public debt checked in its growth and paid off,
it becomes necessary to check and pay off the debts
of citizens.

The debts of individuals are of two kinds, debts
secured by mortgage, when they are for a long term
and are secured by a pledge of real estate or mortgage,
and commercial debts, when they are guaranteed only
by a simple note of hand.

Add to these the bonds of stock companies, whereof
the interest differs somewhat from dividends, and is
carried every year to the debit of the companies.

The interest paid for these two kinds of debts may
be estimated at $240,000,000; the whole public debt,
estimated as capitalized at 5 per cent., would be then
only one=third of the private debts.

It is with the private debts as with the public debt,
the debtors not only desire to decrease the rate of
interest, but seek to do so. The schemes presented to

the Constituent Assembly by the most honored pro=
prietors, such as Messrs. Flandin, Pougeard, and
others, who in this matter gave evidence of real revolu=
tionary spirit, had no other aim, under the title of
Organization of Land Banks, but to furnish money to
agriculture, to property, to industry, at a low price,
and to deliver them gradually from usury. The reduc=
tion which these well=meaning and moderate republicans
hoped to obtain for their constituents by their reform,
was not less than 6 per cent. average, upon the totality
of interest. Instead of the 9 per cent. which money
costs at the State Bank, the Land Banks would have
asked only 3 per cent. That would accomplish to a
slight degree what I propose to accomplish com=
pletely by the dissolution of the Bank of France; it was,
more or less, to begin the Revolution. But nobody
thought then that such an institution would have
been spoliation of the established lenders. The critics
confined themselves to saying that people would lack
confidence, that credit notes would be subject to
depreciation, &c. I cannot either approve or disapprove
the various modes of putting this plan into execution
which were advanced and rejected. I confine myself
to noting that the idea was eminently revolutionary;
and that it was rejected chiefly because it was revo=
lutionary. The corporation of money robbers thought
that interest at 9 per cent. was better for them
than interest at 3 per cent., that privilege was good for
the privileged, that the Land Bank led straight to
Socialism, &c. *Having is keeping, and a fool for
asking,* says the proverb. They who wanted to clip
the claws of usury, not being in the majority in the
Constituent Assembly, were beaten, naturally. Since
in our governmental system politics takes precedence
of justice, and the ballot of truth, what was done was
well done, and we have nothing to complain of.

Nevertheless the matter may come up again. A
simple change in the majority may change the law:
it is with this anticipation that I publish this
programme.

The propriety of the reform in mortgage = secured loans being thus placed beyond question, I mean the reduction of interest on loans upon mortgage, the questions that remain are: 1st. At what rate shall the interest be fixed? and 2nd. How long will it be before the new system will be substituted for the old every= where?

Whatever system may be adopted, on the rate of interest, on the conditions of loan, on the form of the document, and on the amount of issues, it is clear that, once entered upon this path, the tendency of society will have changed in all that concerns loans and debts: from the retrograde tendency which now prevails, on account of the obstacles to credit and the high rate of interest, it will have become revo= lutionary, through the facility of obtaining loans and the moderation of the cost. The greater or less rapidity of the movement will not affect its nature: whether you leave Paris for Dunkirk by rail or by wagon, you turn your back upon Bayonne in either case.

Suppose that the Land Bank of Messrs. Flandin, Pougeard, &c., existed, with an interest rate of 3 per cent.; after a time, by its issues, this bank would have become the regulator of the rate of interest for mortgages, and of interest generally, and it would fall everywhere, as far as the influence of the institution extended.

Suppose again that the Bank limits its issues, that is to say, the amount of its credits, to $100,000,000 a year; the total of indebtedness, national, municipal, and private, being by hypothesis $5,000,000,000, in less than 50 years the turnover of the bank will have entirely absorbed this mass, unless the present creditors maintain their claims by the postponement of maturity and voluntary reduction of interest.

According to this calculation, the revolution in credit, in the proportion of 9 to 3 per cent., would be com= pleted in half a century.

Would you prefer, on the other hand, to continue the present system, and further strengthen it? The way is simple. Do nothing: reject all plans relating to credit, as did the Constituent Assembly. Debts will continue to accumulate: the Country will be crushed; property will be ruined; labor subjugated; the Nation, together with the State, will be sunk in slavery, until it emerges from it by the usual route, bankruptcy.

Thus there is no middle way between Reaction and Revolution. But Reaction is mathematically impossible: we are not free to remain unrevolutionized; our only choice is how fast it shall occur. For myself, I prefer the locomotive.

My advice then is to treat private debts as we have treated the public debt and the Bank; that is to say, to clear the course at a single leap, and reach the goal without stopping by the way.

To this end, without worrying about government, or constitution, prorogation or revision, nor about association, we should proceed by general measures, and make use of the State, since the State, although already encroached upon by our first scheme, is still the mainspring of society.

"By decree of the National Assembly.

"Whereas previous decrees have fixed the rate "of discount at the Bank and of interest on the public "debt at ½ per cent., the interest on all debts, including "mortgages, notes of hand and bonds, is fixed at the "same rate.

"Repayment of the principal may be claimed only by "annuity payments.

"The annuity for all sums below $400 shall be 10 per "cent.; above that, 5 per cent.

"To facilitate the reimbursement of creditors, and "fulfil the function of the former money-lenders, a "department of the National Bank of Discount will "make loans on mortgage. The maximum total of "such loans annually shall not exceed $100,000,000."

Who could complain of a reform at once logical and beneficent, in its universality as well as its radicalism?

The lenders? They are not one in a thousand. Still, no matter how few they are, we must come to an understanding with them. Might does not make right.

Certainly he who lends at 6, 8 or 9 per cent. will not complain that the borrower is robbing him, because he prefers to borrow at 3 per cent.: on this point the capitalists will make no objections. But this is what they will say to mortgagors and to the State:

You can reduce interest, and even make the reduction general, if by a sudden flow of capital or financial scheme you can find credit below the present rates. But what you have no right to do is to postpone repayment of the principal. You would be violating the sanctity of contracts. Either reimburse the principal forthwith, or pay the interest. That is the dilemma.

And as the whole indebtedness, not including National or municipal, amounts to about $3,600,000,000, while there is at the most only $200,000,000 in circulation, it is clear that immediate repayment is impossible. They have got us.

I was in Lyons in 1846—47, employed in a commission and shipping concern. The house had a large number of consignors, and purchasers with annual accounts, from the South and the East. The charges for transportation were a fixed sum, and included the rights of navigation on the canals as well as on the rivers. An order for reduction in favor of cereals having issued, the amount of the charges for rights of navigation was deducted from the bills of lading, so that the customers, not the carriers, profited by the deduction. The contrary would have occurred if the Minister, instead of lowering the charges, had increased them. In both cases there was supreme power, arising from the act of a prince, which had to be complied with, regardless of the contract, inasmuch as it was outside of the provisions of the contract.

Let us apply this rule.

If by an unexpected event, resulting from improvement on the exchange, and the intervention of authority, the legal rate of interest is lowered to 3,

2, 1 or ½ per cent., it is clear that, at the same moment, the stipulated interest in existing contracts must be proportionally reduced. The price of money, like that of transportation and merchandise, is composed of various elements, whereof the multiplication causes a rise, the absence in consequence produces a fall. Up to this point the comparison is exact.

But the creditor, who is no longer willing to give credit, demands repayment; that is to say, he profits by the scarcity of money to evade the law and maintain his interest. The dishonesty is flagrant; nevertheless the pretext is specious: it must be answered.

Upon what does the money market rest? Upon the scarcity of money. If the quantity of gold and silver were increased ten times, twenty times, the value of these metals would be ten times, twenty times less; in consequence, the rate of interest ten times, twenty times lower. It would end by our esteeming gold and silver no more than iron and copper: they would no longer be lent at interest. The scarcity of money is therefore essential to the nature of its function.

But this scarcity is not the less an evil, because in the last analysis it is always of this scarcity that agriculture, commerce and industry complain; so that, by a singular contradiction, labor and exchange are condemned to suffer from the scarcity of merchandise which is necessary to them, and which cannot be otherwise than scarce.

However, the citizens by their agreement, or the State which represents them until the new order is established, have found a method by which money, without becoming less scarce, and thus losing nothing of its value, can no longer place their interests in peril, nor be a menace to commerce and production: this method is to centralize circulation, and render loans reciprocal.

After that, is it not evident that to take advantage of the scarcity of money in order to demand an impossible reimbursement, or failing that, an illegal rate of interest, is to argue from the very fact whereof the legislator desired to destroy the malign influence, and to lay down as a principle precisely that which is in question; more than that, which has been settled?

We may say to the capitalists: You demand from us three and a half billions of specie; how is it that there is but half a million in existence? How, with half a million dollars, have you managed to make us your debtors for three and a half billions? You say it is by the turnover of money and the renewal of loans. Then it is by the turnover of money and the renewal of annuities that we will discharge our indebtedness to you. You have taken time to lend; we will take time to repay. Are you not happy to preserve the value of your principal, even though you do lose the interest?

But reasoning will avail nothing. The eagle defends his eyrie, the lion his den, the hog his trough, capital will not relinquish its interest. And we, poor sufferers, we are ignorant, unarmed, divided: there is not one of us who, when one impulse urges him to revolution, is not held back by another.

In '89 the affair at least was clear: on one side the nobility, the clergy, the Crown; on the other, the Third Estate, forming by itself ninety-nine hundredths of the nation. Today, interests are divided and complicated to infinity: the same individual may represent in his own person a dozen different interests, a dozen contradictory opinions. When the Republic of February entered this thicket, it was like the dragon with many heads; it stayed in the underbrush. The more efforts it made, the more involved it became. There is only one way to put an end to it: to set fire to the woods.

---

4. Immovable Property, *Buildings*.

Whatever may be my personal conclusions, whatever radicalism I may profess in my propositions, it will nevertheless be observed that I always start from a generally admitted principle, from a recognized tendency, from an expressed desire of respectable people; moreover that I constantly proceed by way of direct consequences, supposing the progress to be as slow and imperceptible as you like. The Revolu= tion for me is one thing; the putting of it into exe= cution is quite another. The first is assured, unconquer= ably entrenched; as for the second, though I think it prudent and advisable to hasten it as much as possible, I shall not regard him as an adversary who differs with me on this point.

Let us take up this great question of property, the source of such intolerable pretensions, and of such ridiculous fears. The Revolution has two things to accomplish about property, its dissolution and its reconstitution. I shall address myself first to its disso= lution, and begin with buildings.

If by the above described measures, property in buildings were relieved of mortgages; if the owners and builders found capital at a low price, the former for the buildings they wanted to put up, the latter for the purchase of materials; it would follow, in the first place, that the cost of construction would diminish considerably, and that old buildings could be cheaply and advantageously repaired; and furthermore, that a drop in the rental of buildings would be perceived.

On the other hand, as capital could no longer be invested with advantage in government securities and in banks, capitalists would be led to seek investments in real estate, especially in buildings, which are always more productive than land. There would thereupon occur in this matter also an increase of competition; the supply of buildings would tend to outrun the demand, and the rentals would fall still lower.

It would fall so much the more as the reduction of interest collected by the Bank, and paid to the credi= tors of the State was greater; and if, as I propose, the interest of money were fixed at zero, the returns of capital invested in buildings would soon be zero also.

Then, as the rental of buildings is composed of but three factors, the reimbursement of the capital spent in their construction, the keeping up of the building, and the taxes, a lease would cease to be a *loan for use*, and would become a sale by the builder to the tenant.

Finally, as speculation would no longer seek buildings as an investment, but only as an object of industry, the purely legal relation of landlord and tenant, which the Roman law has transmitted to us, would give place to a purely commercial relation between the seller and the tenant: there would be the same relation, and in consequence the same law, the same jurisdiction, as between the forwarder of a package and the consignee. In a word, house rent, losing its feudal character, would become an ACT OF COMMERCE.

It is always the law of contract and reciprocity which guides us, to the exclusion of all reminiscence of government.

Now, is it true that the lowering of rentals, in so far as it is caused by the low price of capital and of services, is a sign of the increase of wealth and of comfort for the people?

Is it true that Society naturally desires this reduction, and is frustrated in its desires only by the economic chaos wherein the old Revolution has plunged it?

Is it true, finally, that for three years past the idea of organizing cheap rentals of dwellings has been taken up officially, notably in the movement for *Workmen's Villages*, to which the first subscriber was the President of the Republic?

If these facts are undeniable, legitimate, worthy in every respect of the desires of the government and people, it follows that society wishes to change the legal position of property in buildings; and that if, since the Revolution of February, society had been able to turn itself in this direction, if the impulse given from above could have continued, we should be this day, as far as relates to buildings, well on the revolutionary road. If there has been a change of opinion in regard to this, it is due to the warmth with which the factotums of M. Louis Bonaparte have opposed every idea of amelioration, to the lack of intelligence and energy of the republican party, and to the poverty and ignorance of the working classes.

Instead of demanding reduction of rent, a movement arose for the reduction of the selling price of real estate: it was the owners who suffered. While rentals remained almost stationary, selling values declined 50, 60 and 80 per cent. The Revolution would have maintained property: the Reaction, in its frenzy, caused it to suffer irreparable depreciation.

This understood, let us suppose that the City of Paris resuming the abandoned project of Workmen's Settlements, should reopen the campaign against the cost of dwellings; should buy houses that were for sale at the lowest price, contract with associations of building trades for repairing them and keeping them in repair, then lease them, according to the rules of competition and equal exchange. After a while the City of Paris would own most of the houses of which it is composed, and would have all its citizens for tenants.

In this as always, the tendency is noticeable and significant: the right is incontestable. If after the taking of the Bastille, the City of Paris had set aside for such acquisition the sums which it has spent on public festivals, royal coronations, and celebrations of the births of princes, it would already have paid for several hundred millions worth of property. Let the Country be the judge: let it decide in how many years it intends to revolutionize this first class of properties: what it resolves, I shall hold to be wisely resolved and I accept it in advance.

While waiting, permit me to formulate a scheme.

The right of property, so honorable in its origin, when that origin is none other than labor, has become in Paris, and in most cities, an improper and immoral instrument of speculation in the dwelling places of citizens. Speculation in bread and food of prime necessity is punished as a misdemeanor, sometimes as a crime: is it more permissible to speculate in the

13

habitations of the people? Our consciences, selfish, lazy, blind, most of all in matters that touch our pockets, have not yet noticed this similarity: all the more reason that the Revolution should denounce it. If the trumpet of the last judgment should resound in our ears, which of us at that moment would refuse to make his confession? Let us make it then, for I vow the last hour is approaching for the ancient abuse. It is too late to talk of purgatory, of gradual penitence, of progressive reform. Eternity awaits you. There is no middle ground between heaven and hell. We must take the leap.

I propose to manage the dissolution of rentals in the same manner as that of the Bank, of the public debt, and of private debts and obligations.

"From the date of the decree which shall be passed "by future representatives, all payments made as rental "shall be carried over to the account of the purchase "of the property, at a price estimated at twenty times "the annual rental.

"Every such payment shall purchase for the tenant "a proportional undivided share in the house he lives "in, and in all buildings erected for rental, and serving "as a habitation for citizens.

"The property thus paid for shall pass under the "control of the town administration, which shall take "a first mortgage upon it, in the name of all the "tenants, and shall guarantee them all a domicile, in "perpetuity, at the cost price of the building.

"Towns may bargain with owners for the purchase "and immediate payment for rented buildings.

"In such case, in order that the present generation "may enjoy the benefit of reduction in rental, the said "towns may arrange for an immediate diminution of "the rental of the houses for which they have nego= "tiated, in such manner that complete payment may be "made within thirty years.

"For repairs, management and upkeep of buildings, "as well as for new constructions, the towns shall deal "with masons' Unions, or associations of building "trades, according to the rules and principies of the "new social contract.

"Proprietors who occupy their own houses shall "retain property therein, as long as suits their "interests."

Let the Country enter upon this course, and the safety of the people is assured. A guaranty stronger than all laws, all electoral combinations, all popular sanctions, will assure lodging to the workers forever, and render a return to speculation or rents impossible. Neither government, nor legislation, nor code is needed, a simple agreement among citizens suffices, with the execution of it confided to the town: the producer is housed by a simple business transaction; something which neither kings nor dictator will ever accomplish.

5. Property in Land.

Through the land the plundering of man began, and in the land it has rooted its foundations. The land is the fortress of the modern capitalist, as it was the citadel of feudalism, and of the ancient patriciate. Finally, it is the land which gives authority to the governmental principle, an ever-renewed strength, whenever the popular Hercules overthrows the giant.

To-day the stronghold, attacked upon all the secret points of its bastions, is about to fall before us, as fell, at the sound of Joshua's trumpets, the walls of Jericho. The machine which is able to overthrow the ramparts has been found; it is not my invention; it has been invented by property itself.

Everybody has heard of the land banks that have been in use for a long time among the land owners of Poland, Scotland, and Prussia, of which French proprietors and farm owners are demanding so insistently the introduction into our own country. In a previous article, speaking of the liquidation of mortgage secured debts, I had occasion to recall the attempts made by several honorable conservatives in

13*

the National Assembly to endow France with this beneficent institution. I showed, in connection therewith, how the land bank might become an instrument of revolution with regard to debts and interest. I am about to show how it may be the same with regard to landed property.

The special characteristic of the land bank, after the low price and the facility of its credit, is the *reimbursement by annuities.*

Suppose that the proprietors, no longer waiting for the Government to act, but taking their affairs into their own hands, follow the example of the workmen's associations, and get together to found a Bank by subscription, or mutual guaranty.

Suppose that in this credit concern the amount of issues were fixed at $80,000,000 a year, as much as comes to a capital of $400,000,000, and the annuity fixed at one-twentieth, payable in advance, plus a small interest in addition.

It is easily seen that, with the aid of this bank, property, which now borrows at an average rate of 9 per cent., could arrange every year the conversion of $80,000,000 of mortgages, that is to say, pay off $80,000,000 worth of its mortgages at 9 per cent. by an annuity subscription at 5½, 6, or 7 per cent.

At the end of five years the capital of $400,000,000 would be exhausted; but the bank, with its returns from annuities and the discounts which it makes on credits, would have in hand, as the result of its dealings, a sum of $400,000,000, which it will replace anew. The operation will continue thus until at the end of twenty years landed property will have converted four times $400,000,000, that is $1,600,000,000 of mortgages; and in thirty years it will be delivered from usurers.

Once again I say that I do not intend to approve any of the plans for a land bank that have been advanced. I believe that it is possible to organize such an institution, and I base my reasoning on this assumption, which is to me more than a hypothesis.

Nothing is easier than to apply to the repurchase of land the mechanism of this system of credit, which is usually regarded only as a protection against excessive interest, and an instrument for the conversion of mortgages.

The average revenue of landed capital is 3 per cent.

When it is is said that the land brings in 2, 3, 4 or 5 per cent., it means that after the cost of labor is paid (the farmer, peasant or slave must live), the surplus, whatever it may be, in other words, the share of the owner, is held to represent the twentieth, twentyfourth, thirtieth or fortieth of the value of the land.

Thus thirtyfour years of farm rent at 3 per cent., or forty years at 2½ per cent., cover the value of the property.

The farmer or peasant can them pay for the land that he cultivates in twentyfive, thirty, thirtyfour or forty years, if the owner will agree to it: he can pay for it in twenty, eighteen or fifteen years, if he can buy it by the system of annuities. What then prevents the peasant from becoming everywhere the owner of the soil, and freeing himself from farm rent?

What prevents him is that the owner demands to be paid in cash; and that if cash is not forthcoming, he *lets* the land; that is to say, he requires payment in perpetuity.

In that case, you will say, why does not the tenant borrow?

Ah! that is because the loan of money on mortgage agrees exactly with farm rent. The interest required for this kind of loan serves not in the least to extinguish the debt, and is even higher than the farm rent. The peasant therefore finds himself enclosed in a circle: he must cultivate to eternity, but never possess. If he borrows, he gives himself a second master, double interest, double slavery. There is no way of escape without the aid of a fairy.

Well, the fairy exists: it remains only for us to test the virtue of her wand: the fairy is the land bank.

A young peasant, about to start housekeeping, wants
to buy a farm: the farm is worth $3,000.

Suppose that this peasant, with the marriage
portion of his wife, a trifle inherited, and some
savings, can raise a third of this sum: the Land Bank
upon a pledge of $3,000 will not hesitate to lend $2,000,
payable, as we have said, by annual instalments.

This will be as if the cultivator had to pay rent for
15, 20 or 30 years, in order to become the owner of
property worth $2,000. Thus the farm rent is not
perpetual: it is annually charged off the price: it gives
a title to property. And as the price of real estate
cannot be raised indefinitely, since it is only the
capitalization of twenty, thirty or forty fold of the
part of the product which is in excess of the cost of
working the land, it is evident that the peasant cannot
fail to obtain the property. With the Land Bank the
farmer is released; it is the proprietor who is caught.
Do you understand now why the conservatives of the
Constituent Assembly were unwilling to permit a
Land Bank?

Thus what we call farm rent, left to us by Roman
tyranny and feudal usurpation, hangs only by a thread,
the organization of a bank, demanded even by property
itself. It has been demonstrated that the land tends to
return to the hands that cultivate it, and that farm rent,
like house rent, like the interest of mortgages, is but
an improper speculation, which shows the disorder
and anomaly of the present economic system.

Whatever may be the conditions of this Bank, which
will come into existence on the day when those who need
it desire it; whatever be the rate of charge for its
services, however small its issues, it can be calculated
in how many years the soil will be delivered from
the parasitism which sucks it dry, while strangling
the cultivator.

And when once the revolutionary machine shall
have released the soil, and agriculture shall have
become free, feudal exploitation can never reëstablish
itself. Property may then be sold, bought, circulated,

divided or united, anything; the ball and chain of the
old serfdom will never be dragged again; property
will have lost its fundamental vices, it will be trans≠
figured. It will no longer be the same thing. Still,
let us continue to call it by its ancient name, so dear
to the heart of man, so agreeable to the ear of the
peasant, PROPERTY.

What is at that I ask now: that a Land Bank
should be founded at once? That would be something,
no doubt. But why should we not cover at one stride
what it might take a Land Bank a century to
accomplish?

Our tendency is our law; and although there may
be never any lack of continuity among our ideas,
although the mind may always be able, at need, to
insert as many middle terms as it chooses between one
idea and another, yet sometimes Society likes to form
rapid inferences, to take great leaps. What more
puerile than to make a third, a quarter, a tenth of a
revolution? Has not capital had enough? Is capital so
honorable, so generous, so pure, that we still owe it
fifty years of sacrifice? We are in the line of progress;
universal practice pleads for us. What, then, are we
waiting for? Forward! and at full speed, against land
rent.

I propose to decree:

"Every payment of rent for the use of real estate
"shall give title to the farmer for a share of the real
"estate, and shall be a lien upon it.

"When the property has been entirely paid for, it
"shall revert immediately to the town, which shall take
"the place of the former proprietor, and shall share
"the fee≠simple and the economic rent with the farmer.

"Towns may bargain directly with owners who wish
"to do so for the repurchase of rentals and the im≠
"mediate purchase of the properties.

"In that case, provision shall be made for the
"supervision of the towns, for the installation of
"cultivators, and for the fixing of the boundaries of
"possessions, taking care to make up by an increase

"in quantity for any deficiency in the quality of the
"land, and to proportion the rent to the product.

"As soon as all landed property shall have been
"completely paid for, all the towns of the Republic
"shall come to an understanding for equalizing among
"them the quality of tracts of land, as well as accidents
"of culture. The part of the rent to which they are
"entitled upon their respective territories shall serve
"for compensation and for general insurance.

"Beginning with the same date, the former
"proprietors who have held their title by working their
"properties themselves, shall be placed on the same
"footing as the new, subjected to the same rental
"payments, and invested with the same rights; in
"such a manner that the chance of locality or of suc=
"cession may favor no one, and that the conditions
"of culture shall be equal for all.

"The tax on land shall be abolished.

"The rural police are placed under the control of
"the municipal councils."

I suppose that I need not write a commentary to
show that this plan, which is the necessary sequel
to the others, is still only the application on a large
scale of the idea of contract; that the central authority
appears only for the execution of the popular will,
which I assume has already been expressed by vote
of the electors; that when once the reform has been
put in practice, the hand of power will forever
disappear from agricultural and farm land affairs. Such
repetition would be tiresome. It is more advantageous
just now, I think, to adduce certain urgent
considerations in support of my plan.

In many provinces the attention of country dwellers
has been awakened in relation to the probable
consequences of the Revolution of February, in con=
nection with farm property. They understand that
this Revolution ought to put an end to their precarious
holding, and procure for them, not only a market for
their produce, not only money at a low rate, but, above
all, property.

In connection with this, one of the ideas which have obtained favor among the peasants is the *Right* of the cultivator to *improvements* in the property that he cultivates.

A farm worth $8,000 is leased to a farmer for $240 a year; that is, at 3 per cent.

At the end of ten years this farm, under the intelligent management of the farmer, has gained 50 per cent. in value: instead of $ 8,000, it is worth $12,000. This improvement, which is the exclusive work of the farmer, not only profits him nothing, but when the lease has expired, the idler, the proprietor, comes along, and raises the rent to $360. The farmer has created $4,000 for somebody else; more than that, in augmenting the fortune of his master by a half, he has increased proportionally what he himself must pay; he has given his master a stick to beat him with, as they say.

The peasant understands this injustice; and, rather than fail to obtain reparation for it, he will, sooner or later, overthrow government and property, as in '89 he burned the charters. This may be expected at any time. From another side, certain owners also have felt the necessity that labor should reap the reward of its own work: they have even gone beyond the demands of their farmers, and have begun the work of reparation spontaneously. The *Right to the value of Improvements* is one of the first which the legislator must recognize, at least in principle, on pain of revolt and perhaps a peasants' war.

As for myself, I do not believe that such an innovation is practicable in our system of laws and the condition of property; and I doubt whether the hopes of the peasants can triumph over the innumerable difficulties and complications that are involved. I am the first to recognize the legitimacy of the right to the value of improvements; but it is one thing to *recognize a right*, and another to *grant* it; the latter is incompatible with all the laws, traditions, and usages which control property. Nothing

less is needed than a complete recasting of the second
and third books of the Civil Code, with suppressions,
additions and modifications at each sentence, almost
at each word; *seventeen hundred and sixty-six* articles
to revise, discuss, analyze, abrogate, replace, and
develop; more work than a National Assembly could
do in ten years.

All that concerns the recognition of goods, the right
of accession, usufruct, servitude, succession, contract,
prescription, mortgages, must be harmonized with the
right to the value of improvements, and remodelled
from bottom to top. However willing the representatives, whatever light they can shed, I doubt whether
they can devise a law which will satisfy their constituents or themselves. A law which separates, consecrates
and regulates, under all conditions, the right to the
value of improvements, and the consequences which
follow it, is simply an impossible law. It is one of the
cases in which the Right, although perfectly clear,
escapes the definitions of the legislator.

Just as farm land does not increase in value but by
the labor of the farmer, so it does not maintain its
value without labor.   Abandoned or ill-worked land
loses in value or deteriorates, while if properly worked,
it increases in value. To preserve farm land is to
create it, because it means to make it over again
every day, in proportion to its loss. Therefore if it
is just to recognize a share in the value of improvements for the farmer, it is also just to recognize his
share in the value of maintenance.   After recognizing
the right to the value of improvements, we must further
admit the right to the value of conservation. Who will
make this new ruling? Who can embrace it in legislation:
who enshrine it in the Code?

To raise such questions is to cast a plummet into an
abyss. The right to the value of improvements, so
dear to the heart of the peasant, and admitted by the
fairmindedness of many owners, is impracticable
because it lacks generality and depth, in a word,
because it is not sufficiently radical. It is with it as

with the RIGHT TO LABOR, of which no one in the
Constituent Assembly contested the justice, but of
which the codification was equally impossible. The
Right to Labor, the Right to Life, the Right to Hap=
piness, the Right to Love, all these formulas, capable in
an instant of arousing the masses, are entirely without
practical sense. If they betray a real need among the
people, they show even more clearly the incompetence of
their authors.

Let us now proceed to tell the peasant, as we told
the workmen in 1848, that there is nothing to be done;
that the right to the value of improvements, like the
right to labor, like all the evangelical rights, is a
charming thing, no doubt, but quite impossible to
realize; that the world has always been so, and will
always be so; that Providence has made some people
proprietors and some tenants, as he has created oaks
and hawthorn bushes; and all the normal common=
places of Malthusianism, that have been refuted a
hundred times. The information may be ill received;
it may be doubted whether the peasants, any more
than the workmen, will be persuaded by it. Before
long, there must be a solution; if not, take care! ...
I see coming universal expropriation, without public
gain and without preliminary indemnity.

I bring this study to an end, leaving it to my readers
to follow it out in detail, and contenting myself with
having touched upon the general points.

A general liquidation is the obligatory preliminary
of every revolution. After sixty years of mercantile
and economic chaos, a second night of the 4th of
August is indispensable. We are still masters of the
situation, and free to proceed with all the prudence,
all the moderation, that we may think advisable: later,
our fate may not depend upon our free choice.

I have proved at length that in the aspirations of the
Country, in the ideas that are current among capitalists
and proprietors, as well as among peasants and work=
men, everything tends toward this liquidation:
coöperative associations, accumulation of coin at the

Bank, discount houses, credit notes, land banks, work=
men's villages, right to value of improvements, &c., &c.
I have analyzed and deduced these ideas, and I have
found at the bottom of them always the principle of
reciprocity and contract, never that of government.
Finally, I have shown how liquidation could, on each
point, be made to work as rapidly as might be desired;
and if I have pronounced myself in favor of the
easiest and quickest way, it was not, as might be
supposed, because I held extreme opinions, but because
I was convinced that this method is the wisest, the
most just, the most conservative, the most advan=
tageous to all interested, debtors, creditors, house
owners, tenants, land proprietors and tenant farmers.

I in favor of extreme opinions! Do you think, then,
that there is nothing more radical, more summary, than
the plan of conciliation which I prefer and propose?
Have you forgotten the saying of Frederick the Great
to the miller of Sans Souci:

"Do you know that I could take it without paying
for it?"

Between reimbursement by annuities and confiscation,
there are many degrees. Let the counter=revolution
persist in its course, and perhaps before a year is
over the lower classes will demand from the rich,
as reparation and indemnity, a quarter, a third, a half of
their property, and, after some years, the whole. And
the lower classes are stronger than Frederick the Great.
Then the peasants and workmen will not demand the
Right to Labor, nor the Right to the Value of Im=
provements: it will be, the Right to War, and the
Right of Reprisal. What will the answer be?

SIXTH STUDY.

Organization of Economic Forces.

ROUSSEAU said truly: No one should obey a law to which he has not consented; and M. Rittinghausen too was right when he proved that in consequence the law should emanate directly from the sovereign, without the intermediary of representatives.

But it was in the application that both these writers failed. With suffrage, or the universal vote, it is evident that the law is neither direct nor personal, any more than collective. The law of the majority is not my law, it is the law of force; hence the government based upon it is not my government; it is government by force.

That I may remain free; that I may not have to submit to any law but my own, and that I may govern myself, the authority of the suffrage must be renounced: we must give up the vote, as well as representation and monarchy. In a word, everything in the government of society which rests on the divine must be suppressed, and the whole rebuilt upon the human idea of CONTRACT.

When I agree with one or more of my fellow citizens for any object whatever, it is clear that my own will is my law; it is I myself, who, in fulfilling my obligation, am my own government.

Therefore if I could make a contract with all, as I can with some; if all could renew it among themselves, if each group of citizens, as a town, county, province, corporation, company, &c., formed by a like contract, and considered as a moral person, could thereafter, and always by a similar contract, agree with every and all

other groups, it would be the same as if my own will
were multiplied to infinity. I should be sure that the
law thus made on all questions in the Republic, from
millions of different initiatives, would never be anything
but my law; and if this new order of things were called
government, it would be my government.

Thus the principle of contract, far more than that of
authority, would bring about the union of producers,
centralize their forces, and assure the unity and solidarity
of their interests.

The *system of contracts*, substituted for the *system
of laws*, would constitute the true government of the
man and of the citizen; the true sovereignty of the
people, the REPUBLIC.

For the contract is Liberty, the first term of the
republican motto: we have demonstrated this
superabundantly in our studies on the principle of
authority and on social liquidation. I am not free when
I depend upon another for my work, my wages, or the
measure of my rights and duties; whether that other
be called the Majority or Society. No more am I free,
either in my sovereignty or in my action, when I am
compelled by another to revise my law, were that other
the most skilful and most just of arbiters. I am no
more at all free when I am forced to give myself a
representative to govern me, even if he were my most
devoted servant.

The Contract is Equality, in its profound and
spiritual essence. — Does this man believe himself my
equal; does he not take the attitude of my master and
exploiter, who demands from me more than it suits me
to furnish, and has no intention of returning it to me;
who says that I am incapable of making my own law,
and expects me to submit to his?

The contract is Fraternity, because it identifies all
interests, unifies all divergences, resolves all contradictions, and in consequence, gives wings to the feelings
of goodwill and kindness, which are crushed by
economic chaos, the government of representatives,
alien law.

The contract, finally, is order, since it is the organization of economic forces, instead of the alienation of liberties, the sacrifice of rights, the subordination of wills.

Let us give an idea of this organism; after liquidation, reconstruction; after the thesis and antithesis, the synthesis.

1. Credit.

The organization of credit is three-quarters done by the winding up of the privileged and usurious banks, and their conversion into a National Bank of circulation and loan, at $\frac{1}{2}$, $\frac{1}{4}$ or $\frac{1}{8}$ per cent. It remains only to establish branches of the Bank, wherever necessary, and to gradually retire specie from circulation, depriving gold and silver of their privilege as money.

As for *personal credit*, it is not for the National Bank to have to do with it; it is with the workingmen's unions, and the farming and industrial societies, that personal credit should be exercised.

2. Property.

I have shown above how property, repurchased by the house rent or ground rent, would come back to the tenant farmer and house tenant. It remains for me to show, especially in relation to property in land, the organizing power of the principle which we have invoked to bring about this conversion.

All the Socialists, Saint Simon, Fourier, Owen, Cabet, Louis Blanc, the Chartists, have conceived agricultural organization in two ways.

Either the laborer is simply a workman associate of a great farming association, called the Commune, or the Phalanstery;

Or each cultivator becomes a tenant of the State, which is the only proprietor, the only landlord; all land having been taken by it. In this case, the ground rent becomes part of the taxes, and may replace them entirely.

The first of these two systems is governmental and Communist at the same time: through this double principle it has no chance of success. It is a utopian conception, still-born. The Phalansterians will talk for a good while yet of their model community: the Communists are not ready to give up their rural fraternity. They may have this consolation. If the idea of a farming association or of cultivation by the government were ever brought forward as a serious proposal during the Revolution, supposing that a government could still exist in a revolution directed chiefly against itself, the chances of insurrection would be laid before the peasant. There would be the menace of tyranny for him, even from those who called themselves Socialists.

The second system seems more liberal: it leaves the cultivator his own master in his work, subjects him to no orders, imposes upon him no rules. In comparison with the present lot of farmers, it is probable that, with the greater length of leases and moderation of rents, the establishment of this system would encounter little opposition in the country. I admit, for my part, that I hesitated for a long time over this idea, which grants some liberty, and which I could reproach with no injustice.

Nevertheless I have never been completely satisfied with it. I find in it always a character of governmental autocracy which is disagreeable to me: I see in it a barrier to liberty of transactions and of inheritances; the free disposition of the soil taken away from him who cultivates it; and this precious sovereignty, this *eminent domain,* as the lawyers say, forbidden to the citizen, and reserved for that fictitious being, without intelligence, without passion, without morality, that we call the State. By this arrangement, the occupant has less to do with the soil than before; the clod of earth seems to stand up and say to him: You are only a slave of the taxes; I do not know you!

But why should the rural laborer, the most ancient, the most noble of all, be thus discrowned? The peasant loves the land with a love without limit; as Michelet poetically says: he does not want a tenancy, a concubin: age; he wants a marriage.

It is asserted that mankind, as a race, has an anterior, imprescriptible, inalienable right to the soil. It is thence deduced, as by the Physiocrats formerly, that the City or the Country should share in the economic rent. It is said that this economic rent should be taken in taxes. And from all this results the enfeoffment of the land by perpetual, unchangeable tenancy; and, what is more serious, the non-circulation, the immobility, of a whole class of capital, the largest in volume, and the most valuable, through its security.

This doctrine appears to me fatal; opposed to all the teachings of science, and of dangerous tendency.

1. What is called *economic rent* in agriculture has no other cause than the inequality in the quality of the land: without this inequality there would be no economic rent, since there would be no means of comparison. Therefore if anybody has a claim on account of this inequality, it is not the State, but the other land workers who hold inferior land. That is why in our scheme for liquidation we stipulated that every variety of cultivation should pay a proportional contribution, destined to accomplish a balancing of returns among farm workers, and an assurance of products.

2. The industrial occupations, in favor of which the ground rent seems to be reserved, have no more right to it than the State, for the reason that they do not exist apart from agricultural work and independently of it: they are a subdivision of it. The farm worker cultivates and harvests for all: the artisan, the merchant, the manufacturer, work for the farm worker. As soon as the dealer has received the price of his merchandise, he is paid his share of the economic rent, as well as of the gross product of the soil; his account is settled. To make the farm worker only pay the taxes, under the pretext that they are economic rent,

14

would be to exempt other industries from taxation, to their profit, and to permit them to receive the whole of the rent, without reciprocity on their part.

3. As for the drawbacks in non-circulation of real estate, I shall show how serious they are before long.

4. Finally, this universal, absolute, irrevocable farm tenantry, so opposed to the clearest hopes of the times, seems to me, in the present juncture, supremely impolitic. The people, even those who are Socialists, whatever they may say, want to be owners; and, if I may offer myself as a witness, I can say that, after ten years of careful examination, I find the feelings of the masses on this point stronger and more resistant than on any other question. I have succeeded in shaking their opinions, but have made no impression on their sentiments. And one thing is to be noted which shows how far, in the minds of the people, individual sovereignty is identified with collective sovereignty, that the more ground the principles of democracy have gained, the more I have seen the working classes, both in the city and country, interpret these principles favorably to individual ownership.

Therefore while maintaining my criticism, upon the aim of which no one can hereafter misunderstand me, I have been obliged to conclude that the hypothesis of general farm tenancy did not contain the solution that I sought; and that, after having settled for the land, it would be necessary to seriously consider reassigning it in full sovereignty to the worker, because, without that, neither his pride as a citizen nor his rights as a producer could be satisfied.

This important solution, without which nothing stable can be produced in society, I believe I have found; and, as always, as much more simple, more practical, and more fruitful, as it was nearer at hand: it is none other than the principle which has served us for liquidation, transformed into the principle of acquisition.

"Every payment of house rent or farm rent," we have said, "acquires for the house tenant, farmer or peasant a proportional share in ownership."

Make of this idea, apparently quite negative, and which at first seemed a mere fancy, for the need of the cause — make of it a positive, general, fixed rule, and property becomes constituted. It will receive its organization, its rules, its police, its sanction. It will have fulfilled the Idea beneath it, its charter for all and accepted by all, in a single clause; whence all the rest is deducible by the light of common sense.

With this simple contract, protected, consolidated and guaranteed by the commercial and agricultural association, you may, without the slightest apprehension, permit the proprietor to sell, transmit, alienate, circulate, his property at will. Property in land, under this new system, property deprived of rent, delivered from its chains and cured of its leprosy, is in the hands of the proprietor like a five franc piece or a bank note in the hands of the bearer. It is worth so much, neither more nor less, it can neither gain nor lose in value by changing hands; it is no longer subject to depreciation; above all, it has lost that fatal power of accumulation which it had, not in itself, but through the ancient prejudice in favor of caste and nobility which attached to it.

Thus from the point of view of equality of conditions, of the guaranty of labor and of public security, property in land cannot cause the slightest perturbation to social economy: it has lost its vicious character; there remain to be seen the good qualities which it must have acquired. It is to this that I call the attention of my readers, notably of the Communist, whom I beg to weigh well the difference between association, that is to say, government, and contract.

If landed property should come back to the State, as some propose, and should consequently become fixed in the hands of the State, leaving the cultivators either associated or tenant farmers, it would come about that property would disappear, not merely as a right, as a legal principle, but as a *value.*

Suppose that, as things are, the Government should order a complete inventory of all the wealth of the

14*

country, both personal and real. After having taken into account the money, the merchandise in store, the standing crops, furniture, tools, houses and shops, there would be added the land, what is commonly called property. And we would say: The land is worth 16 billion dollars, which, added to 10 billions of products, merchandise, &c., makes a total of 26 billions.

With the system of universal tenantship, on the contrary, these 16 billions of value in land would have to be entirely cut off from the inventory; since, being neither sold nor exchanged, entering into comparison with no other value, belonging to everybody, that is to say, to nobody, they could not, under any classification, any more than the air and the sunlight, enter into the wealth of the nation.

It will perhaps be said that this is only a bookkeeper's artifice; that it does not affect the real wealth of the country, the positive prosperity of the people. A mistake: the people have lost 16 billions, because they have lost the right to dispose of it. In fact, according to the declaration of '93, property is the power of *free disposition*. Property, or the power of free disposition, in a man, is precisely what we call value in a thing; so that he who loses either one, loses both: this is according to the usual practice. Follow this thread carefully.

According to the Constitution of 1848, which in its turn confirmed the right of property, deriving it from labor, he who clears a field, encloses it, tills it, enriches it, buries in it his sweat, his blood, his soul, has not only the right to the crop, which is his already; he has earned in addition a field, a *value*, which constitutes for him an additional reward, which he counts among his possessions, and calls his property. This property he can exchange or sell, and obtain for it a price, according to its importance, on which he may live, without labor, for several years.

Corresponding with this practice, consecrated by all our constitutions, we have laid down a similar rule in the authority granted to our Land Bank: "Every "payment of house rent or farm rent acquires for the "tenant a proportional part of the property."

Suppose then that the farmer, profiting by the advantage conferred upon him by the revolution, has acquired by twenty years of rent payments a property worth $4000, do you think that he would find it the same thing to be able to say, under a Communistic governmental system: The Revolution gives me a longer lease and a lower rent, it is true. But it permits me to acquire nothing, I shall never own this land: naked I came to it, and naked I shall leave it. And as my trade is to hoe the soil, and I cannot do anything else, my condition is incapable ofchange; here I am fixed for life and for the life of my children, attached to the soil. Thus have our rulers willed, our rulers, whom we have chosen to make laws for us, who represent and govern us.

Or under the system of reciprocal contract:

The Revolution has freed me from rent. Each year that I pay rent purchases a part of this farm for me; in twenty years the property will be mine. In twenty years, I, who have nothing, I, who never expected to have anything, I, who would have died without leaving my children anything but the memory of my weariness and my resignation, in twenty years I shall be the owner of this farm, which is worth $4000. I shall be its master, its proprietor! I shall sell it, if I choose, for gold, or for silver, or for bank notes: I shall move to another part of the country if I choose; I shall make my son a merchant if commerce suits him; I shall marry my daughter to a teacher if she likes; and, as for myself, when I am old and unable to work, I shall buy for myself an annuity. My property is my refuge in my old age.

Do you think, I ask, that the peasant would hesitate an instant which to choose?

No doubt the COLLECTIVE wealth of the nation neither gains nor loses in either case: what matters it to society whether the 16 billions of real estate which constitute individual fortunes are included or not in

the total? But for the farmer, in whose hands the soil
is mobilized, and becomes a circulating value, a sort of
money, as it were, I ask again, is it the same thing?

What I say is to no other end than to form opinion,
and to prevent ruinous experiments, as far as in me
lies. As for the outcome, it will be such in its last
result as I have outlined: the greatest of powers, the
necessity of things, in harmony with the human heart,
have so willed. The farmer who did not recognize any
other proprietor than the State, would soon put himself
in the place of the State: he would treat his possessions
as a real proprietor. He would establish among farm
workers for the transmission of farms the same usage
that prevails among notaries, clerks, &c., for the sale
of offices; and, as the peasants in France will always
be the strongest, they will soon have consecrated, by
their powerful decree, what it pleases certain Utopians
to call a usurpation.

Let us then anticipate the unavoidable solution, which
the interest of the country, the preservation of the soil,
the equilibrium of fortunes, and the liberty of transfer
call for; and financial reform points to and demands.
It is ridiculous to want to subject masses of men, under
the name of individual sovereignty, to laws repugnant
to their instincts; on the contrary, it is just and really
revolutionary to propose to them what appeals to
their self-regard, what they can acclaim with enthusiasm. The self-regard of the people in political matters
is the first law.

Let the Assembly of 1852, whether Constituent or
Legislative, make a beginning: let it put a stop to farm
rent, and at the same time to this absurd small parcelling which is a disaster for public welfare: let it
profit by the general liquidation of the land to
recompense inheritances, and prevent their dissipation
hereafter. With facility of purchase by annual
payments, the value of real estate may be indefinitely
divided, exchanged, undergo all imaginable transfers,
without ever cutting up the land. The rest is a matter
of detail, we need not concern ourselves about it.

3. Division of Labor, Collective Forces, Machines, Workingmen's Associations.

In France, two-thirds of the inhabitants are interested in land owning; and even this proportion must increase. Next to credit, which controls everything, it is the greatest of our economic forces; through it, therefore, we must proceed to the revolutionary organization in the second place.

Agricultural labor, resting on this basis, appears in its natural dignity. Of all occupations it is the most noble, the most healthful, from the point of view of morals and health, and as intellectual exercise, the most encyclopaedic. From all these considerations, agricultural labor is the one which least requires the societary form; we may say even more strongly, which most energetically rejects it. Never have peasants been seen to form a society for the cultivation of their fields; never will they be seen to do so. The only relations of unity and solidarity which can exist among farm workers, the only centralization of which rural industry is susceptible, is that which we have pointed out which results from compensation for economic rent, mutual insurance, and, most of all, from abolishing rent, which makes accumulation of land, parcelling out of the soil, serfdom of the peasant, dissipation of inheritances, forever impossible.

It is otherwise with certain industries, which require the combined employment of a large number of workers, a vast array of machines and hands, and, to make use of a technical expression, a great division of labor, and in consequence, a high concentration of power. In such cases, workman is necessarily subordinate to workman, man dependent on man. The producer is no longer, as in the fields, a sovereign and free father of a family; it is a collectivity. Railroads, mines, factories, are examples.

In such cases, it is one of two things; either the workman, necessarily a piece-worker, will be simply the employee of the proprietor-capitalist-promoter; or he will participate in the chances of loss or gain of the establishment, he will have a voice in the council, in a word, he will become an associate.

In the first case the workman is subordinated, ex= ploited: his permanent condition is one of obedience and poverty. In the second case he resumes his dignity as a man and citizen, he may aspire to comfort, he forms a part of the producing organization, of which he was before but the slave; as, in the town, he forms a part of the sovereign power, of which he was before but the subject.

Thus we need not hesitate, for we have no choice. In cases in which production requires great division of labor, and a considerable collective force, it is necessary to form an ASSOCIATION among the workers in this industry; because without that, they would remain related as subordinates and superiors, and there would ensue two industrial castes of masters and wage= workers, which is repugnant to a free and democratic society.

Such therefore is the rule that we must lay down, if we wish to conduct the Revolution intelligently.

Every industry, operation or enterprise, which by its nature requires the employment of a large number of workmen of different specialties, is destined to become a society or company of workers.

That is why I said one day, in February or March, 1849, at a meeting of patriots, that I rejected equally the construction and management of railroads by companies of capitalists and by the State. In my opinion, railroads are in the field of workmen's com= panies, which are different from the present commercial companies, as they must be independent of the State. A railroad, a mine, a factory, a ship, are to the workers who use them what a hive is to the bees, at once their tool and their home, their country, their territory, their property. It is surprising that they who so zealously maintain the principle of association should have failed to see that such was its normal application.

But where the product can be obtained by the action of an individual or a family, without the co=operation of special abilities, there is no opportunity for association. Association not being called for by the nature of the work, cannot be profitable nor of long continuance: I have given the reasons elsewhere.

When I speak of either *collective force* or of an extreme division of labor, as a necessary condition for association, it must be understood from a practical point of view, rather than in a rigorous logical or mathematical sense. Liberty of association being unrestricted, it is evident that if the peasants think well to associate, they will associate, independently of the considerations against it; on the other hand, it is not less clear that if one must live up to the rigorous definitions of science, the conclusion would be that all workers must associate, inasmuch as collective force and division of labor exist everywhere, to however slight a degree.

We must supplement the deficiencies of language, and do for political economy what naturalists do in their classifications, that is to select always not doubtful but marked characteristics, upon which to base our definitions.

I mean to say, therefore, that the degree of associative tendency among workers must be in proportion to the economic relations which unite them, so that where these relations are inappreciable or insignificant, no account need be taken of them; where they predominate and control, they must be regarded.

Thus I do not consider as falling within the logical class of division of labor nor of collective force the innumerable small shops which are found in all trades, and which seem to me the effect of the preference of the individuals who conduct them, rather than the organic result of a combination of forces. Anybody who is capable of cutting out and sewing up a pair of shoes can get a license, open a shop, and hang out a sign, *"So=and=So, Manufacturing Shoe Merchant,"* although there may be only himself behind his counter. If a companion, who prefers journeyman's wages to running the risk of starting in business, joins with the first, one will call himself the employer, the other, the hired man; in fact, they are completely equal and completely free. If a youth of fourteen or fifteen wants to learn the trade, there may be a certain division of labor with him; but this division of labor is the condition of apprenticeship, there is nothing remarkable about it. If orders come in freely, there may be several journey= men and apprentices, besides helpers, perhaps a clerk: then it will be what is called a shop, that is, six, ten, fifteen persons, all doing about the same thing, and working together merely to increase the product, not at all to contribute to its perfection by their different abilities. If suddenly the employer's affairs fall into confusion, and he goes into bankruptcy, they whom he employed will have only the trouble of finding another shop; as for his customers, they run no risk, each of the journeymen, or all of them together, may resume the business.

In such a case, I see no reason for association, unless for individual preference. What collective force there is counts for too little; it does not counterbalance the risks of the venture. Journeymen may wish to be admitted to the advantages of a prosperous establish= ment: I see no difficulty, if the employer consents, and the law does not forbid it. It may be that all, both employer and journeymen, find it to their advantage; that brings it among special cases, which cannot enter into consideration here. But according to the economic law which guides us, such participation cannot be demanded: it is entirely outside of the provision of the new rule of right. To order or prescribe association under such conditions, would be to re=erect, through a mean and jealous spirit, the unfortunate feudal corporations which the Revolution abolished: it would be unfaithful to progress, and a backward step, which is impossible. That is not the future of association, considered as an economic and revolutionary institution. I cannot but repeat what I have already said elsewhere,

that the workingmen's associations which have formed
at Paris for industries of this nature, as well as the
heads of concerns who have given their employees a
share in their dividends, ought to consider themselves
as serving the Revolution from an entirely different
point of view, and for a different object. I shall speak
of this again shortly.

But when the enterprise requires the combined aid of
several industries, professions, special trades; when
from this combination springs a new product, that could
not be made by any individual, a combination in which
man fits in with man as wheel with wheel; the whole
group of workers forms a machine, like the fitting of
the parts of a clock or a locomotive; then, indeed, the
conditions are no longer the same. Who could arrogate
the right to exploit such a body of slaves? Who would
be daring enough to take one man for a hammer,
another for a spade, this one for a hook, that one for a
lever?

The capitalist, you will cry, alone runs the risk of the
enterprise, like the employing shoemaker of whom we
spoke just now. No doubt that is true, but the
comparison holds no further. Could the capitalists alone
work a mine or run a railroad? Could one man alone
carry on a factory, sail a ship, play a tragedy, build the
Pantheon or the Column of July? Can anybody do
such things as these, even if he has all the capital
necessary? And the one who is called the employer, is
he anything more than a leader or captain?

It is in such a case that association seems to me
absolutely necessary and right.

The industry to be carried on, the work to be
accomplished, are the common and undivided property
of all those who take part therein: the granting of
franchises for mines and railroads to companies of
stockholders, who plunder the bodies and souls of the
wage-workers, is a betrayal of power, a violation of
the rights of the public, an outrage upon human dignity
and personality.

Certainly the Parisian workmen, who were the first to mark the course of the Revolution, and assert the principle of identity of interests, were unable at the outset to carry out such a method. It was not for them to organize themselves into manufacturing companies and railroads. Heaven forbid that I should reproach them for it! The position was captured (it will again be captured) and held by thousands of bayonets. The capital which it would be necessary to reimburse was enormous; institutions of credit, indispensable in such a case, did not exist. The workmen could do nothing in this direction: the force of circumstances threw them into industries in which association is least useful. Moreover their work was wholly one of devotion, and provisional in character, nor had it any other aim than to put down usurious commerce, to drive out parasitical speculation, and to form a chosen body of artisans, who would be able to renew the tactics of industrialism, and organize victory for the lower classes, like the young generals of the old revolution.

Thus the outline of the Revolution begins to display itself: already its aspect is grandiose.

On the one hand, the peasants, at last masters of the soil which they cultivate, and in which they desire to take root. Their enormous, unconquerable mass, aroused by a common guaranty, united by the same interests, assures forever the triumph of the democracy, and the permanence of *Contract*.

On the other hand there are myriads of small manufacturers, dealers, artisans, the volunteers of commerce and industry, working in isolation or in small groups, the most migratory of beings; who prefer their complete independence to the sovereignty of the soil; sure of having a country wherever they can find work.

Finally appear the workingmen's associations, regular armies of the revolution, in which the worker, like the soldier in the battalion, manoeuvres with the precision of his machines; in which thousands of wills, intelligent and proud, submit themselves to a superior will, as the hands controlled by them engender, by their concerted action, a collective force greater than even their number.

The cultivator had been bent under feudal servitude through rent and mortgages. He is freed by the land bank, and, above all, by the right of the user to the property. The land, vast in extent and in depth, becomes the basis of equality.

In the same way the wage-worker of the great industries had been crushed into a condition worse than that of the slave, by the loss of the advantage of collective force. But by the recognition of his right to the profit from this force, of which he is the producer, he resumes his dignity, he regains comfort; the great industries, terrible engines of aristocracy and pauperism, become, in their turn, one of the principal organs of liberty and public prosperity.

Our readers must understand by this time that the laws of social economy are independent of the will of any man or any legislator: it is our privilege to recognize them, our honor to obey them.

This recognition and this submission, in the present state of our prejudices, and under the rule of the traditions which beset us, can be brought about only by the mutual consent of the citizens, in a word, by contract. What we have done for credit, housing, agriculture, we must do for the great industries: in this case, as in the others, legislative authority will intervene, only to write its last will and testament.

Let us then lay down the principles of the agreement which must constitute this new revolutionary power.

Large-scale industry may be likened to a new land, discovered, or suddenly created out of the air, by the social genius; to which society sends a colony to take possession of it and to work it, for the advantage of all.

This colony will be ruled by a double contract, that which gives it title, establishes its property, and fixes its rights and obligations toward the mother-country; and the contract which unites the different members among themselves, and determines their rights and duties.

Toward Society, of which it is a creation and a dependence, this working company promises to furnish always the products and services which are asked of it, at a price as nearly as possible that of cost, and to give the public the advantage of all desirable betterments and improvements.

To this end, the working company abjures all combinations, submits itself to the law of competition, and holds its books and records at the disposition of Society, which, upon its part, reserves the power of dissolving the working company, as the sanction of its right of control.

Toward the individuals and families whose labor is the subject of the association, the company makes the following rules:

That every individual employed in the association, whether man, woman, child, old man, head of department, assistant head, workman or apprentice, has an undivided share in the property of the company;

That he has a right to fill any position, of any grade, in the company, according to suitability of sex, age, skill, and length of employment;

That his education, instruction, and apprenticeship should therefore be so directed that, while permitting him to do his share of unpleasant and disagreeable tasks, they may also give variety of work and knowledge, and may assure him, from the period of maturity, an encyclopaedic aptitude and a sufficient income;

That all positions are elective, and the by-laws subject to the approval of the members;

That pay is to be proportional to the nature of the position, the importance of the talents, and the extent of responsibility;

That each member shall participate in the gains and in the losses of the company, in proportion to his services;

That each member is free to leave the company, upon settling his account, and paying what he may owe; and reciprocally, the company may take in new members at any time.

These general principles are enough to explain the spirit and scope of this institution, that has no precedent and no model. They furnish the solution of two important problems of social economy, that of *collective force*, and that of the division of labor.

By participation in losses and gains, by the graded scale of pay, and the successive promotion to all grades and positions, the collective force, which is a product of the community, ceases to be a source of profit to a small number of managers and speculators: it becomes the property of all the workers. At the same time, by a broad education, by the obligation of apprenticeship, and by the co-operation of all who take part in the collective work, the division of labor can no longer be a cause of degradation for the workman: it is, on the contrary, the means of his education and the pledge of his security.

We may add that the application of these principles at an epoch of transition would entail that at which every man of heart, every true revolutionary, should rejoice, the privilege of beginning the reform for the middle class, and its fusion with the lower class.

It must be admitted that, although the laboring class, by its numerical preponderance, and by the irresistible pressure which it is able to exercise upon the decisions of an assembly, is quite capable, with the aid of a few enlightened citizens, of bringing about the first part of the revolutionary programme, social liquidation and the settlement of property in land; it is, nevertheless, by the narrowness of its view and its inexperience in business, incapable of carrying on such large interests as those of commerce and great industry; and in consequence cannot attain its true destiny.

Men are lacking in the lower class, as well as in the democracy: we have seen it but too clearly for three years. They who have reached the greatest celebrity as officials are the last to merit the confidence of the people in matters relating to labor and social economy.

Ask the Parisian associations, enlightened by their experience, what they think to-day of the crowd of little great men, who recently waved the banner of fraternity before them. It would be unavoidable then, in what relates to the carrying on of large industries, that some commercial and industrial experts should be associated with the liberated workers, to teach them the management of affairs. They can be found in abundance: there is not one of the mercantile class, acquainted with commerce and industry and their innumerable risks, who would not prefer a fixed salary and honorable position in a working association to all the worries of a private business; there is not an exact and capable clerk who would not leave a precarious position to accept an appointment in a great association. Let the workers consider it; let them get rid of a mean and jealous spirit; there is room for everybody in the sunlight of the Revolution. They have more to gain by such self-conquest than by the interminable and always destructive squabbles which are inflicted upon them by their leaders, who are sincere, no doubt, but incapable.

4. Constitution of Value. Organization of Low Prices.

If commerce or exchange, carried on after a fashion, is already, by its inherent merit, a producer of wealth; if, for this reason, it has been practised always and by all the nations of the globe; if, in consequence, we must consider it as an economic force; it is not the less true, and it springs from the very notion of exchange, that commerce ought to be so much the more profitable if sales and purchases are made at the lowest and most just price; that is to say, if the products that are exchanged can be furnished in greater abundance and in more exact proportion.

Scarcity of product, in other words, the high price of merchandise, is an evil in commerce: the imperfect relations, that is to say, the arbitrary prices, the anomalous values, are another evil.

To deliver commerce from these two diseases that eat into and devour it, would be to increase the productivity of commerce, and consequently the prosperity of society.

At all times speculation has taken advantage of these two scourges of commerce, scarcity of product and arbitrary value, in order to exaggerate them, and bring pressure upon the unhappy people. Always also the public conscience has rebelled against the exactions of mercantilism, and struggled to restore the equilibrium. We all know of the desperate war waged by Turgot against the monopolizers of grain, who were supported by the courts and by precedent: we can also remember the less fortunate efforts of the Convention, and its laws establishing maximum prices. In our own day, the tax on bread, the abolition of the slaughter house privilege, the railroad rate scale, and those of ministerial offices, &c., &c., are so many attempts in the same direction.

It must always be remembered with shame that certain economists have nevertheless aspired to erect into a law this mercantile disorder and commercial disturbance. They see in it a principle as sacred as that of the family or of labor. The school of Say, sold out to English and native capitalism, the chief focus of counter-revolution next to the Jesuits, has for ten years past seemed to exist only to protect and applaud the execrable work of the monopolists of money and necessaries, deepening more and more the obscurity of a science naturally difficult and full of complications. These apostles of materialism were made to work in with the eternal executioners of conscience: after the events of February, they signed an agreement with the Jesuits, a compact of hypocrisy and a bargain with starvation. Let the reaction which unites them hasten to cause them to retrace their steps, and let them get to cover quickly, for I warn them that if the Revolution spares men, it will not spare deeds.

No doubt Value, the expression of liberty, and growing out of the personality of the worker, is of all
15

human things the most reluctant to submit to formulas. Therein lies the excuse of the misleading routine arguments of the economists. Thus the diciples of Malthus and of Say, who oppose with all their might any intervention of the State in matters commercial or industrial, do not fail to avail themselves at times of this seemingly liberal attitude, and to show themselves more revolutionary than the Revolution. More than one honest searcher has been deceived thereby: they have not seen that this inaction of Power in economic matters was the foundation of government. What need should we have of a political organization, if Power once permitted us to enjoy economic order?

But precisely because Value is in the highest degree difficult to formulate, it is eminently transactional, seeing that it is always the result of a transaction between the seller and the buyer, or as the economists say, between *supply* and *demand*.

In fact, the price of things is the fundamental question in agreements; the one natural and constant element in all contracts between man and man. Whence it follows that the theory of Value is the basis of commutative justice: it should be found at the head of all legislation, as it were a decalogue, since without some pre-existing Value there can be neither sale, nor exchange, nor hire, nor society, nor interest, nor bonds, nor mortgages, &c. Therefore it is not a mere theoretical determination of Value that is needed; it is a practical method of arranging an honest transaction in respect of value.

Who could believe, if the evidence were not before our eyes, that for the six thousand years since men began to govern by law, not one law has been made in the whole world having for its object, not to fix the value of things, which is impossible, but to teach traders how to approximate it? Rules for the *form* of contracts abound and vary infinitely; as to their *matter*, no question has been raised. Therefore we have laws by hundreds of thousands, and not one principle. It is a world upside down, a world at war, such a world as lawyers and judges have made it, and such as Jesuits and Malthusians want to keep it.

It must be understood that I cannot here undertake the full discussion of the theoretical and practical questions which value raises; a discussion without end; which, without exaggeration, might well include the whole of political economy, the whole of philosophy and the whole of history. I reserve this interesting study for some other occasion; for the present, I must be brief, categorical, positive. I should despair of my task if the People had not shortened it by nine-tenths, through its practical, and at the same time revolutionary instinct. I am about to try to formulate their most recent practice. The People is the god who inspires true philosophers. May they recognize their own ideas in my quick words!

Everybdoy knows that from the earliest period EXCHANGE has been separated into two elementary operations, *Sale* and *Purchase*. Money is the universal commodity, the tally, which serves to connect the two operations, and to complete the exchange.

In order therefore to regulate exchange and to systematize commerce, it would be enough to effect methodically one or the other of the two acts of which it is composed, Sale or Purchase.

Let us take Sale for example.

According to what we have just said, Sale will be genuine, normal, fair, from the point of view of economic justice and of value, if it is made at a *just price*, as far as human calculation permits this to be established.

What then is the *just price* for all kinds of service or merchandise?

It is that which represents with exactitude: Ist, the total cost of production, according to the average experience of free producers; 2nd, the wages of the merchant, or indemnity for the advantage of which the seller deprives himself in parting with the thing sold.

If everything which constitutes the material of contracts were sold, hired or exchanged according to
15*

this rule, the whole world would be in repose; peace on earth would be inviolable; there would have been neither soldiers nor slaves, neither conquerors nor nobles.

But, unfortunately for humanity, things are not done so in commerce. The *price* of things is not proportionate to their VALUE : it is larger or smaller according to an influence which justice condemns, but the existing economic chaos excuses — Usury.

Usury is the arbitrary factor in commerce. Inasmuch as, under the present system, the producer has no guaranty that he can exchange his product, nor the merchant any certainty of reselling, each one endeavors to pass off his merchandise at the highest possible price, in order to obtain by the excess of profit the security of which labor and exchange fail sufficiently to assure him. The profit thus obtained in excess of the cost, including the wages of the seller, is called Increase. Increase — theft — is therefore compensation for insecurity.

Everybody being given to Increase, there is reciprocal falsehood in all relations, and universal deceit, by common consent, as to the value of things. Of course this it not written out in black and white in contracts, although the courts would be quite capable of accepting it! But in the spirit of justice, and in the opinion of the parties, it is a perfect understanding among them.

If increase were equal as well as reciprocal, the equity of agreements, the equilibrium of commerce, and therefore the prosperity of society would not suffer. Two equal quantities increased by an equal quantity are still equal: it is a mathematical axiom.

But Increase is without rule, it is chance; and it is against the nature of chance to produce equality or order. Hence it results that the reciprocity of Increase is but the reciprocity of rascality; and that this pretended *law* of the economists is the most active cause of spoliation and poverty.

This is what the Revolution proposes.

Since there is a universal tacit agreement among all producers and traders to take from each other increase for their products or services, to work in the dark in their dealings, to play a sharp game; in a word, to take each other by surprise by all the tricks of trade; why should there not as well be a universal and tacit agreement to renounce increase, that is to say, to sell and pay at the only just price, which is the average cost?

Such an agreement would not be illogical: such alone can secure the prosperity and security of mankind. Sooner or later it can, it must, come to pass; and for my part, I have no doubt that, with a little perseverance on the part of the people, it will come to pass.

But it is hard to stem the current of ages, and to make prejudice retrace its path: a long time, generations perhaps, will pass before the public conscience reaches such a height. While awaiting this marvellous change, there is but one way, that is, to obtain by special formal agreements what will hereafter result from tacit and universal consent, without other special agreement.

Selling at a just price! the old hands will exclaim; that has been known for a long time. What good has it done? Dealers who sell at a just price do not make their fortunes any more, or ruin themselves any less than the rest of us; and, as for the purchasers, they are not better served, nor do they pay less than before. All that talk, they will say, is but empiricism, the revival of worn-out ideas, illusion, despair.

That is precisely what I deny. Sale at a just price is unknown: it has never been put into practice, and for the good reason that it has not been understood.

What will surprise more than one reader, and what seems at first sight contradictory, is that a *just price*, like any sort of service or guaranty, must be PAID FOR: the low price of merchandise, like the merchandise itself, must have its recompense: without this premium offered to the merchant, the just price becomes impossible, the low price a chimaera.

Let us look into this truth, one of the most profound of political economy.

If the dealer usually refuses to sell his goods at cost, it is, on the one hand, because he has no certainty of selling enough to secure him an income; on the other, because he has no guaranty that he will obtain like treatment for his purchases.

Without this double guaranty, sale at a just price, the same as sale below the market price, is impossible: the only cases in which it occurs arise from failures and liquidations.

Do you wish then to obtain goods at a just price, to gain the advantage of a low price, to practise a truth-telling commerce, to assure equality in exchange?

You must offer the merchant a sufficient guaranty.

This guaranty may take various forms: perhaps the consumers, who wish to have the benefit of a just price, are producers themselves, and will obligate themselves in turn to sell their products to the dealer on like terms, as is done among the different Parisian associations; perhaps the consumers will content themselves, without any reciprocal arrangements, with assuring the retailer of a premium, the interest, for example, of his capital, or a fixed bonus, or a sale large enough to assure him of a revenue. This is what is generally done by the butchers' associations, and by the *Housekeeper* society, of which we have already spoken.

These different kinds of guaranties, with the aid of the action of representatives in the Assembly and of an allowance in the budget, might quickly become general, and produce extraordinary effects immediately.

Suppose that the Government, or the Constituent Assembly, to which the proposition was made, had really wanted to revive business, to relieve commerce, industry and agriculture, to stop the depreciation of property, to assure work to laborers.

It might be done by guaranteeing to, say, the first ten thousand employers, manufacturers, dealers, &c., in the whole Republic, the interest at 5 per cent. of

the capital which each of them might put into business,
up to an average amount to each of $20,000.

I say by guaranteeing, not by paying interest:
it would have been agreed that if the net profit of the
business amounted to 5 per cent. or more, the State
should make no payment for interest.

The capital thus guaranteed for ten thousand
establishments would amount to $200,000,000. The
interest to be paid, if paid on the whole of this sum,
would be $10,000,000. But it is evident that the State
would never have to part with any such sum: ten
thousand commercial establishments cannot operate
simultaneously without serving as a support to one
another: what one produces another consumes; labor
is the outlet. The State would not have to pay over
$2,000,000 interest of the $10,000,000 which it
guaranteed.

Can it be thought that such a sum can be compared
with the deficit in production caused by the withdrawal
of capital and the insecurity of employers, with the
enormous depreciation of property, with the proverty
and struggle which have decimated the lower classes?

In a published memorial, speaking in the name of a
mercantile house of Lyons, I made a proposition of
a different nature to the Government, — that we would
guarantee transportation of all merchandise and
passengers from Avignon to Chalons-sur-Marne, for
from 60 to 80 per cent. less than the railroad charges,
stipulating that the State should guarantee to the con-
structors interest at 5 per cent. on their investment.

That would be to obtain, for $60,000, a saving of
several millions.

Do you know what the answer was?

The Government directorate of the Paris to Lyons
railroad, under the pretext that it did not want to *cut
into prices* by favoring a monopoly, preferred to treat
with some friendly speculators for its connection, at
a higher price than that of the railway could be. So
that if in two or three years this railway is built, the
company or the State will still seem to be benefiting

the Country. It is thus that a Government acts that
knows its business. Louis V was the heaviest
stockholder in the starvation pact: the historians,
friends of authority, have condemned his memory to
infamy. He speculated in food. The ministers of the
Republic and their assistants will retain their reputation
for integrity. They speculate only in transportation.

I say plainly that the associations of workmen of
Paris and of the provinces hold in their hands the
salvation of the people and the future of the Revolution. They are able to accomplish everything if they
use skill. It must be that a renewal of activity on their
part will bring light to the darkest minds, and will
compel the placing of the *Constitution of Value* at the
head of the list in the platform for the elections of 1852.

This constitution can result, as I have said, only from
universal consent freely obtained and freely expressed.
To prepare for it, and to bring it about with the least
delay possible, it will suffice if instructions are given
through the new organization of representatives to the
State and to the towns, each to the extent of its
authority and to the limit of its resources, to advise
with a certain number of employers, machinists,
manufacturers, farmers, cattle raisers, coachmen, mes-
sengers, &c., &c., about the submission of bids upon
the following basis:

"The State, in the name of the interests which it
"provisionally represents, and the Provinces and Towns,
"in the name of their respective inhabitants, desiring
"to assure to all fair prices and good quality of
"products and services, and to prevent fraud, monopoly
"and increase, offer to guarantee to the bidders who
"shall submit the most advantageous conditions, either
"interest upon the capital and plant used in their
"business, or a fixed bonus, or, if practicable, a sufficient
"volume of orders.

"Bidders will undertake in return to furnish their
"products and services, as described in their bids, to

"satisfy the needs of consumers — full latitude however
"to be allowed for competition.

"They must state the basis of their prices, the mode
"of delivery, the period of their engagement, and their
"means of execution.

"Sealed bids having been deposited within the
"prescribed period, will be forthwith opened and
"published for a week, a fortnight, a month, three
"months, according to the importance of their subject,
"before an award is made.

"At the termination of each contract, new bids will
be received."

The constitution of Value is the contract of contracts.
It includes all others, realizing the idea which we have
explained in another essay, that the social contract
should include all persons, all interests.

When, by the liquidation of debts, the organization
of credit, the deprivation of the power of increase of
money, the limitation of property, the establishment of
workingmen's associations and the use of a just price,
the tendency to raising of prices shall have been
definitely replaced by a tendency to lower them, and
the fluctuations of the market by a normal commercial
rate; when general consent shall have brought this
great about=face in the sphere of trade, then Value,
at once the most ideal and most real of things, may be
said to have been constituted, and will express at any
moment, for every kind of product, the true relation of
Labor and Wealth, while preserving its mobility through
the eternal progress of industry.

The constitution of Value solves the problem of
competition and that of the rights of Invention; as the
organization of workmen's associations solves that of
collective force and of the division of labor. I can
merely indicate at this moment these consequences of
the main theorem; their development would take too
much space in a philosophical review of the Revolution.

5. Foreign Commerce. Balance of Imports and Exports.

By the suppression of custom houses, the Revolution, according to theory, and regardless of all military and diplomatic influences, will spread from France abroad, extend over Europe, and afterwards over the world.

To suppress our custom houses is in truth to organize foreign trade as we have organized domestic trade; it is to place the countries with which we trade on even terms with ourselves in our trade legislation; it is to introduce among them the constitution of Value and of Property; it is, in a word, to establish the solidarity of the Revolution between the French People and the rest of the human race, by making the new social compact common to all nations through the power of Exchange.

I am about to give a glimpse of this movement in few words.

For what end have custom houses been established?

For the protection of the labor of the nation.

In what does this protection consist?

The State, which is the guardian of the portals of the country, requires foreign merchandise, at its entrance into France, to pay a greater or less tax, which raises the price and favors the sale of home products.

Why not prefer foreign products, you will ask, if it is true that they are cheaper than our own?

Because products can be bought only with products; and if foreign competition should crush our industry in all or in the greater number of directions, it would come to pass that we would be unable to balance our imports by our exports, and would have to pay for them with money, and, when our money was gone, to borrow money abroad, thus giving foreigners a mortgage upon our property, and, what is worse, paying them interest, profit and rent.

Such is the wise and good reason for the establishment of custom houses. All nations understand it, and all nations protect themselves. Let us not dispute as to the efficacy of the means; let us take it for what it is meant to be, with its official significance.

From this definition of the tariff it follows that if it protects the producer, it is not to be understood as making him an exploiter and idler among his fellow citizens; but simply as assuring him of employment, and safeguarding the independence of the country from foreign control. It is with this intention that the tariff, as it perceives that an industry is developing and making profits, reduces its rates and calls in foreign competition, in order to protect the interests of the consumer as much as those of the producer.

Once more, let us not ask whether all these measures which good sense suggests perform the service that is expected of them; whether they are carried out with justice, or whether any irregularity slips in. The ques= tion now is not one of morality, nor of the capacity of the State to act as a protector; but solely of the aim of the institution, and of the necessity which requires it.

Then, as there is progress in every industry, a tendency to reduce the cost of production, and thus to increase the profits, there should be also a tendency to diminish the customs tariff.

The ideal of the system would be that labor should be everywhere guaranteed, competition everywhere established, sales everywhere assured, and prices maintained at their lowest. Such is the true meaning and intention of the tariff.

From what we have said in connection with social liquidation, as well as in connection with the constitu= tion of property, the organization of workingmen's societies and the guaranty of low prices, it follows that if the charge for loans at the Bank should diminish, if the interest on the public debt and upon private obligations were proportionally reduced, if thereupon house rent and ground rent were lowered in like proportion, if a tabulation were made of values and properties, &c., &c., the cost price of all sorts of products would decrease notably, and in consequence the tariff might be lowered to the advantage of all.

That would be a step in general progress such as
has never yet been seen, because a government is
incapable of bringing it about.

If this general movement, as I have more than once
observed, should only make a beginning, if the tariff,
driven by credit, should move on this line however
little, the ancient order of things in all that concerns
our foreign relations would be suddenly changed, and
international economics would enter upon the road to
revolution.

In the matter of the tariff, as in everything else, the
statu quo, indicated by rising prices, is reaction;
progress, indicated by falling prices, is the Revolution.
A famous aristocrat, Robert Peel, understood it thus,
and put it thus in practice; showing himself as far
from the theories of Cobden, as from the selfishness
of the property holders. The tariff reforms of Robert
Peel had for their basis and preliminary condition the
superabundance and low price of capital in England;
while with us the free traders, aided by the Mountain=
ists, are asking for the abolition of the tariff, as
compensation of the national capital, which amounts
to foreign invasion, to repair our deficiencies; exploita=
tion by English, Swiss, Dutch, American, Russian
capitalists, to help the emancipation of our proletarians!
We did not need this example to discover that if the
French nation is sold out to the foreigner, if the
Revolution is betrayed, if a conspiracy is organized
against Socialism, it has been done chiefly by the
organs and representatives of the Republican party.
But we must pardon them: they do not know any
more what they are doing, than what they want.

As for me, I, who oppose the free traders because
they favor interest, while they demand the abolition of
tariffs, — I should favor lowering the tariff from the
moment that interest fell; and if interest were done
away with, or even lowered to ¼ or ½ per cent., I
should be in favor of free trade.

I believe in free trade, even without reciprocity, as a consequence of the abolition of interest, not otherwise; and here is what I base my opinion upon.

If to-morrow the Bank of France should reduce the rate of discount to ½ per cent., both interest and commission included, the manufacturers and dealers of Paris and of the provinces who had no account with the Bank of Paris would immediately be compelled to obtain notes of the Bank for their transactions, since its notes would cost only ½ per cent., instead of 6, 7, 8 or 9 per cent., which money would cost at private bankers.

But it would not be French dealers only who would enter into this arrangement: foreign dealers would join in also. As the notes of the Bank of France would cost only ½ per cent., while those of other countries cost ten and twelve times as much, the former would be preferred; all the world would take advantage of the use of this money in payments.

In order to obtain a greater quantity of these notes, foreign producers would lower the prices of their goods, which would increase the quantity of our imports. But as these notes could no longer be used to buy bonds, since we have liquidated the national debt, nor invested in mortgages on the land, since we have liquidated all mortgages and changed the form of property; as they could be used only in payment for our own products, it is clear that we should no longer have to protect ourselves against imports; on the contrary, we should welcome them. The relation would be reversed; we should no longer need to reduce our purchases, but foreigners would have to be careful not to buy too much.

How can a nation refuse to sell? Such an idea is repugnant: with the universal development of industry, and the division of labor among nations, it implies a contradiction.

To re-establish the balance and to protect themselves against these tactics, foreigners would be obliged to abolish their own custom houses and to reform their banking systems, to constitute value, to emancipate their lower classes; in a word, to bring about revolution. Free trade would then become equal exchange the diversity of interests among nations would gradually result in unity of interest, and the day would dawn when war would cease among nations, as would law‌suits among individuals, from lack of litigable matter and absence of cause for conflict.

Without exceeding the limits which I have been obliged to lay down for myself, I cannot extend this exposition of the industrial organism, especially of that which relates to the new principle of order, the free contract. Those of my readers who have followed for ten years past the course of my revolutionary argu‌ment, will easily fill out what is missing. In resuming the series of economic negations, they will have no difficulty in separating the affirmations and deducing the synthesis.

It is for republican jurisconsults, such men as Crémieux, Michel (of Bourges), Martin (of Strasbourg), Jules Favre, Marie, Bethmont, Grévy, Dupont (of Bussac), Madier de Monjau, Desmarest, Marc‌Dufraisse, Ledru‌Rollin, to open up this new path to the spirit of the century, by developing the revolutionary formula resulting from the opposition of the Social Contract to Government. Long enough politics has been a stumbling block for legal luminaries; and it is not without good reason that the peasant and the soldier, seeing the politicians at work, deride their eloquence and their patriotism. What can there be in common between the man of *Law* and the man of *Force?* The revival of despotism fifty‌two years ago was marked by the expulsion of the barristers; and with propriety. The Constitution of the year V was a bad case for lawyers. As soon as they admitted the principle of government, they had to give way to the representatives of mere force; legal reasoning has nothing to do with the exercise of authority.

In concluding this study, may I be permitted a word in answer to the reproach of pride which has so often

and so mistakenly been made on account of the motto
which I put at the head of my book on *"Contradictions"* — *Destruam et aedificabo* — I destroy and I will
rebuild.

This antithesis, taken from Deuteronomy, is nothing
but the formula of the revolutionary law which serves
as the basis of the present essay, to wit, that every
negation implies an affirmation, and that he only is
the real rebuilder who is first a real destroyer.

SEVENTH STUDY.

Absorption of Government by the Economic Organism.

1. Society without Authority.

GIVEN:
  Man, *The Family*, SOCIETY.

An individual, sexual and social being, endowed with reason, love and conscience, capable of learning by experience, of perfecting himself by reflection, and of earning his living by work.

The problem is to so organize the powers of this being, that he may remain always at peace with himself, and may extract from Nature, which is given to him, the largest possible amount of well-being.

We know how previous generations have solved it.

They borrowed from the Family, the second component part of Humanity, the principle which is proper to it alone, AUTHORITY, and by the arbitrary use of this principle, they constructed an artificial system, varied according to periods and climates, which has been regarded as the natural order and necessary for humanity.

This system, which may be called the system of order by authority, was at first divided into spiritual and temporal authority.

After a short period in which it preponderated, and long centuries of struggle to maintain its supremacy, sacerdotalism seems at last to have given up its claim to temporal power: the Papacy, with all its soldiery, which the Jesuits and lay brothers of to-day would restore, has been cast out and set below matters of merely human interest.

For two years past the spiritual power has been in a way to again seize supremacy. It has formed a coalition with the secular power against the Revolution, and bargains with it upon a footing of equality. Both have ended by recognizing that their differences arose from a misunderstanding; that their aim, their principles, their methods, their dogmas, being absolutely identical, Government should be shared by them; or rather, that they should consider themselves the complements of each other, and should form by their union a one and indivisible Authority.

Such at least would have been the conclusion which Church and State would have perhaps reached, if the laws of the progress of Humanity rendered such reconciliations possible; if the Revolution had not already marked their last hour.

However that may be, it is desirable, in order to convince the mind, to set alongside each other the fundamental ideas of, on the one hand, the politico-religious system (Philosophy, which has for so long drawn a line between the spiritual and the temporal, should no longer recognize any distinction between them); on the other hand, the economic system.

Government then, that is to say, Church and State indivisibly united, has for its dogmas:

1. The original perversity of human nature;
2. The inevitable inequality of fortunes;
3. The permanency of quarrels and wars;
4. The irremediability of proverty.

Whence is deduced:

5. The necessity of government, of obedience, of resignation, and of faith.

These principles admitted, as they still are, almost universally, the forms of authority are already settled. They are:

a. The division of the people into classes or castes, subordinate to one another; graduated to form a pyramid, at the top of which appears, like the Divinity upon his altar, like the king upon his throne, AUTHORITY;

16

b. Administrative centralization;
c. Judicial hierarchy;
d. Police;
e. Worship.

Add to the above, in countries in which the demo=
cratic principle has become preponderant:

f. The separation of powers;

g. The intervention of the People in the Govern=
ment, by vote for representatives;

h. The innumerable varieties of electoral systems,
from the Convocation by Estates, which prevailed in
the Middle Ages, down to universal and direct
suffrage;

i. The duality of legislative chambers;

j. Voting upon laws, and consent to taxes by the
representatives of the nation;

k. The rule of majorities.

Such is broadly the plan of construction of Power,
independently of the modifications which each of its
component party may receive; as, for example, the
central Power, which may be in turn monarchical,
aristocratic or democratic; which once furnished publi=
cists with a ground for classification, according to
superficial character.

It will be observed that the governmental system
tends to become more and more complicated, without
becoming on that account more efficient or more
moral, and without offering any more guaranties to
person or property. This complication springs first from
legislation, which is always incomplete and insufficient;
in the second place, from the multiplicity of function=
aries; but most of all, from the compromise between
the two antagonistic elements, the executive initiative
and popular consent. It has been left for our epoch
to establish unmistakeably that this bargaining, which
the progress of centuries renders inevitable, is the
surest index of corruption, of decadence and of the
approaching dissolution of Authority.

What is the aim of this organization?

To maintain *order* in society, by consecrating and sanctifying obedience of the citizen to the State, subordination of the poor to the rich, of the common people to the upper class, of the worker to the idler, of the layman to the priest, of the business man to the soldier.

As far back as the memory of humanity extends, it is found to have been organized on the above system, which constitutes the political, ecclesiastical or governmental order. Every effort to give Power a more liberal appearance, more tolerant, more social, has invariably failed: such efforts have been even more fruitless when they tried to give the People a larger share in Government; as if the words, Sovereignty and People, which they endeavored to yoke together, were as naturally antagonistic as these other two words, Liberty and Despotism.

Humanity has had to live, and civilization to develop, for six thousand years, under this inexorable system, of which the first term is *Despair* and the last *Death.* What secret power has sustained it? What force has enabled it to survive? What principles, what ideas, renewed the blood that flowed forth under the poniard of authority, ecclesiastical and secular?

This mystery is now explained.

Beneath the governmental machinery, in the shadow of political institutions, out of the sight of statesmen and priests, society is producing its own organism, slowly and silently; and constructing a new order, the expression of its vitality and autonomy, and the denial of the old politics, as well as of the old religion.

This organization, which is as essential to society as it is incompatible with the present system, has the following principles:

1. The indefinite perfectibility of the individual and of the race;
2. The honorableness of work;
3. The equality of fortunes;
4. The identity of interests;
5. The end of antagonisms;

16*

6. The universality of comfort;
7. The sovereignty of reason;
8. The absolute liberty of the man and of the citizen.
I mention below its principals forms of activity:

a. Division of labor, through which classification of the People by INDUSTRIES replaces classification by *caste;*

b. Collective power, the principle of WORKMEN'S ASSOCIATIONS, in place of *armies;*

c. Commerce, the concrete form of CONTRACT, which takes the place of *Law;*

d. Equality in exchange;

e. Competition;

f. Credit, which turns upon INTERESTS, as the governmental hierarchy turns upon *Obedience;*

g. The equilibrium of values and of properties.

The old system, standing on Authority and Faith, was essentially based upon *Divine Right.* The principle of the sovereignty of the People, introduced later, did not change its nature; and it is a mistake to-day, in the face of the conclusions of science, to maintain a distinction which does not touch underlying principles, between absolute monarchy and constitutional monarchy, or between the latter and the democratic republic. The sovereignty of the People has been, is I may say so, for a century past, but a skirmishing line for Liberty. It was either an error, or a clever scheme of our fathers to make the sovereign people in the image of the king-man: as the Revolution becomes better understood, this mythology vanishes, all traces of government disappear and follow the principle of government itself to dissolution.

The new system, based upon the spontaneous practice of industry, in accordance with individual and social reason, is the system of *Human Right.* Opposed to arbitrary command, essentially objective, it permits neither parties nor sects; it is complete in itself, and allows neither restriction nor separation.

There is no fusion possible between the political and economic systems, between the system of laws and the system of contracts; one or the other must be chosen. The ox, while it remain an ox, cannot be an eagle, nor can the bat be at the same time a snail. In the same way, while Society maintains in the slightest degree its political form, it cannot become organized according to economic law. How harmonize local initiative with the preponderance of a central authority, or universal suffrage with the hierarchy of officials; the principle that no one owes obedience to a law to which he has not himself consented, with the right of majorities?

If a writer who understood these contradictions should undertake to reconcile them, it would prove him, not a bold thinker, but a wretched charlatan.

This absolute incompatibility of the two systems, so often proved, still does not convince writers who, while admitting the dangers of authority, nevertheless hold to it, as the sole means of maintaining order, and see nothing beside it but empty desolation. Like the sick man in the comedy, who is told that the first thing he must do is to discharge his doctors, if he wants to get well, they persist in asking how can a man get along without a doctor, or a society without a government. They will make the government as republican, as benevolent, as equal as possible; they will set up all possible guaranties against it; they will belittle it, almost attack it, in support of the majesty of the citizens. They tell us: You are the government! You shall govern yourselves, without president, without representatives, without delegates. What have you then to complain about? But to live without government, to abolish all authority, absolutely and unreservedly, to set up pure *anarchy*, seems to them ridiculous and inconceivable, a plot against the Republic and against the nation. What will these people who talk of abolishing government put in place of it? they ask.

We have no trouble in answering.

It is industrial organization that we will put in place of government, as we have just shown.

In place of laws, we will put contracts. — No more laws voted by a majority, nor even unanimously; each citizen, each town, each industrial union, makes its own laws.

In place of political powers, we will put economic forces.

In place of the ancient classes of nobles, burghers, and peasants, or of business men and working men, we will put the general titles and special departments of industry: Agriculture, Manufacture, Commerce, &c.

In place of public force, we will put collective force.

In place of standing armies, we will put industrial associations.

In place of police, we will put identity of interests.

In place of political centralization, we will put economic centralization.

Do you see now how there can be order without functionaries, a profound and wholly intellectual unity?

You, who cannot conceive of unity without a whole apparatus of legislators, prosecutors, attorneys-general, custom house officers, policemen, you have never known what real unity is! What you call unity and centralization is nothing but perpetual chaos, serving as a basis for endless tyranny; it is the advancing of the chaotic condition of social forces as an argument for despotism — a despotism which is really the cause of the chaos.

Well, in our turn, let us ask, what need have we of government when we have made an agreement? Does not the National Bank, with its various branches, achieve centralization and unity? Does not the agreement among farm laborers for compensation, marketing, and reimbursement for farm properties create unity? From another point of view, do not the industrial associations for carrying on the large-scale industries bring about unity? And the constitution of value, that contract of contracts, as we have called it, is not that the most perfect and indissoluble unity?

And if we must show you an example in our own history in order to convince you, does not that fairest monument of the Convention, the system of weights and measures, form, for fifty years past, the cornerstone of that economic unity which is destined to replace political unity?

Never ask again then what we will put in place of government, nor what will become of society without government, for I assure you that in the future it will be easier to conceive of society without government, than of society with government.

Society, just now, is like the butterfly just out of the cocoon, which shakes its gilded wings in the sunlight before taking flight. Tell it to crawl back into the silken covering, to shun the flowers and to hide itself from the light!

But a revolution is not made with formulas. Prejudice must be attacked at the foundation, overthrown, hurled into dust, its injurious effects explained, its ridiculous and odious nature shown forth. Mankind believes only in its own tests, happy if these tests do not addle its brains and drain its blood. Let us try then by clear criticism to make the test of government so conclusive, that the absurdity of the institution will strike all minds, and Anarchy, dreaded as a scourge, will be accepted as a benefit.

2. Elimination of Governmental Functions — Worship.

The old revolution did not attack public worship: it was content with threatening it: a double error, which has been repeated in our day, and which is explained, on both occasions, as a surviving desire for reconciliation between the powers, temporal and spiritual.

There lurks the enemy nevertheless. God and King, Church and State; these have ever been the soul and body of conservatism. The triumph of liberty in the Middle Ages lay in separating them, and even in accepting their separation as a principle, showing the stupidity of both. Nowadays we can confess it without danger; but philosophically this separation is inadmissible. He who denies his king, denies his God, and *vice versa;* hardly anybody but the republicans of yesterday refuses to understand this. But let us grant this compliment to our enemies, the Jesuits know it; for while, since '89, real revolutionaries have not ceased to combat both the Church and the State, and to array them against each other, the Holy Congregation has always had it in mind to reunite them, as if faith could rejoin what reason has separated.

Robespierre was the first who in 1794, gave the signal for the return to God by society. This despicable rhetorician, in whom the soul of Calvin seemed to be born again, and whose *virtue* has done us more harm than all the vices of the Mirabeaus, the Dumouriezs, the Dantons, the Barras, put together, had all his life but one thought, the restoration of Power and of Worship. He prepared quietly for this great work, sometimes by sending to the guillotine unfortunate atheists or harmless Anarchists, sometimes by giving serenades to the Supreme Being, and teaching the people the catechism of authority. He deserved what the Emperor, who understood him, said about him: *That man has more method than you think!* Robespierre's *method* was simply to reestablish authority by religion and religion by authority. Eight years before the First Consulate, Robespierre, celebrating auto-da-fe's *To the Glory of the Great Architect of the Universe,* reopened the churches and paved the way for the Concordat. Bonaparte only revived the politics of the pontiff of Prairial. But as the Victor of Arcola had little faith in the efficacy of Masonic dogmas, and besides, did not feel that he was strong enough to found a new religion, like Mahomet, he confined himself to reestablishing the old; and, with this object, made a treaty with the Pope.

From that time the fortunes of the Church were restored: its acquisitions, its encroachments, its influence advanced at the same pace as did the usurpations of power. That was natural: religion is unquestionably the oldest manifestation of government and the highway for authority. Finally, the Revolution of February raised the pride and pretensions of the clergy to the highest point. Certain disciples of Robespierre, following the example of their master, invoked the benediction of God upon the Republic, and handed it over, for the second time, to the priests. Despite the murmurs of the public conscience, one does not know to-day whether the Jesuits or the Representatives have most influence.

Nevertheless Catholicism must submit: the supreme work of the Revolution in the nineteenth century is to do away with it.

I say this, not in a spirit of incredulity nor of malice: I was never a mocker, and I hate no one. I merely express a logical conclusion. Since the subject permits, I will even make a prediction. Everything is in conspiracy against the priest, even M. Foucault's pendulum. Unless conservatism succeeds in rehabilitating society from bottom to top, in its body, its soul, its ideas, its tendencies, Christianity has not twenty-five years to live. Perhaps in half a century the priest will be chased out of his profession as a swindler.

M. Odilon Barrot disclaimed having said that the law in France was atheistic: he gave a different turn to his thought. M. Odilon Barrot made a mistake in retracting: atheism is the first article of our law. As soon as the State fails to openly accept a doctrine, it has no longer any faith: it denies God and religion. I know that it is a contradiction that this should be so; but it is so, despite the contradiction; and that it should be so is not the least of the triumphs of the Revolution. Religion cannot exist as a mere vague and indefinite sentiment of piety: it is positive, dogmatic, definite, or it is nothing. That is why Jean-Jacques Rousseau, Bernardin de St. Pierre, Jacobi, no matter what they say, are as much atheists as Hegel, Kant, and Spinoza. Is not this indifference atheism, or, better, anti-theism, which causes us to protect equally both Jew and Christian, Mahometan, Greek Catholic, Papist, and Protestant? Is not this philosophic spirit atheism, and the most refined atheism, which considers facts by themselves, in their evolution, their series, their relations, without giving a thought to a first principle, or to the cause of causes? If one may join two such words, is it not an atheistic theology, this rational criticism, which classes ideas of cause, substance, spirit, god, future life, &c., &c., as forms of our understanding, or symbols of our consciousness; and which conse≠ quently explains in a way that compels our assent, all religious manifestations, theologies and theogonies, as the unfolding of concepts?

We ask in vain what sphere in this world can be found for a religion of which the doctrines are all diametrically opposed to the most legitimate and approved tendencies of society, of which the morality is founded upon expiation, absolutely at variance with our ideas of liberty, equality, perfectibility and happiness; of which the revelations, long since proved false, would be beneath contempt, were it not that philosophy, in ex≠ plaining their legendary origin, shows us the primitive form of the intuitive ideas of the human mind. In vain we seek a reason for public worship, a function for the priest, a pretext for the faith: it is impossible to obtain any answer, however slightly favorable, unless we voluntarily blind ourselves. Certainly religion would long ago have been nothing in society, nothing even in our private consciences, if our tolerance had not been greater than our belief, if our practice had not been broader than our reason. Public worship antagonizes our ideas, our morals, our laws, our nature: it would have been done away with, if the first Constituent Assembly, which ordered the sale of the property of the clergy, had not, by an incomprehensible scruple, conceived itself under obligation to pension them as compensation.

What supports the Church among us, or rather what serves as a pretext for keeping it, is the cowardice of self≠styled republicans, who are almost all of the religion of the Savoyard vicar. Like the Abyssinians, of whom Doctor Aubert told me, who, when they are troubled with tape≠worm, get rid of a portion, but are careful to retain the head, our deists cut off from religion whatever discommodes or shocks them: they would not for the world upset the principle of religion, the eternal source of superstition, robbery, and tyranny. No worship, no mysteries, no revelations; that suits them well enough. But don't touch their God: they would accuse you of parricide. So superstition, usurpation, pauperism, grow again unceasingly, like the links of the tapesworm. And such people pretend to govern the Republic! General Cavaignac, whose remnant of piety offered to the Pope the hospitality of the nation, is a candidate for the Presidency! Would you give your daughter to a man who carries such a monster in his bosom?

More than eighteen centuries ago a man tried, as we are trying to-day, to renegerate humanity. In the sanctity of his life, in his prodigious intelligence, in his bursts of indignation, the Genius of Revolutions, the Adversary of the Eternal, thought that he recognized a son. He appeared to him and said, while pointing to all the kingdoms of the earth: All these will I give thee, if thou wilt recognize me as thy father and adore me. No, replied the Nazarene, I adore God and serve him only. The illogical reformer was crucified. After him again came Pharisees, publicans, priests, and kings, more oppressive, more rapacious, more infamous than ever; and the Revolution, twenty times begun, twenty times abandoned, still remains in doubt. Aid me, Lucifer, Satan, whoever you are, demon opposed to God according to the faith of my fathers! I will speak for you; and I ask nothing from you.

I know very well that it is with religion as it is with the State, that it does not suffice to show its emptiness and incapacity; that we must offer something to fill the place left vacant by it. I know that they who ask what we offer in place of government will not fail to ask what we will give in place of God.

I do not draw back in the face of any difficulty. I even admit with sincere conviction, what the atheists of former days did not admit, that such should be the task of philosophy. I grant that, just as it does not suffice to do away with government, without replacing it with something else, so we cannot entirely dislodge God, without showing the unknown which is to succeed him in the order of human conceptions and social developments.

Without attempting at present to concern myself with this substitution, who does not see that it would already be well advanced, if the theoretical and practical insufficiency of the divine principle, if its economic unfitness, if its incompatibility with the present revolution had become plain to everybody? Who does not see that the new THESIS would be comprehended so much the better and so much the more quickly, as its analogue should be generally understood; that is to say, that the theory of free contract, which takes the place of the governmental theory, should the sooner become common property, and consequently the necessity of the following equation rendered more striking: *The Supreme Being is to X as the governmental system is to the industrial system.* As every negation in society implies a subsequent affirmation, the contrary also obtains, and every affirmation implies a preliminary elimination. Do you want to bring down the new principle, called by the Socialists of every age, and announced by Jesus Christ himself under the name of the *Paraclete?* Begin by sending the Eternal Father back to heaven. His presence among us holds by but a single thread, the budget. Cut that thread, and you will find out what the Revolution should put in place of God.

Moreover I cannot understand the delicacy of certain democrats in matters that touch the ecclesiastical budget. The example of the old Constituent Assembly paralyzes them. The civil list of the clergy was established in 1799, they think, to replace the Church property, which was sold to pay for the needs of the nation. Would it not be confiscation to abolish the ecclesiastical budget?

There is a misunderstanding here which it is desirable to clear up; not only on account of the intriguers who make use of it, but above all for the sake of the timorous souls who are misled by it.

During the centuries of faith, when there was neither centralized government nor budget, when money was scarce, and the only guaranty of a living was immovable property, the priests received their property from the piety of the faithful, not as mere individuals, but as the ministers of public worship. It was the religious institution that was endowed; the sacerdotal body was but a usufructuary. This usufruct it naturally ought to lose, when public finances permitted the cost of public services to be otherwise defrayed, or when the endowment became purposeless, the religious institution being about to perish. In '89, it was with the Church as with the secular power: it had become corrupt, and faith in it was shaken. The piety of the people, who thought that they could purchase heaven, enriched a multitude of do-nothings. The sovereign, willing to meet the wishes of those who gave, but not desiring to enter into the question of the utility or inutility of religion at the moment, decided that the revenue of the Church in future should be in proportion to services rendered; that only those among the clergy who performed parochial functions should be remunerated. Certainly the Constituent Assembly would have done right to show itself more rigorous. The Church, having put itself outside of the Revolution, as it has done since 1848, there were good grounds to take from it both its property and its stipends. Far from indemnifying the clergy, it would have been but just to sue it for damages for its underhand opposition to the revolution. The Constituent Assembly treated it with moderation, holding, though mistakenly, that public worship was still a necessary institution. It needed it for its own government.

We are impelled to say more by the progress of thought which took place when public feeling had been calmed, and by the more and more openly declared hostility of a sacerdotalism which permits neither philosophic reasoning, nor political freedom, nor social

progress; which knows only alms-giving as an alleviation
of poverty, thereby adding insult by Providence to
injury by Hard Luck; a sacerdotalism which is destroyed
by the diffusion of science and the increase of prosperity.

I grant that worship should be free, and that he who
serves at the altar should live from the altar. But I add
that to do exact justice, the participants in the sacrifice
should pay the sacrificial priest. When the tax for public
worship shall have been remitted, and the 8 million
dollars which it requires shall have been deducted from
the township assessments, and when perpetual and
inalienable endowments shall have been prohibited, and
the acquisitions made by the clerical body since 1789
sequestrated, order will again prevail. The townships
perhaps, or religious associations, will provide for their
priests as they choose. Why should the State be the
banker for the towns in respect to the clergy? Why
interfere between pastors and their parishioners? Does
the Government take account of pious works; does it
concern itself about holy images, about the heart of
Mary, about the holy sacrament; does it need masses
and Te Deums?

If public worship really has any material or moral
value; if it is a service that the public needs and
demands; I have no objection. *Let it alone, let it go.*
Let public worship, like industry, be free. I only
mention that traffic in holy things, like any other traffic,
should be subject to demand and supply, and not be
coddled and subsidized by the State; that it is a matter
of exchange, not of government. In this, as in everything
else, the free contract should be the supreme law. It is
all right that each one should pay to be baptized, to be
married, to be buried. Let them who would adore
assess themselves for the cost of their adorations,
nothing is more just. The right to assemble for prayer is
equal to the right to assemble to talk politics or
economics; the oratory, as well as the club, is inviolable.

But talk no more to us of the religion of the State,
nor of the religion of the majority, nor of salaried Public
Worship, nor of the neo-Christian Republic. These are

so many apostasies from reason and right: the Revolution cannot compound with Divinity. Above all, propound to the people no more questions such as the following, under the pretext of direct legislation; to which I am sure they will answer by a thundering *Yes*, and the most conscientious Yes in the world:

Shall God be recognized?
Shall there be a Religion?
Shall this Religion be administered by priests?
Shall these priests be paid by the State?

Do you want the counter=revolution to be finished in two days, — complete — replete? Talk to the people not of King nor Emperor nor Republic, nor of land reform, nor free banking, nor universal suffrage: the People knows pretty nearly what these things mean: they know what they want, and what they don't want. Do as Robespierre did: talk to them about the *Supreme Being* and the *immortality of the soul.*

3. Justice.

Justice — Authority, incompatible terms, which nevertheless the ordinary man persists in regarding as synonymous. He talks of the *authority of the law*, just as he talks of a *government of the people;* phrases instilled into him by the powers that be; so that he does not perceive the contradictions involved. Whence arises this distortion of ideas?

Justice, like order, began with force. At first it was the law of the prince, not of the conscience. Obeyed through fear rather than through love, it is enforced, rather than explained: like the government, it is the more or less intelligent use of arbitrary power.

Without going farther back than the history of France, justice, in the Middle Ages, was a privilege of the lords, and was administered sometimes by him in person, sometimes by a tenant farmer, or by a superintendent. One was amenable to the justice of the lord, just as one was liable to him for certain days of labor, just as one is still liable for taxes. One had to pay for a judgment, just as he had to pay to have his grain ground or his bread baked; and he who paid the most, had the best chance of winning. Two peasants, convicted of having settled their difference through an arbiter, would have been treated as rebels, and the arbiter prosecuted as a usurper. Administer another man's justice? what an abominable crime!

Little by little, the Nation grouped itself about the chief baron, who was the king of France, and all justice was deemed to spring from him, whether granted as a concession of the Crown to feudatories, or delegated to guilds for the administration of justice, of which the members paid for their privileges in hard cash, as still is done by registrars and attorneys.

At last, since 1789, justice has been exercised directly by the State, which alone gives enforceable judgments, and which receives as pin-money, not counting fines, an appropriation fixed at $5,400,000. What have the people gained by this change? Nothing. Justice remains what it was before, an emanation from authority; that is to say, a formula for coercion, fundamentally void, and open to challenge in all its decisions. We do not even know what real justice is.

I have often heard this question discussed: Has Society the right to punish with death? Beccaria, an Italian of no great talent, made himself a reputation in the last century by the eloquence with which he refuted the advocates of the death penalty. And in 1848 the people thought that they were doing a wonderful thing, while waiting for better, in abolishing the death penalty for political offences.

But neither Beccaria nor the revolutionaries of February have touched even the first word of the question. The use of the death penalty is only one special manifestation of criminal justice. The real question is not whether society has a right to inflict the death penalty, or to inflict any penalty at all, however trifling, or even to acquit or to pardon, but whether it has any right to pronounce judgment at all.

Let society defend itself if attacked: that is within its right.

Let it avenge itself, taking the risk of reprisals, if that seem for its advantage.

But that it should judge, and after judging should punish, that is what I deny, that is what I refuse to grant to any authority.

The individual alone has the right to judge himself, and, if he thinks expiation would be good for him, to demand punishment. Justice is an act of conscience, essentially voluntary, as the conscience cannot be judged, condemned, or acquitted but by itself: all else is war, the rule of authority, and barbarism, the abuse of force.

I live in the company of *unfortunates*, that is the name they call themselves, whom Justice drags before it for theft, counterfeiting, bankruptcy, indecent assault, infanticide, assassination.

Most of them, as far as I can learn, are three-quarters convicted, without any admission on their part, *rei sed non confessi*[27]; and I think that I do not slander them in saying that in general they do not seem to be above reproach.

I understand that these men who are at war with their fellows should be summoned and compelled to repair the damage they have caused, to bear the cost of the injury which they have occasioned; and, up to a certain point, to pay a fine in addition, for the reproach and insecurity of which they are one of the causes, with more or less premeditation. I understand, I say, this application of the laws of war between enemies. War also may have, let us not say its justice, that would be to profane the word, but its rules.

But that beyond this, these same people should be shut up, under pretext of reforming them, in one of those dens of violence, stigmatized, put in irons, tortured in body and soul, guillotined, or, what is even worse, placed, at the expiration of their term, under

---

[27] Accused but not confessed.

17

the surveillance of the police, whose inevitable revelations will pursue them wherever they may have taken refuge; once again I deny, in the most absolute manner, that anything in society or in conscience or in reason can authorize such tyranny. The Code is constructed, not for justice, but for the most iniquitous and atrocious vengeance; the last vestige of the ancient hatred of the patrician for the servile classes.

What agreement have you made with these men, that you arrogate the right to hold them accountable for their misdeeds by chains, by violence, by public stigma? What promises have you made them of which you can avail yourself? What conditions have they accepted which they have violated? What limit placed upon the overflow of their passions, and recognized by them, have they overpassed? What have you done for them that they should do anything for you; what do they owe you? I am looking for the free and voluntary contract which binds them; and I see only the blade of justice, the sword of power, suspended over their heads. I ask for the written, reciprocal obligation, signed by their hand, which proclaims their default; and I find only threatening and one-sided prohibitions of a self-styled legislator, who needs the aid of the executioner to have any authority.

Where there has been no contract there can be neither crime nor misdemeanor before a court. And here I hold you by your own maxims: *All that is not prohibited by law is permitted*, and *The law applies to the future only, it has no retroactive force*.

Well then, the law (and this is written after sixty years under your institutions) — the law is the expression of the sovereignty of the People; that is to say, if I am not much mistaken, it is the social contract, the personal obligation of the man and the citizen. In so far as I have not wanted the law, in so far as I have not consented to it, voted for it, signed it, I am under no obligation to it; it has no existence. To use it before I have recognized it, and to avail yourself of it against

me, despite my protest, is virtually to give it retroactive
effect and to violate the law itself. Every day it
happens that a decision is reversed for an error in form.
But there is not one of your acts which is not marked
by invalidity, and by the most monstrous of invalidities,
the assumption that the accused knew the law. Souf-
flard, Lacenaire, and all the criminals whom you have
sent to execution, turn in their graves and accuse you
of false judgment. What have you to reply?

Talk not of tacit consent, of the eternal principles of
society, of the moral standard of nations, of the
religious conscience. It is precisely because the
universal conscience does recognize right, morality, the
claims of society, that you should have explained its
principles, and asked for the acquiescence of all. Did
you do this? No, you enacted whatever you chose, and
you called this edict of yours the rule of conscience,
and the expression of general consent. There is too
much partiality in your laws, too many implications and
equivocations, upon which we are not agreed. We
protest against both your laws and your justice.

General consent! That recalls another pretended
principle, which you present to us as another of your
triumphs, that every accused person should be tried
by his equals, who are his natural judges. Ridiculous!
Has this man who has never been asked to take part in
the discussion of the law, who has never voted for it,
never even read it, who would not understand it if he
should read it, who has not been consulted upon the
choice of a legislator, — has he any natural judges?
Are these capitalists, these proprietors, these rich men,
who are in touch with the government, who enjoy its
protection and favor, are they the natural judges of the
poor? Are these the "honest and free men," who will
declare him guilty, "on their honor and conscience"
(what a guaranty for the culprit!), "before God" (of
whom the accused has never heard), "before men" (among
whom he is not counted); and if he advances in protest
the wretched condition to which society has reduced
him, if he reminds them of the poverty of his life and
17*

all the hardships of his existence, will reply by bringing up the tacit consent and the conscience of the human race?

No, no, magistrates, you shall no longer enact this part of violence and hypocrisy. It is enough that there is nothing that calls your good faith in question; and that, because of that good faith, the future will pardon you; but you shall go no further. You have no right to judge; and this lack of right, this invalidity of your tenure, was implicitly asserted on the day when, in the face of the world, in a federation of all France, the principle of the sovereignty of the People was proclaimed, which is nothing else than individual sovereignty.

Remember, there is but one way to do justice; it is that the culprit, or merely the defendant, should do it himself. And he will do it when each citizen shall have appeared at the social compact; when, at this solemn assemblage, the rights, the obligations, and the functions of each shall have been defined, guaranties exchanged, and assent signed.

Then justice, springing from liberty, will no longer be vengeance: it will be reparation, As there will be no more opposition between social law and the will of the individual, litigation will be cut off, there will be nothing for it but acknowledgment.

Moreover the machinery of lawsuits then will reduce itself to a simple meeting of witnesses; no intermediary between the plaintiff and defendant, between the claimant and the debtor, will be needed except the friends whom they have asked to arbitrate.

Then indeed, according to the democratic principle that the judge should be elected by the litigants, the State will have no more to do with judicial matters than the duel: the right to justice granted to everybody is the best guaranty of the judgments.

The complete, immediate, abolition of courts and tribunals, without any substitution or transition, is one of the prime necessities of the Revolution. Whatever delay may occur in other reforms, if social liquidation, for example, should not take place for twenty-five years, or the organization of economic forces for half a century, in any case the suppression of judicial authority cannot be postponed.

As for the principle involved, justice as now established is never anything but a formula for despotism, and the negation of liberty and right. Wherever you allow a jurisdiction to survive, you erect a monument to counter-revolution, whence, sooner or later, will arise a new political or religious autocracy.

As for the policy, it would risk everything to leave the interpretation of the new social compact to the ancient magistracies, saturated as they are with baneful ideas. We see but too clearly that if the administrators of justice are pitiless toward Socialists, it is because Socialism is the negation of the juridical function, as well as of the law that stands behind it. When the judge pronounces the fate of a citizen, arrested for revolutionary thoughts, words or writings, it is not a culprit but an enemy whom he strikes. For the sake of justice, suppress this official, who, administering justice, is fighting for his robe and fireside.

Moreover, the way has been mapped out: the commercial tribunals, the councils of arbiters, the recognition of arbitration, and the appointment of experts, so frequently ordered by the courts, are so many steps already made toward the democratization of justice. To carry the movement to completion, nothing is needed but a decree giving authority to all arbiters, appointed at the request of any one whomsoever, to send for witnesses, and to put their decisions into execution.

4. Administration, Police.

Everything in our society is contradictory: that is why we can never come to an understanding, are always ready to fight. Public administration and the police will afford us another proof.

If there is anything to-day which seems improper, sacrilegious, a direct attack upon liberty of Reason and of Conscience, it is a government which, usurping the domain of faith, pretends to control the spiritual duties of its subjects. Even in the eyes of Christians, such tyranny would be intolerable; if there were not insurrection, martyrdoms would reply. The Church, instituted and inspired from above, asserts its own right to govern souls, but refuses this right to the State; which is noteworthy, and constitutes of itself a beginning of liberalism. Touch not the censer, it cries to rulers. You are the guardians of the outward: we are the guardians of the inward. Before you, faith is free: religion does not derive from your authority.

On this point opinion, at least in France, is unanimous. The State may still be willing to pay for public worship, and the Church to accept the subsidy, but the State does not interfere at all with dogmas and ceremonies. Believe or not; worship or not; that is your affair. The Government has decided not to enter any more into matters of conscience.

Of two things one: either the Government, in making this sacrifice of its right of initiative, has committed a grievous error; or it has intended to take a step backward, and to give us a pledge of its retreat. Why indeed, if the Government does not think that it has the right to force religion upon us, should it think that it has the right to force law upon us? Why, not content with legislative authority, should it exercise judical authority in addition? Why police authority? Why administrative authority?

What indeed! does the Government leave to us the care of our souls, the most important part of us, upon the control of which hangs order in this life, together with our happiness in the other, but intervenes in our material affairs, commercial business, relations with our neighbors, the most ordinary matters? Power is like the curate's maid; it leaves souls to the devil; all it wants is the body. If it can get its hands into our purses, it scorns our thoughts. What a disgrace! Can we not take care of our possessions, arrange our accounts, settle our differences, provide for our common needs, at least as well as we can look after our salvation and care for our souls? What business have we with the legislation of the State, with the judiciary of the State, with the police of the State, with the administration of the State, any more than with the religion of the State? What reason, what pretext even, can the State advance for this exception to local and individual liberty?

Will it be said that the contradiction is only apparent; that the authority of the State is universal and excepts nothing; but that for its more complete operation, it has had to divide itself into two equal and independent powers; the one the Church, to which is confided the care of souls, the other the State, to which belongs the government of bodies?

To this I reply, in the first place, that the separation of the State from the Church was not made for better organization, but on account of the incompatibility of the interests which they control; in the second place, that the results of this separation have been most deplorable; seeing that the Church, having lost its power over temporal matters, is no longer listened to in spiritual matters; while the State, assuming to interfere only in material questions, and solving them only by force, has lost the respect and aroused the condemnation of all. And it is precisely for that reason that the State and the Church, convinced too late of their inseparability, are now trying to reunite themselves in an impossible fusion, at the moment when the Revolution has pronounced the downfall of both.

But neither can the Church, lacking political sanction, maintain its control of thought; nor can the State, deprived of higher principles, aspire to the control of material interests; while, as for their fusion, it is even more chimerical than that of an absolute monarchy with a constitutional monarchy. What liberty has separated, authority cannot reunite.

My question thus stands untouched: by what right does the State, which cares nothing for thought nor for public worship, the State, which is as godless as the law, assume to rule material interests?

To this question, which is entirely one of law and morality, reply is made:

1st. That individuals and communities, not being able to look at general interest, seeing that their own interests are opposed, need some sovereign ruler.

2nd. That as affairs cannot be carried on harmoni≠ously if each locality, each association, each group of interests, is left to its own individual impulse; if public functionaries receive as many different and contra≠dictory orders as there are individual interests, it is essential that a single power should give the orders, and consequently that functionaries should be appointed by the Government.

You cannot get out of it: there is inevitable and fatal antagonism of interests; that is the premise; there must be centralized, official command; that is the conclusion.

It was from such reasoning that our fathers, in '93, after having destroyed divine right, feudal rule, distinc≠tion of classes, baronial courts, &c., reestablished a government based upon electoral mandate, and disagreed with the Girondists, who, without being able to say how they expected to secure unity, nevertheless, it is said, opposed centralization.

We now see the fruits of this policy.

According to M. Raudot, the total number of Govern≠ment officials for the State and municipalities is 568,365. The army is not included in this figure. There is there≠fore, in addition to the soldiers, whose number varies from 400,000 to 500,000, a mass of 568,365 agents, super≠visors, inspectors, &c., who enmesh the country, whom the Government supports at the expense of the nation, and of whom it makes use perhaps to watch over the morals of the people, perhaps to defend itself against the attacks of the discontented, or, more terrible still, the assaults of antagonistic thought.

This is the Rule that centralization inflicts upon us. Do you not think that complete Anarchy would be better for our peace of mind, our labor and our prosperity, than this million of parasites armed to attack our liberties and our interests?

And this is not all.

As there are 568,365 employees of the State at the command of the ministry, the opposition, whether monarchical or democratic matters little, has on its side an army twice, thrice, four times as numerous, composed of men who are without employment, dis= contented with their position, who covet government situations; and who, in order to obtain them, work as hard as they can, under their district leaders, to overthrow the Governmental heads of departments. Thus on the one hand war between officialdom and industry; on the other, war between the ministry and the opposition. What do you think of this kind of order?

At this game of puss=in=the=corner our unhappy country has passed its life since '93, and the end is not yet. If I may tell what is known to everybody, *Republican Solidarity,* a society established to assert, propagate, and defend the Revolution, at the same time aimed, not at overthrowing the Government, but at having ready a complete staff, which if the exigency required could take the places of the old· employees, and carry on the work without crippling the service. That is the way in which the revolutionaries of to=day understand their part. What a good thing it was for the Revolution that the government of Louis Bona= parte ·dissolved the *Republican Solidarity!*

As a State religion is the rape of the conscience, so a State political administration is the castration of liberty. Deadly devices, wrought by the same madness for oppression and intolerance; whose poisonous fruits show their identity. State religion produced the Inqui= sition; State administration produced the police.

It is easily understood that the priesthood, at first, like the Chinese mandarins, only a scientific and

literary caste, may have nursed thoughts of religious
control, while science, intolerant of error, has legitimate aspirations to instruct the reason. The priesthood
enjoyed this prerogative, as long as it taught science,
of which the characteristic is to be experimental and
progressive: it lost it when it placed itself in opposition
to progress and experience.

But that the State, whose only science is force, and
whose only doctrine, along with its etiquette and its
lackeys, is the theory of the platoon and battalion —
that the State, I say, treating the Nation forever as a
child, should undertake, at the nation's expense and
against its will, under pretext of discordance between
its desires and its needs, to administer its property, to
judge what is suitable for its interests, to dole out to
it the power of movement, liberty, life; that would
indeed be inconceivable, would indicate some infernal
machination did we not know, through the history of
all governments, that if power has always ruled the
People, it is because through all time the People,
ignorant of the laws of order, has been the accomplice
of Power.

If I were talking to men who had love of liberty
and respect for themselves, and I wanted to excite
them to revolt, I should confine myself in my speech
to reciting the powers of a prefect.

According to their authors:

"The prefect is the agent of the central power: he is
"also the intermediary between the Government and
"the Department: he procures administrative action:
"he provides for the public service directly, by his
"own action.

"As the *agent of the central power*, the prefect per-
"forms those acts that relate to the property of the
"State or of the Department; and fulfils the functions
"of police.

"As intermediary between the Government and the
"Department, he causes the laws sent to him by the
"ministers to be published and put into execution, and
"gives executive force to the taxrolls; *vice versa*, he

"forwards claims, information, &c., to the central
"Government.

"*As procurer of administrative action*, he fulfils
"diverse functions towards those in his charge and
"towards his subordinates: these are, *instruction,*
"*direction, initiation, inspection, supervision, estimation*
"*or appreciation, control, censorship, reformation,*
"*redress, finally, correction or punishment.*

"As *provider for the needs of the public service*, the
"prefect acts sometimes as clothed with *guardianship,*
"sometimes as with *military command,* sometimes as
"having *judicial jurisdiction.*"

In charge of the business of the Department and the
State, officer of the judicial, intermediary and pleni-
potentiary police, instructor, director, initiator, inspec-
tor, supervisor, estimator, controller, censor, reformer,
redresser, corrector, guardian, commander, superintendent, aedile, judge — that is the prefect, that is the
Government. And you tell me that a people that will
submit to such a rule, a people thus held in leading
strings, under collar and bridle, under rod and whip,
is a free people! that such a people understands liberty,
that it is capable of tasting liberty and receiving it!
No, no, such a people is less than a slave; it is nothing
but a war-horse. Before freeing it, it must be raised
to the dignity of a man, by reconstructing its understanding. It will say to you itself, in the simplicity of
its belief: What would become of me without saddle
or bridle! I have never known any other rule of life
nor any other condition. Clear up my ideas, gratify
my affections, balance my interests, then I shall need
no master, I can get along without a rider.

Thus society, by its own confession, turns in a circle.
This government, which society holds up as a guiding
principle, it admits is nothing but the supplement of
its reason. Just as between the guidance of his conscience and the tyranny of his instincts, man has given
himself a mystical controller — the priests; just as
between his own and his neighbor's liberty he has
placed as arbiter the judge; just so between his own

and the public interest, supposed by him to be as
irreconcilable as his reason and his instinct, he has
sought another mediator, the prince. Man has thus
deprived himself of his moral character, and of his
judicial dignity, and he has cast away his right of
initiative; by this loss of his powers he has made
himself the poor slave of impostors and tyrants.

But since Jesus Christ, Isaiah, David, Moses himself,
it has been admitted that the just man has need neither
of sacrifice nor of priest; and we have but now proved
that the setting up of a judge superior to the judged
is a contradiction in principle and a violation of the
social compact. Would it be more difficult, for the
accomplishment of our social and civic duties, to
dispense with the lofty intervention of the State?

We have shown that the industrial system is the
harmony of interests resulting from social liquidation,
free currency and credit, the organization of economic
forces, and the constitution of value and property.

When that is accomplished, what use will there be
any more for government; what use punishment;
what use judicial power? The CONTRACT solves all
problems. The producer deals with the consumer, the
member with his society, the farmer with his township,
the township with the province, the province with the
State, &c. &c. It is still the same interest which passes
along, transforms itself, balances itself, is reflected to
infinity: still the same idea which issues from each
faculty of the soul as a centre toward the periphery
of its attractions.

The secret of this equalizing of the citizen and the
State, as well as of the believer and the priest, the
plaintiff and the judge, lies in the economic equation
which we have hereinbefore made, by the abolition of
capitalist interest between the worker and the employer, the farmer and the proprietor. Do away with
this last remnant of the ancient slavery by the reciprocity of obligations, and both citizens and communities
will have no need of the intervention of the State to
carry on their business, take care of their property,

build their ports, bridges, quays, canals, roads, establish markets, transact their litigation, instruct, direct, control, censor their agents, perform any acts of super= vision or police, any more than they will need its aid in offering their adoration to the Most High, or in judging their criminals and putting it out of their power to do injury, supposing that the removal of motive does not bring the cessation of crime.

Let us make an end of it. Centralized government can be understood under the old monarchy, when the king, called the first baron of the realm, was the fountain, in virtue of his divine right, of all justice, all power of action, all property. But after the declara= tions of the Constituent Assembly, after the still more explicit and positive amplifications made by the Con= vention, to pretend that the Country, that is to say each locality for its own concerns, has not the right to rule, administer, judge and govern itself; to take from the people the disposition of their forces, under the pretext that the Republic is one and indivisible; to reestablish despotism by metaphysics, after having overthrown it by insurrection; to treat as *Federalists*, and as such to mark for proscription, all who speak in favor of liberty and local sovereignty; all this is to be false to the true spirit of the French Revolution and its most assured intentions; it is to deny progress.

I have said, and I cannot repeat too often, that the system of centralized government which prevailed in '93, thanks to Robespierre and the Jacobins, was nothing but feudalism transformed; it was the applica= tion of algebra to tyranny. Napoleon, who gave the last touch to it, bore witness to this.

Let M. Ledru=Rollin consider this: his last statement in favor of direct government is a first step beyond Jacobin tradition, back to the true revolutionary tradi= tion; just as the protest of M. Louis Blanc against what he calls *Girondism*, is the first note of governmental reaction. The Constitution of '93 is the Gironde and Danton; the representative system is the Jacobin Club and Robespierre. But Robespierre and the Jacobins are discredited: sixty years of experience have taught us what the unity and indivisibility of their republic was worth.

As for the Constitution of '93, even if it did mark the movement toward a new order of ideas, it cannot serve as an example to us now, although it may be well to recall its terms and tendencies. The revolution= ary spirit has advanced since then: we are indeed in harmony with that Constitution, but we have lived sixty years beyond it·

5. Public Instruction; Public Works; Agriculture and Commerce; Finances.

Propose the following questions to the people, and you can be quite sure of the replies in advance:

Question. Shall instruction be free and compulsory? Answer. Yes.

Q. Who shall give the instruction? A. The State.

Q. Who shall bear the cost? A. The State.

Q. Shall there be a minister of Public Instruction? A· Yes.

Nothing easier, you see, than to make the People legislate. Everything depends on the way in which the questions are put· It is the method of Socrates, arguing against the Sophists.

Q. Shall there be also a Minister of Public Works? A. Certainly, since there will be public works.

Q. Also a Minister of Agriculture and Commerce? A. Yes.

Q. A Minister of Finance? A. Yes.

How marvellous! The People talks like the child Jesus in the midst of the elders. However little you may like it, I am going to make it say that it wants tithes, the right of the first night, and the kingdom of Dagobert·

Let us once more examine the plea which serves as a pretext for the existence of the State.

The People, because they are so many, are supposed not to be able to carry on their own affairs, neither instruction, nor proper behavior, nor protection; like a great lord who does not know what his fortune is, and who is not quite right in his mind; but who pays for the management of his property, for his domestic economy, and for the care of his person, agents, sub-ordinates and superintendents of all kinds; some who take account of his revenues and regulate his expenses, others who deal in his name with supply merchants and bankers, still others who watch over the safety of his person, &c., &c.

Thus the budget of expenses of the sovereign is composed of two parts: 1st. Real services and actual materials of which are composed his support, his pleasures and his luxuries. 2nd. The remuneration of servants, aids, commissioners, representatives, assis-tants, almoners, solicitors, guards, who act for him.

The second part of the budget is much the largest: it is composed:

1st. Of interest due to bankers with whom the People holds a current account; interest which to-day, together with the sinking fund, amounts to $69,200,000, and constitutes the public debt.

2nd. Salaries of the important officers, direct repre-sentatives of the sovereign, and heads of each branch. These amount to $1,800,000.

3rd. Salaries of employees, clerks, assistants, menials of every grade and degree. Of the $161,000,000 allowed for the various ministers, at least three-quarters are used for such payments.

4th. Cost of excise, assessment, and collection of the public revenues. These come to $29,800,000.

5th. Pensions paid by the public to old employees, after thirty-five years of service, of which the total is $9,000,000.

6th. Finally, unexpected expenditures, uncollected returns, nominal receipts, all charged to the account of profit and loss, $16,000,000.

Thus, for from forty to sixty millions, at most, of real services and actual materials of which the yearly expenditure of the People is composed, the governmental system makes them pay $286,800,000, say 200 to 240 millions of profit, that the servants of the People draw from their appointments. And in order to assure themselves forever of this immense prey, in order to prevent any notion of reform and emancipation from entering their master's head, the said servants have made their master declare himself in perpetual minority, and incapable of executing his civil and political rights.

The worst of this system is not so much the inevi‍table ruin of the master, as the hatred and scorn which his servants bear toward him; not knowing him, knowing only his head superintendents, from whom they receive their appointments and take their orders, and whose part they always take against the sovereign People.

Attacking this system on the front, we have said:

The People is a collective entity.

They who have exploited the People from time immemorial still hold it in servitude, stand upon this collectivity of its nature, and deduce from this its legal incapacity, which requires their personal control. We, on the contrary, from the collectivity of the People, draw proof that it is completely and perfectly capable, that it can do anything, and needs no one to restrain it. The only question is how to give full play to its powers.

Thus, in speaking of the public debt, we have shown that the People, precisely because it is multiple, could organize its own credit very well, and has no need to enter into relations with money lenders. And we have done away with debts: no more loans, no more ledger account, no more intermediaries, no more State, between the capitalists and the People.

Public worship has been disposed of in the same way. What is the priest? we have asked. An inter‍mediary between the People and God. What is God himself? Another supernatural and imaginary inter‍mediary between the natural instincts of man and his reason. Cannot man do what his reason points to, without being constrained by respect for a Creator? That would be a contradiction. In any case, faith being free and optional, and each one constructing his own religion, worship becomes a matter for the inward tribunal, an affair of conscience, not of material use. Almsgiving has been suppressed.

The judiciary too has gone. What is Justice? Mutual guaranties; that which for two hundred years we have called the Social Contract. Every man who has signed this contract is fit to be a judge: justice for all; authority for none. As for procedure, the shortest is the best. Down with tribunals and jurisdictions!

Last came administration, accompanied by the police. Our decision was taken quickly. Since the People is multiple and unity of interest constitutes its collectivity, centralization comes about through this unity; there is no need of centralizers. Let each household, each factory, each association, each municipality, each district, attend to its own police, and administer carefully its own affairs, and the nation will be policed and administered. What need have we to be watched and ruled, and to pay, year in and year out, 25 millions? Let us abolish prefects, commissioners, and policemen too.

The next question is of schools. This time there is no idea of suppression, but only of converting a political institution into an economic one. If we preserve the methods of teaching now in use, why should we need the intervention of the State?

A community needs a teacher. It chooses one at its pleasure, young or old, married or single, a graduate of the Normal School or self-taught, with or without a diploma. The only thing that is essential is that the said teacher should suit the fathers of families, and that they should be free to entrust their children to them or not. In this, as in other matters, it is essential that the transaction should be a free contract and subject to competition; something that is impossible under a system of inequality, favoritism, and university monopoly, or that of a coalition of Church and State.

18

As for the so-called higher education, I do not see how the protection of the State is needed, any more than in the former case. Is it not the spontaneous result, the natural focus of lower instruction? Why should not lower instruction be centralized in each district, in each province, and a portion of the funds destined for it be applied to the support of higher schools that are thought necessary, of which the teaching staff should be chosen from that of the lower schools. Every soldier, it is said, carries a marshal's baton in his knapsack. If that is not true, it ought to be. Why should not every teacher bear in his diploma the title of university professor? Why, after the example of what is done in workingmen's associations, as the teacher is responsible to the Academic Council, should not the Academic Council be appointed by the teachers?

Thus even with the present system of instruction, the university centralization in a democratic society is an attack upon paternal authority, and a confiscation of the rights of the teacher.

But let us go to the bottom of the matter. Governmental centralization in public instruction is impossible in the industrial system, for the decisive reason that *instruction* is inseparable from *apprenticeship,* and scientific education is inseparable from professional education. So that the teacher, the professor, when he is not himself the foreman, is before everything the man of the association of the agricultural or industrial group which employs him. As the child is the pledge, *pignus,* betwen the parents, so the school becomes the bond between the industrial associations and families: it is unfitting that it should be divorced from the workshop, and, under the plea of perfecting it, should be subjected to external power.

To separate teaching from apprenticeship, as is done to-day, and, what is still more objectionable, to distinguish between professional education and the real, serious, daily, useful practice of the profession, is to reproduce in another form the separation of powers and the distinction of classes, the two most powerful instruments of governmental tyranny and the subjection of the workers.

Let the working class think of this.

If the school of mines is anything else than the actual work in the mines, accompanied by the studies suitable for the mining industry, the school will have for its object, to make, not miners, but chiefs of miners, aristocrats.

If the school of arts and crafts is anything but the art or craft taught, its aim will soon be to make, not artisans, but directors of artisans, aristocrats.

If the school of commerce is anything but the store, the counting house, it will not be used to make traders, but captains of industry, aristocrats.

If the naval school is anything but actual service on board ship, including even the service of the cabin boy, it will serve only as a means of marking two classes, sailors and officers.

Thus we see things go under our system of political oppression and industrial chaos. Our schools, when they are not establishments of luxury or pretexts for sinecures, are seminaries of aristocracy. It was not for the People that the Polytechnic, the Normal School, the military school at St. Cyr, the School of Law, were founded; it was to support, strengthen, and fortify the distinction between classes, in order to complete and make irrevocable the split between the working class and the upper class.

In a real democracy, in which each member should have instruction, both ordinary and advanced, under his control in his home, this superiority from schooling would not exist. It is contradictory to the principle of society. But when education is merged in apprenticeship; when it consists, as for theory, in the classification of ideas; as for practice, in the specialization of work; when it becomes at once a matter of training the mind and of application to practical affairs in the workshop and in the house, it cannot any longer depend upon the State: it is incompatible with government. Let there

18*

be in the Republic a central bureau of education, another of manufactures and arts, as there is now an Academy of Sciences and an Office of Longitude. I see no objection. But again, what need for authority? Why such an intermediary between the student and the schoolroom, between the shop and the apprentice, when it is not admitted between the workman and his employer?

The three bureaus, of Public Works, of Agriculture and Commerce, and of Finance, will all disappear in the economic organism.

The first is impossible, for two reasons: 1st, the control undertaking such works will belong to the municipalities, and to districts within their jurisdiction. 2nd, the control of carrying them out will rest with the workmen's associations.

Unless democracy is a fraud, and the sovereignty of the People a joke, it must be admitted that each citizen in the sphere of his industry, each municipal, district or provincial council within its own territory, is the only natural and legitimate representative of the Sovereign, and that therefore each locality should act directly and by itself in administering the interests which it includes, and should exercise full sovereignty in relation to them. The People is nothing but the organic union of wills that are individually free, that can and should voluntarily work together, but abdicate never. Such a union must be sought in the harmony of their interests, not in an artificial centralization, which, far from expressing the collective will, expresses only the antagonisms of individual wills.

The direct, sovereign initiative of localities, in arranging for public works that belong to them, is a consequence of the democratic principle and the free contract: their subordination to the State is an invention of '93, and a return to feudalism. This was the especial work of Robespierre and the Jacobins, and the most deadly blow at popular liberty. The fruits of it are well known: without centralized Power, we should never have had the absurd competition of two

roads from Paris to Versailles; without centralized
Power, we should never have had the fortifications of
Paris and of Lyons, with detached forts; without cen=
tralized Power, the radial system of railroads would
never have obtained the preference; without centralized
Power, which always draws to itself the most important
matters, in order to use them, to work them, in the
interest of its creatures and hangers=on, we should not
see every day public property given away, public ser=
vice monopolized, taxes wasted, squandering remuner=
ated, the fortune of the people eagerly sacrificed by
their legislators and ministers.

I may add that, contrary as is the supremacy of the
State to democratic principles in the matter of public
works, it is also incompatible with the rights of
workers created by the Revolution.

We have already had occasion to show, especially
in connection with the establishment of a National
Bank and the formation of workers' societies, that in
the economic order labor subordinated to itself both
talent and capital. This the more, because that under
the operation, sometimes simultaneous, sometimes in=
dependent, of the division of labor and of collective
power, it becomes necessary for the workers to form
themselves into democratic societies, with equal con=
ditions for all members, on pain of a relapse into
feudalism. Among the industries which demand this
form of organization, we have already mentioned rail=
roads. We may add to these the construction and
support of roads, bridges and harbors, and the work
of afforestation, clearing, drainage, &c., in a word, all
that we are in the habit of considering in the domain
of the State.

If it becomes thenceforth impossible to regard as
mere mercenaries the workmen who are closely or
distantly connected with the associations for buildings,
for waters and forests, for mines; if we are to be
forced to see this low mob as sovereign societies; how
can we maintain the hierarchical relations of the
minister to the heads of departments, of heads of

departments to engineers, and of engineers to workers;
how, in short, preserve the supremacy of the State?

The workmen, much elated by the use of the political
rights conferred upon them, will desire to exercise them
in their fullness. Associating themselves, they will
first choose leaders, engineers, architects, accountants;
then they will bargain directly, as one power with
another, with municipal and district authorities for
the execution of public works. Far from submitting to
the State, they will themselves be the State; that is to
say, in all that concerns their industrial speciality, they
will be the direct, active representative of the
Sovereign. Let them set up an administration, open
credit, give pledges, and the Country will find in them
a guaranty superior to the State; for they will be
responsible at least for their own acts, while the State
is responsible for nothing.

Shall I speak of the Ministry of Agriculture and
Commerce? The budget for this department amounts
to $5,500,000, which is squandered in *subsidies, bonuses,
allowances, premiums, remittances, secret funds, super=
vision, central service*, &c. Translated, this means,
favors, corruptions, sinecures, parasitism, robbery.

Thus for instruction in agriculture and its various
aids, I find $640,000. It is safe to say, notwithstanding
my respect for the estimable professors, that
$640,000 worth of *guano* would be of more use to the
peasants than their lessons.

For the veterinary school and the stud, I find $685,000.
Despite these, the horses in France are continually
deteriorating, and there are not enough of them. We
can let the Jockey Club go then, and let the breeders
alone.

For the manufactures of Sevres, Gobelins, Beauvais;
for the Conservatory, the Schools of Arts and Crafts,
the subsidies to commerce and manufactures, $759,615.
What do these manufactures produce? Nothing, not
even masterpieces. What progress do our schools
effect in industry? None. They do not even teach

there the true principles of international economics. What end do these encouragements to commerce serve? None, evidently. The portfolio of the Bank empties itself every day!

For sea fishing, $800,000, intended to encourage the sailor population. There is moreover in the budget $800,000 received for licenses levied upon these same fisheries: it follows that we are paying $1,600,000 extra, that we may eat sea fish, and that without this we could not meet the competition of foreign fishing fleets! Would it not be easier to remove the $1,600,000 of taxes and expenses of every sort, which weigh down the owners of vessels; that is to say, to abolish ministerial action as far as they are concerned?

The most curious of the articles of this department is that which deals with workmen's associations. I am not joking: since 1848, the Government has set itself to pay a license for Socialism. For the supervision of associations, $15,400.

Let the Government give as much to them instead. They will be glad to get it, and the Government will have so much the less trouble.

Finally, to support, direct, suvervise, pay for, all this parasitism, $142,630, for what is called the central ad= ministration. Double that sum: double the budget for Agriculture and Commerce, and let the State refrain from interfering with agriculture, commerce, industry, horse=raising, and fisheries, and let it turn them over to workmen's associations, who will make them worth something, under the direction of men of science and artists; and the State, paid for doing nothing, will for the first time have aided order.

As for the Ministry of Finance, it is evident that its functions are entirely confined to the other Ministries. The finances are to the State what the hayrack is to the ass. Suppress the political machine, and you will have left an administration of which the sole object is to procure and distribute subsistence. Districts and municipalities, resuming the control of their public works, are as capable of paying their own

expenses as of planning them: the financial inter=
mediary disappears: at the most we might retain, as a
general bureau of statistics, the Chamber of Accounts.

6. Foreign Affairs, War, Navy.

He that is guilty of one is guilty of all, says the
Gospel.   If the Revolution allows any portion of
government to remain, it will soon return in its entirety.
But how can we dispense with government in dealing
with foreign affairs?
A nation is a collective being which continually deals
with other collective beings like itself; which therefore
must establish an organ, a representative, in short,
a government, for its international relations.   Here at
least, then, is not the Revolution about to be false to
its own principle; and to justify its lapse by quoting
the stupid pretence that *the exception proves the rule?*
That would be deplorable, and moreover is inadmis=
sible. If the government is indispensable for diplomacy,
it is as much so for war and for the navy; and, as all
is comprised in power and society, we should soon see
governmentalism reestablish itself in the police, then
in the administration, then in the judiciary, and then
where would the Revolution be?
This dwelling upon foreign politics is what best
shows how weak is still the conception of the Revolu=
tion among us. It shows a prejudiced fidelity to the
traditions of despotism, and a dangerous leaning
toward counter=revolution in European democracy,
unceasingly busy in maintaining the balance of power
among the nations.
Let us try, in this as in other matters, to reconstruct
our ideas, and to free ourselves from habit.
After the Revolution has been accomplished at home
will it also be accomplished abroad?
Who can doubt it? The Revolution would be vain
if it were not contagious: it would perish, even in
France, if it failed to become universal. Everybody
is convinced of that. The least enthusiastic spirits do

not believe it necessary for revolutionary France to interfere among other nations by force of arms: it will be enough for her to support, by her example and her encouragement, any effort of the people of foreign nations to follow her example.

What then is the Revolution, completed abroad as well as at home?

Capitalistic and proprietary exploitation stopped everywhere, the wage system abolished, equal and just exchange guaranteed, value constituted, cheapness assured, the principle of protection changed, and the markets of the world opened to the producers of all nations; consequently the barriers struck down, the ancient law of nations replaced by commercial agreements; police, judiciary, administration, every-where committed to the hands of the workers; the economic organization replacing the governmental and military system in the colonies as well as in the great cities; finally, the free and universal commingling of races under the law of contract only: that is the Revolution.

Is it possible that in this state of affairs, in which all interests, agricultural, financial and industrial, are identical and interwoven, in which the governmental protectorate has nothing to do, either at home or abroad, is it possible that the nations will continue to form distinct political bodies, that they will hold themselves separate, when their producers and consumers are mingled, that they will still maintain diplomacy, to settle claims, to determine prerogatives, to arrange differences, to exchange guaranties, to sign treaties, &c., without any object?

To ask such a question is to answer it. It needs no demonstration; only some explanations from the point of view of nationalities.

Let us recall the principle. The reason for the institution of government, as we have said, is the economic chaos. When the Revolution has regulated this chaos, and organized the industrial forces, there is no further pretext for political centralization; it is absorbed in industrial solidarity, a solidarity which is based upon general reason, and of which we may say, as Pascal said of the universe, that *its centre is everywhere, its circumference nowhere.*

When the institution of government has been abolished, and replaced by the economic organization, the problem of the universal Revolution is solved. The dream of Napoleon is realized, and the chimera of the Dean of St. Peter's becomes a necessity.

It is the governments who, pretending to establish order among men, arrange them forthwith in hostile camps, and as their only occupation is to produce servitude at home, their art lies in maintaining war abroad, war in fact or war in prospect.

The oppression of peoples and their mutual hatred are two correlative, inseparable facts, which reproduce each other, and which cannot come to an end except simultaneously, by the destruction of their common cause, government.

This is why nations will inevitably remain at war, as long as they remain under the rule of kings, tribunes, or dictators; as long as they obey a visible authority, established in their midst, from which emanate the laws which govern them: no Holy Alliance, Democratic Congress, Amphictyonic Council, nor Central European Committee can help the matter. Great bodies of men thus constituted are necessarily opposed in interests; as they cannot merge, they cannot recognize justice: by war or by diplomacy, not less deadly than war, must quarrel and fight.

Nationality, aroused by the State, opposes an invincible resistance to economic unity: this explains why monarchy was never able to become universal. Universal monarchy is, in politics, what squaring the circle or perpetual motion are in mathematics, a contradiction. A nation can put up with a government as long as its economic forces are unorganized, and as long as the government is its own, the nationalism

of the power causing an illusion as to the validity of
the principle; the government maintains itself through
an interminable succession of monarchies, aristocracies,
and democracies. But if the Power is external, the
nation feels it as an insult: revolt is in every heart,
it cannot last.

What no monarchy, not even that of the Roman
emperors, has been able to accomplish; what
Christianity, that epitome of the ancient faiths, has
been unable to produce, the universal Republic, the
economic Revolution, will accomplish, cannot fail to
accomplish.

It is indeed with political economy as with other
sciences: it is inevitably the same throughout the
world: it does not depend upon the fancies of men or
nations: it yields to the caprice of none. There is not
a Russian, English, Austrian, Tartar, or Hindoo political
economy, any more than there is a Hungarian, German
or American physics or geometry. Truth alone is equal
everywhere: science is the unity of mankind.

If then science, and no longer religion or authority,
is taken in every land as the rule of society, the sover≠
eign arbiter of interests, government becoming void,
all the legislation of the universe will be in harmony.
There will no longer be nationality, no longer fatherland,
in the political sense of the words: they will mean
only places of birth. Man, of whatever race or color
he may be, is an inhabitant of the universe; citizenship
is everywhere an acquired right. As in a limited
territory the municipality represents the Republic,
and wields its authority, each nation on the globe
represents humanity, and acts for it within the
boundaries assigned by Nature. Harmony reigns,
without diplomacy and without council, among the
nations: nothing henceforward can disturb it.

What purpose could there be for entering into
diplomatic relations among nations who had adopted
the revolutionary programme:

No more governments,

No more conquests,

No more custom houses,
No more international police,
No more commercial privileges,
No more colonial exclusions,
No more control of one people by another, one
State by another,
No more strategic lines,
No more fortresses?

Russia wants to establish herself at Constantinople,
as she is established at Warsaw; that is to say, she
wants to include the Bosphorus and the Caucasus in
her sphere. In the first place, the Revolution will not
permit it; and to make sure, it will begin by revo=
lutionizing Poland, Turkey, and all that it can of
Russian provinces, until it reaches St. Petersburg. That
done, what becomes of the Russian relations at
Constantinople and at Warsaw? They will be the
same as at Berlin and Paris, relations of free and equal
exchange. What becomes of Russia itself? It becomes
an agglomeration of free and independent nationalities,
united only by identity of language, resemblance of
occupations, and territorial conditions. Under such
conditions conquest is meaningless. If Constantinople
belonged to Russia, once Russia was revolutionized
Constantinople would belong to it neither more nor
less than if it had never lost its sovereignty. The
Eastern question from the North ceases to exist.

England wants to hold Egypt as she holds Malta,
Corfu, Gibraltar, &c. The same answer from the Revo=
lution. It notifies England to refrain from any attempt
upon Egypt, to place a limit upon her encroachments
and monopoly; and, to make sure, it invites her to
evacuate the islands and fortresses whence she threatens
the liberty of the nations and of the seas. It would be
truly a strange misconception of the nature and scope
of the Revolution to imagine that it would leave
Australia and India the exclusive property of England,
as well as the bastions with which she hems in the
commerce of the continent. The mere presence of the
English in Jersey and Guernsey is an insult to France;

as their exploitation of Ireland and Portugal is an insult to Europe; as their possession of India and their commerce with China is an outrage upon humanity. Albion, like the rest of the world, must be revolutionized. If necessary to force her, there are people here who would not find it so hard a task. The Revolution completed at London, British privilege extirpated, burnt, thrown to the winds, what would the possession of Egypt mean to England? No more than that of Algiers is to us. All the world could enter, depart, trade at will, arrange for the working of the agricultural, mineral and industrial resources: the advantages would be the same for all nations. The local power would extend only to the cost of its police, which the colonists and natives would defray.

There are still among us *chauvinists* who maintain absolutely that France must recapture her *natural* frontiers. They ask too much or too little. France is everywhere that her language is spoken, her Revolution followed, her manners, her arts, her literature adopted, as well as her measures and her money. Counting thus, almost the whole of Belgium, and cantons of Neufchatel, Vaud, Geneva, Savoy, and a part of Piedmont belong to her; but she must lose Alsace, perhaps even a part of Provence, Gascony and Brittany, whose inhabitants do not speak French, and some of them have always been of the kings' and priests' party against the Revolution. But of what use are these repetitions? It was the mania for annexations which, under the Convention and the Directory, aroused the distrust of other nations against the Republic, and which, giving us a taste for Bonaparte, brought us to our finish at Waterloo. Revolutionize, I tell you. Your frontiers will always be long enough and French enough if they are revolutionary.

Will Germany be an Empire, a unitary Republic, or a Confederation? This famous problem of Germanic unity, which made so much noise some years ago, has no meaning in the face of the Revolution; which proves indeed that there has never been a Revolution.

What are the States, in Germany as elsewhere?
Tyrannies of different degrees of importance, based
on the invariable pretexts, first, of protecting the
nobility and upper class against the lower classes;
second, of maintaining the independence of local
sovereignty. Against these States the German
democracy has always been powerless, and why?
Because it moved in the sphere of political rights.
Organize the economic forces of Germany, and
immediately political circles, electorates, principalities,
kingdoms, empires, all are effaced, even the Tariff
League: German unity springs out of the abolition of
its States. What the ancient Germany needs is not
a confederation but a liquidation.

Understand once for all: the most characteristic, the
most decisive result of the Revolution is, after having
organized labor and property, to do away with political
centralization, in a word, with the State, and as
a consequence to put an end to diplomatic relations
among nations, as soon as they subscribe to the
revolutionary compact. Any return to the traditions
of politics, any anxiety as to the balance of power in
Europe, based on the pretext of nationality and of the
independence of States, any proposition to form
alliances, to recognize sovereignties, to restore
provinces, to change frontiers, would betray, in the
organs of the movement, the most complete failure to
understand the needs of the age, scorn of social reform,
and a predilection for counter-revolution.

The kings may sharpen their swords for their
last campaign. The Revolution in the Nineteenth
Century has for its supreme task, not so much the
overthrow of their dynasties, as the destruction to the
last root of their institution. Born as they are to war,
educated for war, supported by war, domestic and
foreign, of what use can they be in a society of labor
and peace? Henceforth there can be no more purpose
in war than in refusal to disarm. Universal brotherhood
being established upon a sure foundation, there is
nothing for the representatives of despotism to do but

to take their leave. How is it that they do not see that this always increasing difficulty of existence, which they have experienced since Waterloo, arises, not as they have been made to think, from the Jacobin ideas, which since the fall of Napoleon have again begun to beset the middle classes, but from a subterranean working which has gone on throughout Europe, unknown to statesmen, and which, while developing beyond measure the latent forces of civilization, has made the organization of those forces a social necessity, an inevitable need of revolution?

As for those who, after the departure of kings, still dream of consulates, of presidencies, of dictatorships, of marshalships, of admiralties and of ambassadorships, they also will do well to retire. The Revolution, having no need for their services, can dispense with their talents. The people no longer want this coin of monarchy: they understand that, whatever phraseology is used, feudal system, governmental system, military system, parliamentary system, system of police, laws and tribunals, and system of exploitation, corruption, lying and poverty, are all synonymous. Finally they know that in doing away with rent and interest, the last remants of the old slavery, the Revolution, at one blow, does away with the sword of the executioner, the blade of justice, the club of the policeman, the gauge of the customs officer, the erasing knife of the bureaucrat, all those insignia of government which young Liberty grinds beneath her heel . . .

.   .   .   .

EPILOGUE.

SINCE the law of the 31st of May, the Revolution has seemed to keep silence. Not a newspaper has officially espoused its cause: not a voice has boldly and intelligently asserted it. It has moved along only by its own impetus. The Democratic factions which at first rallied to its banner have profited by the forced abstention from revolutionary talk to make a retreat unnoticeably, and to return to their political affiliations. One would say that Socialism, expressed in vaguer and vaguer terms, or represented by vain Utopias, was on the eve of expiring. 1852 was the date set down for its obsequies. The republicans of yesterday undertook to bury it, some in the Constitution of 1848, some in direct government: the Presidency of the Republic was the prize!

But, as the proverb says, the statesman proposes, the Revolution disposes. After universal suffrage had disowned it, as it had already been thrice disowned, it would still not take its departure. It cares as little for the decision of universal suffrage as for the anathemas of Jean Mastaï. Henri V himself, if it were possible that Henri V could reascend the throne, could only assert the Revolution, as did his great-uncle in 1814. It is Necessity in person, while your constitutions, your politics, and your universal suffrage itself are but the tinsel of the circus. 1852 matters no more to it than 1851, 1849, or 1848: it bursts like a torrent, it rises like the tide, without caring whether you have had time to close your sluice gates.

Of what use is it to trifle with the force of circumstances? Will facts be changed or modified because we have not foreseen them? Will our security be greater because we choose to shut our eyes? It is a policy of the brainless, which the people will judge severely, and of which the upper class will pay the cost!

As for myself, free from all struggles of ambition, devoid of self-seeking, but only too clear as to the future, I propose, as in 1848 I proposed, in the interest of all parties, the course which seems best to me, and I ask you to bear witness of my words. In 1789 everybody was revolutionary, and proud of it; it is necessary that in 1852 everybody should again become revolutionary, and be glad of it. Shall I then still be so sorry that the Revolution should seem as much more terrible, as the picture of it from my pen is more true?

Humanity, in the theologico-political sphere, wherein it has been tossed these six thousand years, is like a society which, instead of being placed on the outside of a solid planet, is shut up inside a hollow one, lighted and warmed by a stationary sun in the centre, and apparently in the zenith for the countries curving around it, like the subterranean world of Virgil. Who knows whether there is not such an arrangement in the infinite variety of worlds? The rings of Saturn are not less extraordinary.

Imagine such a world, wherein all positions are the inverse of our own. Distance would prevent the inhabitants from seeing the boundaries of their situation, while barbarism, war, and lack of means of communication would keep them within their respective limits. For a long time they would imagine that the space above, beyond the sun, was the abode of gods, and that the ground under their feet covered the home of the damned far away. What tales the imagination of their poets would hang upon this! What cosmogonies, what revelations their mystagogues would bring forth, founding upon them religion, morality, and laws.

Nevertheless the progress of civilization, even of conquest, would bring great disturbances to these infernal regions, voyages of circumnavigation would be made: the earth would be traversed in every direction,

19

and mathematical and experimental certainty would be reached that this splendid universe, to which the imagination could assign no limits, was only a hollow globe, several thousand miles in diameter inside; wherein the inhabitants, regarding themselves as perpendiculars at every point of the surface toward the centre, must really stand head to head. These strange news must have created a terrible scandal among the doctors of the ancient religions. Doubtless some Galileo paid with his blood for the glory of having discovered that the world was round, and that there were anticephales.

But what occurred to redouble the anxiety was that, at the same time that ancient beliefs were falling away, it was noticed that the habitable space was not proportionate to the activity and fecundity of the race which was therein imprisoned; the world is too small for the humanity which works it; air is lacking, and after some generations, we shall die of hunger!

Then these men who at first had regarded their orb as infinite, and had sung its praises, now found themselves imprisoned like a nest of beetles in a clod of earth; and began to blaspheme God and Nature. They accused the Sovereign Creator of having deceived them; the despair and confusion was frightful. The bolder swore, with terrible imprecations, that they would not stay there. Threatening heaven with eye and fist, they began audaciously to bore into the ground, so well that one day the drill encountering only emptiness they concluded that the concave surface of their sphere corresponded to an external convex surface of an outer world, which they set about visiting.

From the point of view of our political and religious ideas, with which our intelligence is hemmed in as by an impenetrable sphere, we are in exactly the same position as these men, and we have reached the same result.

From the origin of societies, the spirit of man, confined and enveloped by the theologico-political

system, shut up in a hermetically closed box, of which
Government is the bottom and Religion the top, has
taken the limits of this narrow horizon for the limits
of a rational society. God and King, Church and State,
twisted in every way, worked over to infinity, have
been his Universe.   For a long time he has known
nothing, imagined nothing beyond.   At last, the circle
has been traversed; the excitement of the systems
suggested by this has exhausted him; philosophy,
history, political economy, have completed the triang=
ulation of this inner world; the map of it has been
drawn; and it is known that the supernatural scheme
which humanity contemplates as its horizon, and its
limit, is but itself; that, far as humanity may look into
the depths of its consciousness, it sees but itself; that
this God, source of all power, origin of all causality,
of which humanity makes its sun, is a lamp in a cavern,
and all these governments made in his image are but
grains of sand that reflect the faint light.

These religions, these legislations, these empires,
these Governments, this wisdom of State, this virtue
of Pontiffs, all are but a dream and a lie, which all
hang upon one another and converge toward a central
point, which itself has no reality. If we want to get
a more correct idea of things, we must burst this crust
and get out of this inferno, in which man's reason will
be lost, and he will become an idiot.

To=day we have become aware of this. The old
world of thought, which for so many centuries has
absorbed human speculation, is but one side of that
given us to traverse. The drill of philosophy has
pierced it here and there; soon we shall be free and
clear of our embryonic shell. We are about to gaze
on new skies, to see face to face and in its essence, the
infinite, *Sicuti est facie ad faciem.*[28]

When society has turned from within to without, all
relations are overturned. Yesterday we were walking
with our heads downwards: to=day we hold them erect,

---

[28] As it were face to face.

19*

without any interruption to our life. Without losing our personality, we change our existence. Such is the nineteenth century Revolution.

The fundamental, decisive idea of this Revolution is it not this: NO MORE AUTHORITY,   neither in the Church, nor in the State, nor in land, nor in money?

No more Authority! That means something we have never seen, something we have never understood; the harmony of the interest of one with the interest of all; the identity of collective sovereignty and individual sovereignty.

No more Authority! That means debts paid, servitude abolished, mortgages lifted, rents reimbursed, the expense of worship, justice, and the State suppressed; free credit, equal exchange, free association, regulated value, education, work, property, domicile, low price, guaranteed: no more antagonism, no more war, no more centralization, no more governments, no more priests. Is not that Society emerged from its shell and walking upright?

No more Authority! That is to say further: free contract in place of arbitrary law; voluntary transactions in place of the control of the State; equitable and reciprocal justice in place of sovereign and distributive justice; rational instead of revealed morals; equilibrium of forces instead of equilibrium of powers; economic unity in place of political centralization. Once more, I ask, is not this what I may venture to call a complete reversal, a turn-over, a Revolution?

The distance by which the two systems are separated may be judged by the difference in their modes of expression.

One of the most solemn moments in the evolution of the principle of authority was at the promulgation of the Decalogue. The voice of the angel commands the people, prostrate at the foot of Sinai:

Thou shalt adore the Eternal, it said, and nothing but the Eternal;

Thou shalt swear by him only;

Thou shalt observe his feasts, and thou shalt pay his tithes;
Thou shalt honor thy father and mother;
Thou shalt not kill;
Thou shalt not steal;
Thou shalt not commit fornication;
Thou shalt not commit forgery;
Thou shalt not covet nor calumniate;
For the Eternal commands thus, and it is the Eternal who has made thee what thou art. Only the Eternal is sovereign, wise and worthy. The Eternal punishes and rewards: the Eternal can make thee happy or unhappy.

All legislators have adopted this style: all, in speaking to man, use the words of a sovereign. Hebrew commands in the future tense, Latin in the imperative, Greek in the infinitive. The moderns do the same thing. The tribunal of M. Dupin is as infallible and terrible as that of Moses. Whatever may be the law, from whatever lips it may be proclaimed, it is sacred; even when pronounced by that fateful trumpet, which with us is the voice of the majority.

"Thou shalt not assemble,
"Thou shalt not print,
"Thou shalt not read,

"Thou shalt respect thy representatives and function-
"aries whom the fortune of the ballot or the good
"pleasure of the State has given thee,

"Thou shalt obey the laws which their wisdom has
"given thee,

"Thou shalt pay thy taxes faithfully,

"And thou shalt love the Government, thy lord and
"thy god, with all thy heart, with all thy soul, and
"with all thy mind, because the Government knows
"better than thou what thou art, what thou art worth,
"and what is good for thee; and it has the power to
"chastise those who disobey its commandments, as
"well as to recompense to the fourth generation those
"who are agreeable to it."

O, personality of man! Can it be that for sixty
centuries you have grovelled in this abjection? You
call yourself holy and sacred, but you are only the
prostitute, the unwearied and unpaid prostitute, of
your servants, of your monks, and of your soldiers.
You know it, and you permit it. To be GOVERNED
is to be kept in sight, inspected, spied upon, directed,
law‑driven, numbered, enrolled, indoctrinated, preached
at, controlled, estimated, valued, censured, commanded,
by creatures who have neither the right, nor the
wisdom, nor the virtue to do so. .. To be GOVERNED
is to be at every operation, at every transaction, noted,
registered, enrolled, taxed, stamped, measured, num‑
bered, assessed, licensed, authorized, admonished, for‑
bidden, reformed, corrected, punished. It is, under
pretext of public utility, and in the name of the general
interest, to be placed under contribution, trained, ran‑
somed, exploited, monopolized, extorted, squeezed,
mystified, robbed; then, at the slightest resistance, the
first word of complaint, to be repressed, fined, despised,
harassed, tracked, abused, clubbed, disarmed, choked,
imprisoned, judged, condemned, shot, deported, sacri‑
ficed, sold, betrayed; and, to crown all, mocked, ridi‑
culed, outraged, dishonored. That is government; that
is its justice; that is its morality. And to think that
there are democrats among us who pretend that there
is any good in government; Socialists who support
this ignominy, in the name of Liberty, Equality and
Fraternity; proletarians who proclaim their candidacy
for the Presidency of the Republic! Hypocrisy! . . . .
With the Revolution it is another matter.
The search for first causes and for final causes is
eliminated from economic as from natural science.
The idea of Progress replaces that of the Absolute in
philosophy.
Revolution takes the place of Revelation.
Reason, aided by Experience, shows man the laws
of nature and of society, and says to him:
These are the laws of necessity itself. No man has
made them: nobody forces them upon you. They have

little by little been discovered, and I exist only to bear witness of them.

If you observe them, you will be just and righteous;
If you violate them, you will be unjust and wicked.
I propose no other sanction for them.

Already, among your fellows, many have perceived that justice was better for one and all than injustice, and they have agreed among themselves to keep faith and do right; that is to say, to respect the rules for transactions which are pointed out by the nature of things as alone capable of assuring them of comfort, security and peace in the highest degree.

Will you join the compact, and form a part of their society?

Do you promise to respect the honor, the liberty and the property of your brothers?

Do you promise never to appropriate for yourself by violence, nor by fraud, nor by usury, nor by interest, the products or possessions of another?

Do you promise never to lie nor deceive in commerce, or in any of your transactions?

You are free to accept or refuse.

If you refuse, you become a part of a society of savages. Excluded from communion with the human race, you become an object of suspicion. Nothing protects you. At the slightest insult, the first comer may strike you, without incurring any other blame than that of cruelty to animals.

If you agree to the compact, on the contrary, you become a part of the society of free men. All your brothers are bound to you, and promise you fidelity, friendship, aid, service, exchange. In case of infraction, on their part or on yours, through negligence, anger or malice, you are responsible to one another for the damage, as well as for the scandal and insecurity of which you have been the cause. This responsibility may go as far as excommunication or death, according to the gravity and the repetition of the offence.

The law is clear, the sanction still more so. Three articles, which are but one, compose the whole social compact. Instead of swearing fidelity to God and your king, the citizen makes oath upon his conscience, before his brothers and before Humanity. Between these two oaths there is the same difference as between servitude and liberty, faith and science, courts and justice, usury and labor, government and economics, non-existence and existence, God and man.

Shall I remind you now that all the elements of the old society, religion, politics, business, end in this?

"In my verses, Reason leads man to Faith," says Racine the younger. Just the contrary is true. Theology leads men, step by step, to reason: it has never done anything else. All its investigations are experiments in philosophy. There is a *Sacred Physics*, a *Politics from the Holy Scriptures*, a *Canon Law*, a *Scholastics*. What are all these? Rationalism in revelation. Theology, from its earliest day, has sought truth OUTSIDE of itself: theology itself began those researches which were sure to lead us outside the circle with which it had surrounded us. As fast as it set up its dogmas, it undid them itself by its interpretations and glosses: to-day it has reached the point of denying its mysteries, and of talking, as the Apocalypse says, the language of the Beast. Everybody felt this upon reading the last charge of Monseigneur Sibour. Well, the die is cast. It is too late to go back: it would be absurd not to go to the bottom. The stone which covered the sepulchre of Golgotha is removed: Christ came out at dawn: Peter, John, Thomas himself and the women have seen him: nothing remains but the empty spot, with the door open upon the world. Do not try to shut it, citizen Caiaphas, you could more easily stop the crater of Etna.

When religion is convicted of revolutionary ideas, shall politics dare to be more conservative? Is it not politics which, by concession after concession, by system after system, has made us end in the absolute, definite denial of its own principle, government? Was it not from political discussions that once upon a time sprang this illuminating formula:

Liberty, Equality, Fraternity!

Theology, encroaching every day upon the dòmain of philosophy, has taken the direction of the primitive world; politics has traversed it and drawn the map of it. After having explored everything, described everything, it has planted its Columns of Hercules: universal suffrage is its *ne plus ultra*. I have nothing more to give you, it says; nothing more to teach you. If you want anything more, you need not look on the surface: you must look underneath. Talk to my friends, the economists. They are miners by trade; perhaps they will give you satisfaction.

Political economy in fact is the queen and ruler of this age, although its mercenaries are unwilling to admit it. It is political economy which directs everything, without appearing to do so. If Louis Bonaparte fails in his demand for prorogation, *business* is the cause. If the Constitution is not revised, it is the Stock Exchange which forbids. If the law of the 31st of May is revoked, or at least profoundly modi≠fied, it is commerce that has demanded it. If the Republic is invincible, it is because the *interests* protect it. If the peasant, of the earth from of old, embraces the Revolution, it is because the earth, his adored mistress, summons him. If we do not rest on Sunday, it is because industrial and mercantile influ≠ences are opposed to it. . . .

Evidently, social economy, little known divinity, leads the world. Let it show itself boldly, tell its secrets, give its orders, and all nations, all classes, will be at its feet.

The peasant waits for but one sign: he wants the soil, he watches it anxiously: it will not escape his covetousness. To acquire this land, he has gone into debt, loaded himself with mortgages: he pays to Capi≠tal and to the State, I know not how many hundred millions; and up to now, he has gained nothing. All the governments have promised him low prices, credit and riches: all have passed away without keeping their word. The Republic came and completed his ruin.

Thus the peasant is profoundly sceptical about government: in politics, he has not the slightest principle, not the shadow of a conscience, not the most superficial opinion. In 1848, he would have made Louis Bonaparte emperor; in 1852, he will perhaps make Ledru-Rollin king. Do you know why? It is because the peasant is before all things revolutionary: his ideas and his interests require him to be so.

The mechanic is like the peasant. He wants work, instruction, participation, a low price for rent and food. Do not take his pro-constitutional manifestations too seriously. He despises political theories as much as the peasant does. He is thoroughly revolutionary; ready to go from Louis XVI. to Mirabeau, from the Gironde to Marat, from Robespierre to Napoleon, from Cabet to Lamartine. His well-known history matches his sentiments.

The merchant, the manufacturer, the small proprietor, although more circumspect in their language, hold like views. What they want is *business*, transactions, orders, easy money, capital for long terms, ample outlets and no fetters, no duties. In their simplicity they call that being conservative, not revolutionary. It was in this frame of mind that they voted in December, 1848, for General Cavaignac; that they are now supporting the Constitution from attacks, and repudiating the Socialists with their systems. They entirely misunderstand. The merchant, the manufacturer, the agricultural proprietor, all those among the richer and middle classes who are holders of securities and mortgages, or who have an independent business, care little, at bottom, for politics and the form of government. Such people want a living, and a good living: they are revolutionaries in their hearts; only they go to the wrong shop for the Revolution.

Up to now they have been made to believe that political order, order in the street, such as the Government secures, was enough to give them what they asked: they have regarded the supporters of Power as the supporters of their own interests; and they have held aloof from the Revolution, noisy at first, bigoted, exclusive, and, most of all, out at elbows. When will the newspapers beloved by the upper classes make up their minds to undeceive their readers, the *Siecle*, which has languished since the death of Louis Perree, the *Presse*, too often mistaken, the *National*, always hoping. No doubt the necessity of pretending to be revolutionary, from the point of view of the lower class, has kept up a sense of distrust among the upper class: it thought that the question was only one of making the lower class upper, and the upper, lower. To-day, the question has been so much cleared up that separation on such grounds need not be continued.

Who then will show the merchants, the manufacturers, the small proprietors, all the classes whose labor produces more than their capital, that they have nothing to fear from a revolution which, by reducing the cost of credit to ¼ per cent., by paying off the public debt and all mortages, by converting house rent and ground rent into a reimbursement of the owners, by reducing the public expenditure by seven-eighths, relieves production of 45 per cent. of its cost, restores to the worker the whole of his wages, and consequently creates a continually growing market for the manufacturer, in the midst of a home population? It would be like trying to persuade the workman that it would be better for him to continue to lose $40 of his wages, and receive $1.20 interest for the $30 that he deposits in the savings bank. No, no, such blindness cannot last; and the day when it shall be dissipated, perhaps to-morrow, will be the day of the Revolution.

The adversaries of the Revolution, we know them all, are neither the peasants, nor the workmen, nor the merchants, nor the manufacturers, nor the small proprietors. They should not be even the capitalists, if, realizing the impetus to industry which will be given by the reform in credit, they understand that with an immense demand to be satisfied, the stock company can give them, for some years longer, a larger return than bank discounts, mortgages, and national bonds.

The adversaries of the Revolution are they who live on prejudice even more than on parasitism: they are above all they who, more sure that the Revolution must come than are the Revolutionaries themselves, speculate, gamble, and, if I may venture to say so, cultivate resistance to the fall of ancient institutions, in order to make their profit out of it, and at each relaxation of resistance, at each step of progress, reap a new harvest. These men in the front rank of Jesuitism, of monarchy, of the moderate governmentalist Republicans, to whom I must add certain dabblers in social theories, are the real enemies of the Revolution; so much the more guilty in that they are of a less robust faith, and their hostility is only a matter of vanity and self-interest.

But what do I say? Is there to-day a man capable of the crime of counter-revolution? And if by chance such an one should be found, would he not be in great part excusable, on account of the service which his opposition would render to the very cause which he intended to oppose?

Who would have thought of free credit, unless capital had held back? *Capital refuses*, said M. Thiers in 1848: I fear that it will cost it much some day to have refused.

Who would have brought up again the worn-out topic of the *decatholicization* of Europe, had it not been for the war on Rome?

Who would have known of the agrarian revolt, without the affair of Poitiers Street?

Who would have thought of abolishing the courts, if the magistrates had not been so severe?

Who would have raised the question of the passive obedience of the soldier, and talked of doing away with a standing army, had it not been for the declaration of a state of siege, and the attacks upon the people by the National Guard?

Who, without the abuses of government, would have formulated economic organization?

Who, without M. Rittinghausen's *Direct Legislation,* without M. Considérant's *Direct Government,* without the dictatorship of Nauvoo, would have revived the theory of the SOCIAL CONTRACT, and laid down the principle of Anarchism more securely?

Pursue then, Royalists, Jesuits, Bancocrats, Phalans: terians, Icarians, the course of your foolish resistance. Continue to enlighten the people, and to show them the need of a revolution. The farther you go, the more you will serve the people, and I like to think that they will pardon you.

But you, Republicans of the old school, to whom the desire for advance is not lacking, and respect for authority is the only restraint, can you not for once give rein to your instincts? Here are two candidates, M. Cavaignac and M. Ledru:Rollin, whose part it would very soon be, if they were willing, to lead, the one the business class, the other the working class, to the higher world of human rights and economic organiza: tion. Already they have taken the motto of the last Democratic:Socialist congress: *The Republic is above Universal Suffrage.* But M. Cavaignac, defending the Constitution, thought himself more and more to be the friend of *order;* while M. Ledru:Rollin, in his manifesto countersigned by Mazzini, could not refrain from crossing himself, on his forehead, mouth and breast, at the mere word, *Anarchy.* Despising equally their party affiliations, they both fear to fall into the pit of Revolution, which to us is the way to deliverance, as if they expected to find the devil at the bottom. Forward then, cowards! You have half your body on the brink already. You have said: The Republic is above Universal Suffrage. If you understand the formula, you will not avoid the commentary:

THE REVOLUTION IS ABOVE THE REPUBLIC.

TABLE OF CONTENTS.